CORPORATION NATION

I see in the near future a crisis approaching that unnerves me and causes me to tremble for the safety of my country . . . corporations have been enthroned and an era of corruption in high places will follow, and the money power of the country will endeavor to prolong its reign by working upon the prejudices of the people until all wealth is aggregated in a few hands and the Republic is destroyed.

—Abraham Lincoln, 1864

CORPORATION
NATION

How Corporations Are Taking Over Our
Lives and What We Can Do About It

CHARLES DERBER

St. Martin's Press New York

94 CORPORATION NATION. Copyright © 1998 by Charles Derber. All rights
reserved. Printed in the United States of America. No part of this book
may be used or reproduced in any manner whatsoever without written permission except in the case of brief quotations embodied in critical articles or
reviews. For information, address St. Martin's Press, 175 Fifth Avenue,
New York, N.Y. 10010.

Library of Congress Cataloging-in-Publication Data

Derber, Charles.
    Corporation nation : how corporations are taking over our lives and what
we can do about it / Charles Derber. — 1st ed.
        p.   cm.
    Includes bibliographical references and index.
    ISBN 0-312-19288-6
    1. Corporations—Political aspects—United States.   2. Corporations—
United States—Sociological aspects.   3. Social responsibility of business—
United States.   4. Business and politics—United States.   5. Industrial
policy—Moral and ethical aspects—United States.   6. Labor policy—Moral and
ethical aspects—United States.   7. International trade—Moral and ethical
aspects.   8. Democracy.   9. Sovereignty, Violation of.   10. Power (Social
sciences)   I. Title
HD2785.D388   1998
306.3—dc21   98-23514
                                                                    CIP

DESIGN BY JAMES SINCLAIR

First edition: November 1998

10 9 8 7 6 5 4 3 2 1

To
My Father and Mother
who inspired my principles and my love of life

Morrie Schwartz
whose sunny love in life and triumph in death
brightens all my days

and

Elena
for whose strength, nurturance, and heroic perseverance
I am in loving awe

CONTENTS

ACKNOWLEDGMENTS

I am grateful to all the scholars and critics of the corporation who came before me, my colleagues and friends who sustained me, and all the activists around the world who are working to make possible a new world. I am indebted to the participants of a Boston seminar on the corporation, including Tim Costello, Richard Grossman, June Sekera, Charles Edmunson, Severyn Bruyn, Kent Greenfield, Elly Leary, Debra Osnowitz, Yale Magrass, S. M. Miller, and Michael Bettencourt. Grossman and Costello helped me rethink some of my basic assumptions; Osnowitz, Magrass, and Miller read the entire manuscript and gave me valuable substantive and editorial feedback; Greenfield read parts of the manuscript and helped guide me in legal thinking and critique; Edmunson inspired me as an employer-owner who walked the talk and Leary as a labor historian and organizer whose keen thinking and passion for justice burned bright; and Bruyn deepened my vision at every level, from local to global.

My colleagues in the Leadership for Change Program at Boston College helped nurture my belief in—and entertained my skepticism about—democratic change arising from within the corporation itself. These include Severyn Bruyn, Paul Gray, Joe Raelin, Eve Spangler, Bill Torbert, Sandra Waddock, Judy Clair, Charles Edmunson, Laury Hamel, Robert Leaver, Charlene O'Brien, Neil

Smith, Steve Waddell, Lynn Rhenisch, and Leah Egan. I also want to thank Steven Piersanti for his own contributions to corporate responsibility and his close reading and comments on the manuscript, as well as Noam Chomsky, David Korten, Howard Zinn, and Paul Levenson for their intellectual and personal inspiration.

Numerous undergraduate and graduate students were a captive audience for various drafts of this work, and their insights and suggestions made this a much better book. Thanks also to Eunice Doherty, Brenda Pepe, and Roberta Negrin for their office and personal help at Boston College. I also want to express gratitude and enthusiasm for the legion of new populist activists, including David Lewit and the thousands of hopeful citizens joining the Alliance for Democracy, Chuck Collins and his crusaders for equality at United for a Fair Economy, and Tim Costello and all the labor activists committed to making the labor movement a social movement again.

I am deeply grateful to my editor, Cal Morgan, for his excitement about the ideas, for the extraordinary attention he gave to the manuscript, and for the gift of his expert editorial skills.

I cannot express adequately my gratitude to my friends and colleagues, David Karp and John Williamson, who read and commented on the manuscript, indulged my obsessions, and supported me all along the journey. While my dear friend Morrie Schwartz died before this work appeared, his faith in me, belief in the importance of the ideas presented here, and merry, loving presence—which has now touched millions of people—were a daily blessing.

Only Elena fully understands the meaning of living with a writer obsessed. Her close reading and critical commentary on the manuscript, which helped shape both the substance and style of the work, as well as her loving support, made this book possible.

Introduction: The New Problem with No Name

A generation ago, Betty Friedan wrote in her groundbreaking work *The Feminine Mystique* of "a problem that has no name." Millions of housewives with two children in white-picket-fenced houses, she argued, were living out lives of quiet desperation, with no words to communicate their suffering and no sense that they had a right to be anything but grateful for the golden lives mid-century America had bestowed upon them.[1]

Today, most Americans, both male and female, face a different unnamed problem. A mother in Hartford, Connecticut, says, "My son is with Aetna, and he frequently gets transferred back and I said, 'Gee, they're great, they're doing so much for you,' and he said, 'Yeah, Mom, until they lay me off.'"[2]

As she goes on to say about her son's life, "That's a horrible way to have to live."[3] This new problem without a name is creating feelings of powerlessness and insecurity in millions of Americans. Even those fortunate enough to have well-paying corporate jobs sense their lives becoming precarious, vulnerable to a bewildering array of forces beyond their control. Who is responsible for their plight? Can anyone fix it? They are no longer certain.

In my own university, now being "reengineered," a secretary tells me that, as an employee, she feels like one of the women Friedan described in the 1950s. She says that there is a growing sense of vague, unspoken apprehension among the office staff. While the university says it does not want to fire people, she and her fellow secretaries don't know what to expect. She describes herself as at loose ends emotionally, lashing out uncharacteristically at coworkers, and sinking periodically into feelings of depression, acute frustration, and anger.

Many Americans today are like the women described by Friedan who asked themselves, "Why am I so dissatisfied?" And millions resemble other women of that period who were in denial, "sure they had no problem," even though they struggled with feelings of insecurity, powerlessness, and sometimes desperation.[4]

Without a clear sense of who is responsible for their troubling feelings they have little sense of whom to confront, or turn to, about them. They feel at once grateful for what they have—and guilty for feeling otherwise. They have a nagging sense that something is wrong with their lives, yet they have no clear language for expressing it—and no vision of how to change it.

Today's problem with no name bears many similarities to the problem Friedan discussed. It is, for one thing, veiled by a dominant social myth, analogous to the feminine mystique that Friedan dissected: the corporate mystique, as seductive, pervasive, and enduring a phenomenon as the feminine one that still lingers today.

The corporate mystique is a set of cherished beliefs and illusions at the very heart of American culture. We are all, in some measure, captives of the new mystique, which is at the root of the way we think about the most important institutions in our society—chief among them corporations themselves. The corporate mystique dictates how we think about not only what corporations are and the importance of their roles in our lives, but what government and markets, business and democracy, and the good life are all about. It is the main recipe for how to live and think in a corporate world.

Yet the corporate mystique is, at heart, an ideology, which for decades has effectively disguised the rising power of corporations in our lives. Corporate ascendancy is emerging as the universal order of the post-communist world. Its most obvious feature is the reign of vast and much-admired global corporations, from General Electric to Microsoft to Disney. Yet the essence of corporate ascendancy is the quiet shift of sovereignty that is shaking the roots of our democracy.

Corporate ascendancy refers to the rise of a new weakened form of democracy in which the powers of average Americans are being transferred to vast institutions with diminishing public accountability. With the government increasingly unresponsive to popular opinion, and corporations almost entirely unaccountable to the public, corporations have begun acquiring new public powers and acting as unelected partners with governments.

The first part of this book offers a new look at the emerging twenty-first-century corporate order. Our social landscape is now dominated by corporations that are bigger and more powerful than most countries. General Motors has annual sales larger than Israel's Gross Domestic Product; Exxon's annual sales are larger than Poland's GDP. One hundred sixty-one countries have smaller annual revenues than Wal-Mart does. General Electric has hundreds of subsidiaries—giant companies such as GE Capital—which are themselves bigger than most nations.

Two hundred corporations, led by giants such as GE, Time Warner, and Philip Morris, dominate America's economy—and much of the rest of the world. Their combined sales in 1996 were larger than the combined gross national product of all but the nine largest nations. Historians speak of the twentieth century as the age of nations and nationalism. Our end of century and the next century loom as the triumphal age of corporations.

America's biggest companies—and some huge European and Japanese corporations—are an overwhelming force in our national politics. Corporations poured almost $2 billion into political campaigns in 1996 alone—only one of many measures of corporate political power. The relation between corporate power and democracy goes largely undiscussed in newspapers, schools, legislatures, and dinner conversations, as does the very nature of the corporation itself, a question that a hundred years ago was at the center of the national consciousness. It is a testament to the power of the corporate mystique that neither liberals nor conservatives have the vocabulary to raise these questions today.

In a rare effort by opinion makers to broach these issues, Ted Turner, founder of CNN and now a top executive in Time Warner, the world's biggest media corporation, has publicly worried about the democratic implications of corporate concentration in media: "Media concentration is a frightening thing. It's owned more and more by Disney, General Electric . . . Westinghouse, which now owns CBS. You have two of the four major networks owned by people that have huge investments in nuclear power and nuclear weapons—both GE and Westinghouse. What kinds of balanced story are they going to give you on the news about the nuclear issues?" Turner did not note that Time Warner is the second largest book publisher in the world, the largest music company, the owner of many of America's most important magazines—including *Time, Fortune, Life, People, Money, Sports Illustrated,* and *Martha Stewart Living*—and, along with TCI, the owner of television cable systems serving 47 percent of the American cable audience. Turner is implicitly asking whether democracy can survive in a world dominated by companies such as his own.

Corporate ascendancy does not yet threaten to lead to absolute corporate power, but it involves the growing public powers of corporate entities that are defined by the corporate mystique as private enterprise. In addition to capturing huge global markets for traditional products, corporations are invading traditionally public sectors such as medicine, education, social services, and law enforcement. Corporations now own and manage huge domains of the public sector. To speak of the incorporation of America is not to speak metaphorically: There is scarcely any sphere of American life that is not coming under corporate administration.

The corporate mystique has helped to obscure not only the very question of corporate power, but how deeply personal the subject is. The personal identity of today's worker, consumer, and citizen is becoming a corporate construction. Corporations help create our growing obsession with money and success molding both our morality and material lives. We get our dreams and opinions from corporate-owned media such as Time Warner or Disney, our children's education from curricula provided by Microsoft or AT&T, our food from Philip Morris, the world's largest grocer, and our credit from one-stop corporate superbanks such as Citibank and Chase, but this insight only scratches the surface of corporate involvement in our lives. Every citizen has a place in the world of corporate ascendancy, including those not working in the corporation or not working at all. It is impossible to underestimate the extent to which one's own moral integrity and sense of self-respect stem from how one is situated in that world, and the extent to which most of us are involved as both agents and targets of corporate power.

In the past, corporations have served as a shelter from the cold calculus of the market, breeding loyalty and moral commitment among workers and consumers alike. Today, in our new era of greed, the corporation is rushing to shed the last vestiges of community within its walls. Downsizing, outsourcing, and permanent insecurity are the new dread mantras of the corporate world, and they are deeply personal in their impact. The new corporate "morality" is at the heart of a rising uncivil order, which is spreading into every corner of our lives a systemic and sometimes misplaced and abusive market logic. As each of us comes to terms with our unwitting dual complicity—both as perpetrators and victims of corporate abuse—our sense of personal and moral identity will never be quite the same.

The corporate order is undermining the security of American life as our parents knew it, along with the moral certitudes of loyalty and community they lived by. This is not an unambiguous loss; America at mid-century was for many a compromised and constraining place. But the new generation is growing up with an identity it would not have chosen: that of a permanently anxious class with contingency as its new moral code. As jobs have become temporary or otherwise contingent in the new corporate order, so have our communities and, increasingly, our marriages. The crisis of contingency has deeply seared our consciousness; it marks our personal lives with both new opportunities and terrible vulnerabilities. Both advocates and critics of the corporation, as the concluding chapter reveals, have failed to appreciate how deeply corporate morality shapes personal morality, and has engendered today's crisis of values.

Students have often told me that they leave their sociology classes depressed because the sociological analysis they find there seems at once persuasive and without redemption. Social criticism has its role, but too often it has helped undermine itself in the United States by offering no solutions. Critics without constructive approaches get treated as Cassandras and reasonably dismissed as idealists or nihilists. No matter how compelling a critique, it will find little fertile soil if it offers no constructive solutions, no alternatives to inspire and involve them.

I have promised my students—and now my readers—that they will not walk away with this complaint. While the first half of this book is largely diagnostic, the second half offers a new vision and suggestions for programmatic reform that seriously address the political and spiritual problems of corporate ascendancy. I also discuss at some length the kind of personal and political change necessary to put them into practice.

Today, the prospects of change are inhibited by both the vast power of the corporation and the enchantments of the corporate mystique, both of which have effectively removed the issue of corporate sovereignty from national consciousness. But in the Gilded Age, one hundred years ago, and half a century later in the New Deal, the question of the corporation and its moral responsibilities became the centerpiece of American politics, carried by strong populist and labor movements. Although the issue has been buried now for at least two decades, new conditions are arising that could elevate these concerns once again to the forefront of national political debate.

While I argue here for a new positive populism, readers will quickly recognize that I have departed from the populist tradition as well as progressive left and liberal traditions historically associated with challenges to corporate ascendancy. While there is much to learn from populism, New Deal liberalism, and American radical thought, they are inadequate as responses to today's problems. Among their great flaws, as described in the later chapters of this book, is their tendency to confuse a critique of corporate ascendancy with an all-out assault on business as a social enterprise. In the second part of this book, I show that this approach has doomed virtually all American critics of the market order, and has created misleading notions about the change we need. We desperately need a challenge to the culture of greed, materialism, and manic consumerism that the new corporate order has bred. But there will be no solutions to downsizing, inequality, and the morality of contingency—and little hope for a more humane or democratic culture—in a world of declining or failing business. The changes we need must defend society against the new corporate assault—while at the same time protecting the health of business enterprise itself.

Positive populism starts with a recognition of the many benefits that the American corporation—and American business generally—has delivered. Visitors from around the world marvel at the consumer cornucopia that Americans enjoy, and flock to American shopping malls to buy goods that are either unavailable or vastly more expensive in their own countries. American corporations are among the most innovative and productive enterprises in history, and deliver unrivaled creature comforts to their huge consumer base. On my own trips abroad, when I have found German stores closed at night or on the weekend when I wanted to buy food or medicine, when I have had to pay for use of the shopping cart in a British grocery store or for a glass of tap water in a

Belgian restaurant, or when I couldn't use my credit card for ordinary purchases in France, I quickly came to appreciate the many things I took for granted from American business.

The American public has historically rejected populism, in part because it has benefited handsomely from the success of the American corporation. Millions of Americans have been employed their whole lives by corporations and are understandably grateful for the standard of living they enjoy. While poor Americans and even many in the middle class haven't shared in the great corporate profit boom of the last two decades, they still can regard themselves as privileged compared to most of the world's population.

Even Karl Marx, their most famous foe, recognized the dynamism of the emerging corporations in his own time, and celebrated their coming as the precondition for a better life. Marx dedicated his life to a harsh critique of the new capitalist world in the making, but never forgot that the rising corporation was the engine of a radical new prosperity. Only corporate capitalism, he said, could liberate most of the world from centuries of feudal poverty and despotism, and open the door to the rule of law, individual rights, and opportunity. Marx was wrong about many things, but right in recognizing the deep contradictions involved in trying to humanize the rising market order. For even as corporations wreak havoc on the lives of millions of workers and communities here and all over the world, they are still global symbols of opportunity and the central engine of economic growth on which most Americans depend. Americans now harbor deep new grievances toward corporations. We feel betrayed by their frequently cold, calculated influence on our lives, and fear their growing power and wealth. But a new populism cannot take hold until it's demonstrated that it will not hurt business or the larger economy.

The realistic opportunities for change today lie in contradictory principles within contemporary business about how to remain competitive. While most large corporations have taken the same low road as their robber baron forebears a century ago, many of the same companies are seeking to empower employees, and to decentralize the huge bureaucracies that have traditionally protected corporations from public accountability. The new movements for corporate responsibility, while deeply flawed, hint that cooperation and economic democracy—core goals of positive populism—may ironically be emerging as necessary conditions of business success. Many sectors of business can find a place in the positive populist movement—which is not likely to succeed without their embrace.

Positive populism is a movement that affirms the virtues of business even as it seeks to humanize and democratize it. This creates many conundrums, for it is a movement which can succeed only by tapping the deep personal anger and hurt that corporations create among disposable workers and communities—without demonizing either corporations or their leaders. Positive populism seeks to encourage corporations to take the high road to social justice, but also recognizes that the new moral order we need will not always go hand in hand with maximizing profits.

The change we need will have to be championed by many sectors of the business world, but must be led by social movements whose values transcend making money and profit—including a newly assertive labor movement and vocal grassroots movements in communities across the nation. It must call on the strength of both "insider" and "outsider" populist forces—managers and shareholders seeking to democratize the business system from within, and populist labor and social movements acting from outside the corporation to preserve the ideals of democracy. Cooperation between insiders and outsiders is essential to positive populism, but their relation will be a difficult one, and their strategies not always harmonious. How to reconcile them is one of the great challenges of the twenty-first-century progressive agenda.

Since the crisis of corporate ascendancy is both economic and spiritual, so must be the movements that seek reform. Our nation is in need of a transformative movement, one that combines the forces of healthy business, energized workers and unions, and newly activist citizens, in the pursuit of a truly democratic culture. Deep economic and political changes are necessary to achieve corporate responsibility and a society that values people over money. What we need, finally, is a politics of the heart—but one that recognizes that we need more than changes of heart to create a new moral and truly democratic society.

ONE

The End of the Century

On July 31, 1995, the Walt Disney Company, America's most famous entertainment company, announced it would acquire ABC, America's premier news network. A month later, two of America's most powerful financial institutions—Chase Manhattan Bank and Chemical Bank—decided to merge and become the nation's largest bank. Two months after that, Time Warner proclaimed that it was acquiring Ted Turner's Turner Broadcasting Network, thereby marrying the world's biggest media company and the nation's biggest cable system. Just three years later, those gigantic mergers would look almost puny, dwarfed by the 1998 Nationsbank merger with Bank of America, the Chrysler/Daimler Benz merger, and the merger between Citicorp and Traveler's Group, the biggest in history.

Mergers and takeovers, orchestrated by financiers such as junk-bond king Michael Milken, had become the symbol of greed and power in the roaring 1980s. In sheer volume, however, the merger activity of the 1990s makes the eighties look tame. Concentration is a tidal force in banking, insurance, utilities, aerospace, pharmaceuticals, telecommunications, health care, and many other industries. The years from 1994 to 1998 set successive records as the biggest merger years in American history.

While merger mania has periodically seized the American economy, the current frenzy hints at a surprising historical precedent for the current period: the Gilded Age, which extended from shortly after the Civil War to the earliest years of the twentieth century. It was an era when captains of industry and finance such as John D. Rockefeller, Andrew Carnegie, and J. P. Morgan knit American business into national corporate fiefdoms of enormous power. Like today, it was a time of explosive change, fierce competition, and mass mergers, culminating in the famous "trusts" first put together by Rockefeller in Standard Oil.

With the 1990s came a second hint of a new Gilded Age: the revelation that the United States had become the most unequal country in the developed world—with the gap between rich and poor growing disturbingly vast. By the mid-nineties, not only was the gap the largest in fifty years, but as the United Nations reported, "the United States is slipping into a category of countries—among them Brazil, Britain, and Guatemala—where the gap is the worst around the globe."[1]

The Gilded Age, likewise, was marked by the accumulation of great wealth in the midst of overwhelming poverty. While Rockefeller and Morgan were becoming the nation's first billionaires, most Americans, including millions of impoverished immigrants and poorly paid workers, worked twelve-hour days just to stay alive. A hundred years later, America was moving again toward a great divide of vast wealth and mass poverty. In 1998, *one* rich man, Bill Gates, had personal wealth of 50 billion dollars—more than the combined net wealth of the bottom 40 percent of the U.S. population, or 100 million Americans. In 1996, the richest 1 percent of the population enjoyed a median net worth of several million dollars and had accumulated 40 percent of the nation's wealth—the highest proportion since the 1920s. At the same time 40 million Americans—including *one of every four children*—had fallen into poverty, also the highest percentage in decades.[2]

Building a Bridge to the Gilded Age

When President Clinton ran for reelection in 1996, he told Americans he wanted to build a bridge to the twenty-first century. The nation had to prepare for the millennium, he explained. According to the president, entering a brave new world of burgeoning technology meant that we would all have to get on the information superhighway, and travel together across the millennial bridge.

But in a revealing interview at the end of 1996, Clinton hinted that another bridge that we might cross leads straight back to the Gilded Age. Talking with James Fallows in *The Atlantic,* the president spoke of remarkable similarities between the end of the last century and the end of our own. Among the striking comparisons the president described were ". . . labor turmoil, boom-and-bust economies, ethnic changes wrought by immigration of that era and other shocks" that transformed the country. Clinton suggested that just as the Gilded Age saw a shift from an agricultural and craft-oriented economy to an industrial one, today we are "changing our industrial paradigm—we're going from the industrial age to an information-technology age, from the Cold War to a global society." Clinton also observed that, like today, the Gilded Age was a period of contradictions, simultaneously opening up dramatic new economic opportunities while threatening to leave millions of people behind. Then and now, "vast fortunes are being made—people are having opportunities they never dreamed of. But a lot of people have been dislocated."[3]

Clinton's historical speculations deserve serious scrutiny. The great differences between the Gilded Age and the present—including the rise of a large middle class and a vast regulatory state—make clear that we do not live in a clone of the Gilded Age. But the president has hit upon something more fundamental than he was able to flesh out in that *Atlantic* interview. Some of the nation's defining qualities—its corrupted democracy and social Darwinist thinking—seem to have leapfrogged from the end of the last century to the end of this one.

Historian Arthur Schlesinger, Jr., has written of American political history as cyclical. The political pendulum's swing from Gilded Age conservatism to the liberal reaction of twentieth-century progressives to the counterreaction of the Reagan-Gingrich era is part of the picture. But the historical parallels with the Gilded Age go far deeper. They involve seismic shifts in the organization of markets, shocks to traditional notions of fairness and community, the rise of a new culture of greed, and a radical rewriting of the contract between corporations and workers. In both eras, the balance of power in the nation shifted drastically, with corporations gaining great new power relative to contending forces such as unions. Both periods were golden ages of business.

The Gilded Age brought both hope and tragedy. It ushered in the American century, with the United States emerging as the new industrial power that would replace Britain as the guardian of a new world order. Americans—among them millions of immigrants who dreamed of a better future—were never more hopeful about their prospects for prosperity. The booming new industrial economy created by the robber barons—the popular name given to Gilded Age business leaders—allowed many citizens to realize their dreams, and the Gilded Age showed the remarkable potential of American business to harness the resources of the nation.

Yet millions of Gilded Age Americans worked in sweatshops, and the intensity of economic and social exploitation wrought by the robber barons became legendary. The growth of urban slums, the concentration of new monopoly power in the trusts, and the scandalous corruption of politics made many turn-of-the-century Americans feel their nation was losing its democratic promise.

Today's new Gilded Age order stems from an economy fueled by revolutionary advances in market scale and technology. It is dominated by dynamic corporations larger than any in history, and run by men possessed of power, business networks, and personal fortunes far exceeding those of the robber barons. It is defined by a democracy in which popular sovereignty is eroding. And it features a culture in which old-fashioned "virtues" like laissez-faire economies, social Darwinism, and accumulation of wealth are enjoying redoubled popularity. Despite some central differences, the new order and the old reveal parallels at almost every level.[4]

Robber Barons of the Information Age

Every year a group of America's most influential men assemble at the ranch of financier Herbert A. Allen in Sun Valley, Idaho. Most are heads of famous global media and technology corporations: Microsoft's CEO Bill Gates, Sumner Redstone, chairman and CEO of Viacom, Michael Eisner, CEO of Disney. They are part of a group of business leaders who have been dubbed the "new establishment." "Call them the swashbucklers of the Information Age," writes journalist Elise O'Shaughnessy, "or the highwaymen of the infobahn: they are the leaders of the computer, entertainment, and communications industries, whose collective power and influence have eclipsed both Wall Street and Washington."[5]

The new establishment actually extends well beyond the elites of Hollywood, Silicon Valley, and the telecommunications world. It includes Wall Street financiers and the chiefs of giant industrial Fortune 500 companies such as GE and GM. It encompasses descendants of the robber barons themselves, including some members of the Ford, DuPont, and Rockefeller families, many of whom remain part of the Forbes 400 list of richest Americans and still run their ancestral companies, banks, or foundations. The new establishment is neither so new nor so exclusively information-oriented as popular accounts have suggested. Today's most powerful corporate leaders from across the economic spectrum have joined forces in such influential groups as the Business Roundtable. The unofficial executive committee of the new establishment, the

Roundtable includes the heads of the largest U.S. banks, industrial conglomerates, insurance companies, retail chains, and utility corporations—and together they are closely aligned with policy elites and political leadership in every branch of government.

In matters of personal style, the new elites are hardly the charismatic masters of their age that the robber barons were. Today's corporate leaders tend to be anonymous, gray-suited organization men, absorbed within an institutional system larger and more powerful than themselves. While they have great power, their charisma and personal ownership stakes matter far less than those of a Rockefeller or a J. P. Morgan, and they are to a far greater degree the captives of financial markets they do not fully control and of the interlocked business networks over which they preside. The personal power of the robber barons has been subsumed into a global corporate web. While they speak the language of entrepreneurialism, the new business elites are far from the rugged individualists who strode across the Gilded Age landscape.

And yet these two sets of business barons have much in common. Like the robber barons, today's business elites have radically restructured the economy in ways that promise both dynamic technical progress and frightening social polarization. Despite the current rhetoric of social responsibility, they, like their descendants, are presiding over supercharged corporate systems that will be remembered for their irresponsibility.

Like today's new business leaders, the robber barons saw the possibilities of a new economic order and took dramatic action to bring it about. Carnegie, for example, though ruthless in his cost-cutting and technological restructuring strategies, also deserves credit for almost single-handedly midwifing America's steel industry into becoming the world's dominant producer. Such enduring economic achievements—including laying the economic foundations for a prosperous middle class and a century of growth—help explain why the robber barons are admired by many Americans as icons. Though they came to symbolize greed and power to much of the nation, their legendary business success has nevertheless become part of the American creed.

It is the transformation of their society—not just its economy but its politics and its morals—that is the most important parallel between the Rockefellers and Carnegies and America's new corporate establishment. Beyond their economic exploits, the barons of steel, oil, and pork remade the politics and values of their era. "Like earlier invading hosts arriving from the hills, the steppes, or the sea," a leading Gilded Age scholar wrote in the 1940s, the robber barons "overran all the existing institutions which buttress society. . . ." We must understand "how they took possession of the political government, of the School, the Press, the Church, and how finally they laid hands upon the world of fashionable or polite society . . . as well as over the manners and opinions of the people." The same holds true of business leaders today—and, more precisely, of the great corporations they run. Their economic power is linked to far-reaching political influence, and they have had remarkable success in imprinting pro-business values on our collective conscience.[6]

The Corporate Web, Then and Now

President Rutherford B. Hayes, himself a former railroad lawyer, exclaimed in amazement about the Gilded Age: "Shall the railroads govern the country or shall the people govern the railroads? . . . This is a government of the people, by the people and for the people no longer. It is a government of corporations, by corporations and for corporations." In the Gilded Age, and again in our time, the corporation has become the country's economic engine, private government, and holy shrine.[7]

For all practical purposes, late-nineteenth-century leaders in-

vented the modern corporation. They radically changed the pre–
Civil War institution they inherited, turning it into one of the
world's models of efficiency. In conjunction with the government and the judicial system, Gilded Age elites shifted constitutional powers from the public to corporations and their leaders—a
legal and political transformation that continues today in subtle
yet alarming ways. The result was a tension between corporate and
popular sovereignty that exploded violently in epic riots and
strikes at the end of the last century—but is being played out today largely off the public radar screen.

Then as now, corporate elites cooperated to plan joint economic
initiatives and worked together to influence legislation. One of today's corporate leaders acknowledges that most of them "talk to
each other or have a meal with each other all the time, whether
they admit it or not. They are engaged in a constant dialogue."
This is more than idle chatter: their intricate network of connections constitutes what is, in essence, a new worldwide corporate
web.[8]

Corporations, at base, are legal devices for concentrating capital
of the many in the hands of the few. Today as in the Gilded Age,
though, capital is concentrating furiously, beyond the limits of
any individual corporation. Merger mania is just the most extreme
symptom of a much broader dynamic that joins corporations into
far-flung networks of economic and political cooperation. The new
corporate web has unprecedented, intriguing potential to create a
new global family of all peoples. But by turning dominant competitors into increasingly intimate partners, it suggests a Gilded
Age–style set of dangers as well.

The corporate web of today is a byzantine mix of interlocking
board directorships, strategic alliances, and contracting networks
that link virtually every Fortune 500 corporation with every
other. John Malone, CEO of TCI, one of the great cable and media giants, describes his relation to Rupert Murdoch as that of
variously "competitors or partners or co-schemers." What bonds
them, says one veteran observer of America's leading executives,

"is a sense of interlocking ventures and relationships . . . they're inextricably tied with one another because of the deals they've made."[9]

The Gilded Age saw the formation of the first great corporate web. Rockefeller sat on thirty-seven corporate boards, Morgan on forty-eight. Railroad barons such as Commodore Vanderbilt and Jay Gould constantly realigned themselves with each other and with financiers like Morgan in shifting alliances to gain competitive advantage, corner the market, and advance their collective power. The trend was toward ever-larger systems of alliance, building toward huge systems of concentrated power. The culmination came with the marriage of the Morgan and Rockefeller corporate families at the beginning of the twentieth century. By 1912, the Gilded Age web involved 341 interlocking directorships linking more than a hundred of America's top corporations, including Standard Oil, U.S. Steel, Chase National Bank, AT&T, Westinghouse, General Electric, and the country's leading railroads.[10]

Today's new corporate web, like the corporate network a century ago, expands economic cooperation while concentrating corporate power. It can increase both efficiency and profits, and has the potential to create a socially useful form of industrial planning. But as in the Gilded Age, it is also an instrument for controlling markets and leveraging political power for business ends.

Executives today, as in the Gilded Age, constantly reshuffle and expand their partnerships in the corporate dance for power and market share. As financier Herbert Allen says, "It's no different than fighting over railroads." A colleague speaks of John Malone as a new J. P. Morgan, driven by the philosophy that "I'm going to have a piece of everything. Some of it may not work out, but I'm going to have a piece of everything." The fallout for the rest of the population, as in the Gilded Age, is more ambiguous. The new entangled giant corporations bring the promise of wealth in the context of permanent economic insecurity and mass poverty.[11]

Economic Insecurity, Poverty, and the Assault on Labor

As outgoing labor secretary Robert Reich was leaving Washington in 1997, he wrote enthusiastically about the 11 million new jobs created during the first Clinton administration. As in the 1890s, America's leaders could take pride in the economic resurgence of America after many had forecast its collapse. Reich argued strongly that the new global order led by American corporations would bring a new century of affluence.

But Reich was clear about the social costs of success. "The unfinished agenda is to address widening inequality. Almost 18 years ago, inequality of earnings, wealth and opportunity began to increase, and the gap today is greater than at any time in living memory." As Reich commented on the breakdown of the old corporate contract that held that "as companies did better, their workers should as well," he plaintively asked, "Are we, or are we not, still in this together?"[12]

The sad answer is no. The social disuniting of America is the most important parallel between the Gilded Age and today. We may have a much larger and more affluent middle class today, as well as some safety nets that did not exist a hundred years ago. America's class structure and standard of living have changed dramatically. But once again today we are in the grip of a perverse form of economic growth that polarizes America into increasingly separate worlds.

The richest 1 percent of Americans today own more than $4 trillion in assets, enough to pay down the national debt themselves. The bottom 80 percent own only 6 percent of the nation's financial wealth. To find a comparable wealth gap in American history we have to go back before the New Deal era, when new policies were implemented to alleviate poverty and inequality. A leading scholar at the turn of the last century concluded that the poorest "seven-eighths of the families hold but one-eighth of the national wealth, while but one percent of the families hold more than the remaining ninety-nine percent." The 1890 census data suggested that the richest 1 percent of Americans owned 54 percent of national wealth, compared to about 42 percent today.[13]

Wealth became the great corrupting symbol of the Gilded Age, with robber barons, such as the Vanderbilts, Rockefellers, and Fricks, aping the lifestyles of European aristocrats. Their estates were replicas of palaces like Versailles; at their parties one might see "monkeys seated between the guests, human gold fish swimming about in pools, or chorus girls hopping out of pies."[14]

Richard Hofstadter writes that the Gilded Age's wealth and economic dynamism were achieved at "a terrible cost of human values. . . . The land and the people had both been plundered." In slums like Pittsburgh's Painter Mill, people cooked in dark cellar kitchens in houses without ventilation or drinking water. Neighborhoods in New York City had higher population density than that of Bombay, the most densely populated city in the world. More than 80 percent of the Gilded Age workforce was poor.[15]

Today, while the nation's official poverty rate is only 15 percent, it is much higher than in any Western European country or Japan. The parallel with the Gilded Age is especially notable in the huge scale of child poverty, with a million children expected to become newly poor as a result of welfare reform. Dr. Deborah Frank of Boston City Hospital reports that it has become common in the city to see malnourished poor infants "whose mothers were diluting their formula with water because they couldn't afford more."[16] The main cause of poverty, as in the Gilded Age, is not unemployment so much as very low wages; 70 percent of today's poor have jobs. The corporate social contract, while far more protective today, is moving back, as Reich hints, toward the Gilded Age model. The pattern includes not only low wages but the creation of a disposable workforce, harsh working conditions, and a relentless assault on unions.

The bloody 1894 strike at Carnegie's Homestead Steel, which dealt the labor movement a crushing defeat, rightly became a notorious symbol of the Gilded Age, much as President Reagan's

1981 busting of PATCO, the air traffic controllers' union, came to symbolize a new union-free era a century later. After destroying the Homestead union, Homestead's chief executive officer, Henry Clay Frick, sent an exuberant cablegram to Carnegie: "We had to teach our employees a lesson, and we have taught them one that they will never forget. . . . Do not think we will ever have any serious labor trouble again." Carnegie, the sometime robber baron idealist who ten years earlier had angered other robber barons by his acceptance of unions, joyously wired Frick: "Congratulations all around—life worth living again."[17]

The aspiring middle class of 1900 was full of hope for the future, but it was also a very anxious class. It could prosper in booms but in other times its members were not even assured of food or lodging. John "Bet-a-Million" Gates—head of the Steel and Wire Trust—introduced the idea of the "disposable worker" a century ago, laying off thousands of workers during periods of prosperity to create fear in his labor force. Gilded Age workers, like millions of employees today, could never feel confident that their jobs would be there tomorrow.[18]

The consequences for workers of the Gilded Age attack on unions were not surprising. Many worked in sweatshops. The life span of a mill worker in Lawrence, Massachusetts, in the 1890s was twenty-two years shorter, on average, than that of the owner. More than 700,000 workers were killed in industrial accidents between 1888 and 1908; "a brakeman with both hands and all of his fingers was either remarkably skillful, incredibly lucky or new on the job." America's working class today is better off by far than its Gilded Age equivalent. But the current assault on unions, the creation of a new contingent workforce, and the tidal wave of downsizing have combined to make contemporary American workers not much more secure than their Gilded Age forebears.[19]

The Best Government Money Can Buy

When President Clinton spoke about today's parallels with the Gilded Age, he did not mention how his own presidency has helped to make his point. Clinton has privately called himself an "Eisenhower Republican," making the balanced budget his highest priority, ending welfare, and announcing that "the era of big government is over." Such Republican goals might seem curious for the Democratic party, but they reflect, as in the Gilded Age, the nature of American politics in a time of corporate ascendancy.

Clinton was elected president exactly one hundred years after President Grover Cleveland, arguably the nation's first "new Democrat." Cleveland and Clinton are Democrats who won reelection only by embracing the national political agenda of big business. In 1892, railroad baron Jay Gould telegraphed Cleveland, that "I feel . . . that the vast business interests of the country will be entirely safe in your hands." Cleveland, for his part, assured corporate America that "No harm shall come to any business interest as the result of administrative policy so long as I am President." He proved himself by repeatedly using the Sherman Antitrust Act to outlaw labor strikes, which at that time were the only recourse for workers seeking to negotiate a living wage. In 1894, in the famous Pullman strike, he sent in federal troops to attack the workers. Said the president "to those who pleaded on behalf of the workers: 'You might as well ask me to dissolve the government of the United States.'"[20]

Politics was safe for business, no matter who ruled. A Gilded Age business leader wrote, "It matters not one iota what political party is in power or what president holds reins of office."[21] The barons had no sentimental loyalty to either Democrats or Republicans because both had become parties of business, a pattern increasingly in evidence today.

At Clinton's second Inaugural, a protester carried a sign calling the administration "The best government money can buy." Even before the sexual scandals of his second term, Clinton was mired in multiple financial scandals, from Whitewater to possibly illegal domestic and foreign White House campaign solicitations. In the astonishing $2 billion spent on 1996 campaigns, Clinton had showed that Democrats could hold their own with Republicans, winning contributions from most of America's large corporations.

The Clinton protester could just as well have waved his sign one hundred years ago. "Washington was a bad joke. Congress was 'transformed into a mart where the prices of votes was haggled over, and laws, made to order, were bought and sold.'" President Grant's administration, known as the Great Barbecue, presaged the Gilded Age administrations to come, blatantly doling out favors to the highest bidder.

Gilded Age politics, according to Secretary of State William Seward, had turned the political party into "a joint-stock company in which those who contribute the most direct the action,"[22] and as today, the corporations had by far the most to give. The robber barons flooded politics with big money. To elect President McKinley in 1896, GOP chairman Mark Hanna, a business leader himself, raised millions of dollars from corporations—then an unprecedented event and a foreshadowing of the scandalous role of corporate money in politics a century later. Beyond filling the campaign coffers, Hanna also virtually invented the hired lobbyist, who came to assume a defining role in the Gilded Age. Bribery and lobbying allowed the robber barons to write legislation and shape vital commission reports or political platforms. Republican senator Joseph Foraker of Ohio got about $50,000 from Standard Oil during the six-month period he spent preparing the antitrust planks of the Republican party.[23]

The robber barons virtually reinvented politics. Had they been only wealthy captains of industry, they would be today simply a fascinating historical curiosity. But because their economic achievements were based on a political reconstruction of the corporation that eroded the sovereignty of the public, they had a profound and enduring impact on American democracy.

Gilded Age politics can be defined simply: It used the language and machinery of formally democratic government to weaken real democracy. The Gilded Age suffered "a government of Wall Street, by Wall Street and for Wall Street," in the heated 1890 rhetoric of populist orator Mary Ellen Lease. While the robber barons preceded Ronald Reagan in denouncing big government as evil, they quietly expanded the intricate web of connections that linked the corporation and the government, and in the process broke down the barriers between economic and political power on which capitalist democracy presumably rested. Corporations became private governments with quasi-public powers, while government itself became a servant of private interests.

The corporate undermining of democracy was so blatant in the Gilded Age that it gave rise to the Progressive Era and its "clean politics" reforms. While hardly hostile to business, Progressivism and the New Deal restored a modicum of democracy, eliminated the most outrageous corruption, and created a Democratic party not entirely under the sway of business.

"God gave me my money."

We live in a period of moral fervor. The Christian Right, calling for restoration of discipline and faith, wields vast power in the Republican party. President Clinton increasingly uses his bully pulpit to call for V chips, school uniforms, and a general return to "family values."

A new rhetoric of personal responsibility is transforming American politics. The discourse of responsibility has become a central part of President Clinton's lexicon: We all must take responsibility for our own lives, he argues. The focus is on each individual's moral development. This new ethic is seen by many to offer the hope, in this most materialist of ages, of a great moral awakening.

The new politics of responsibility has both liberal and conservative poles. Among liberals, it is associated with personal growth, the revival of civil society, and a grassroots renewal of blighted neighborhoods and a return to community-level democracy. Among conservatives, it takes a more traditional focus on religious revival and a new entrepreneurship. The almost messianic quality of this vision among mainly conservative officials in Washington invests their efforts to cut off welfare with a sense of moral rectitude: The poor should take responsibility for themselves, the argument goes; America's great social programs, including Social Security, should be privatized. Now it will be each person responsible for herself or himself.

Such moralism is hardly new in American life. It has roots in American Puritanism, and is strongly linked to rugged individualism and the American Dream. The rags-to-riches success story is one of America's most enduring myths—it was already familiar by the time the Horatio Alger stories codified it during the Gilded Age—and it constitutes one of the common threads between the new politics of responsibility and the old politics of business. Particularly in its conservative manifestation, the new morality is linked to broader philosophies of individualism and social Darwinism dominant in the Gilded Age.

Gilded Age culture saturated Americans with the morality of business and individual responsibility, equating wealth with virtue. Robber-baron morality might seem an oxymoron; the greed and corruption of the nineteenth-century industrialists set a new low standard in American life. Yet the robber barons were among the nation's most moralistic leaders. They draped themselves in the lofty rhetoric of social Darwinism, which framed the workings of the free market as a blessing from God and subjected the unwashed poor to a religion-fueled moral indignation. John D.

Rockefeller, for example, readily used Darwinist language: "The growth of a large business is merely a survival of the fittest . . . it is merely the working-out of a law of nature and a law of God." Rockefeller could conclude that "God gave me my money."

Social Darwinism dominated the thinking of the Gilded Age. It made poverty, competition, and exploitation all part of the natural struggle for existence. Said one railroad baron, "Society as created was for the purpose of one man getting what the other fellow has."[24] Social Darwinism and rugged individualism intertwined to create a theology that gave spiritual meaning to the terrible gulf between rich and poor. The robber barons' conversion of their own ill-begotten wealth into a symbol of God's favor, and reading of God's mysterious purposes into the misery of the poor, was the great spiritual accomplishment of a passionately commercial and otherwise notably nonspiritual age. It helped engender the public worship of wealth and acceptance of poverty that is among the cruelest of the robber-baron legacies.

Social Darwinism comes to us today in far more nuanced terms. President Clinton is more communitarian than rugged individualist. His "I feel your pain" style of moralism has little resonance with the robber-baron approach. Clinton's style is therapeutic rather than punitive. He urges responsibility for one's fate as a means of personal growth, not as divine retribution.

Even the Gingrich Republicans, the most militantly social Darwinists of contemporary politicians, are careful to blame poverty not on God but on the welfare system. Republican representative Dan Mica of Florida brought this transformation home in a single image: Hailing the looming demise of welfare, he nodded to the familiar sign "Don't feed the alligators," suggesting that any poor family, like a family of zoo-bound alligators, should be able to feed itself when left to fend for itself. The open view of many social Darwinists in the Gilded Age had been that the poor would simply die off; today, more politically canny figures such as Mica exhort the poor to liberate themselves from their politically created dependency to exercise their God-given potential.

Today, as in the Gilded Age, we live in a world where a morality of personal responsibility rubs shoulders with a culture of greed and of flagrant social irresponsibility. Now as then, business has shed its collective responsibility for employees—just as government has for its citizens. Yet this threat to the common good is organized in the name of nurturing responsibility itself. The politics of personal responsibility offers a public moralism that does not disturb the culture of greed or existing relations of power. Making money is again a sign of personal responsibility while the failure to do so suggests a moral lapse.

The specter of moral breakdown that permeates our own times also lingered nearby during the Gilded Age, a sure product of the cynical rhetoric of personal responsibility and the erosion of public hope for social change. Yet such demoralization never gripped much of the population in the Gilded Age, an era of explosive rebellion by labor and populist movements. The populist and labor movements of today are quieter, less incendiary—yet they are resurfacing, and they are, once again, a source of hope.

T W O

The Curse of the Robber Barons

I recently took my Russian in-laws to Newport, Rhode Island, where with thousands of other tourists we marveled at the summer palaces of the old nineteenth-century industrialists. We toured the Breakers, the famous summer home of the Vanderbilts, with its seventy-eight rooms, twenty-three bathrooms, and beautiful terraced verandas overlooking the ocean. Commodore Vanderbilt and his sons, the railroad barons who built the New York Central Railroad and a vast shipping empire, were the second richest family of the Gilded Age. Their wealth in the 1890s amounted to about $6 billion in today's dollars, a paltry sum compared to Bill Gates's $50 billion fortune, but nonetheless startling when one recognizes that 90 percent of the Vanderbilts' fellow Americans lived on the edge of poverty.

A different but still entertaining tour might have pointed out the astonishing parallels between the world of corporate ascendancy that the robber barons built and our current social order. The Gilded Age is a splendid mirror of our own times. But corporate ascendancy today has its own unique features. While headed by powerful and fabulously wealthy individuals such as Bill Gates, the core of our new system is institutional—vast global corporations allied with national governments—that collectively shape our dreams and seek to enforce a business-dominated agenda on all sectors of society.

There are many other changes since the Gilded Age. We now have a vast federal regulatory government that the robber barons didn't confront. Though the federal regulators—recruited disproportionately from the industries they regulate—often seem like foxes in the henhouse, they are a significant counterweight to big companies. Regulation has not stripped away corporate power, but it has curbed corporate autonomy and changed business ideology.[1] And though they are under siege today, there exist now new working and middle classes that enjoy legal rights and entitlements unknown to Americans in the Gilded Age. Middle-class movements—ranging from feminism to environmentalism—have presented twentieth-century corporations with a set of legal, judicial, and political challenges that the robber barons never had to worry about.

Nonetheless, the revolution of the 1980s and 1990s has been a shift in the balance of power back toward the Gilded Age model. Our society is losing its crucial ability to put a check on the encroaching corporation.

Countervailing Power

In an influential book, *American Capitalism,* published in 1952, John Kenneth Galbraith tried to come to terms with the rise of the few hundred huge corporations which already dominated the economy forty years ago: "The comparative importance of a small number of great corporations in the American economy cannot be denied," Galbraith wrote. "In principle the American is controlled, livelihood and soul, by the large corporation"; yet in practice, he continued, the American "seems not to be completely enslaved . . . the danger is in the future; the present is still tolerable." In the 1950s, tyrannical corporate power had for the moment ceased to be an immediate danger—because of the rise of countervailing power, which the giant corporations themselves had called into being.[2]

Galbraith's discussion of countervailing power, though imperfect, offers an illuminating framework for understanding the role corporations should play in our society. Countervailing power, as Galbraith describes, is power exercised by unions, governments, consumers, suppliers, and competitors to keep corporations in check. Galbraith painted the Gilded Age as an era of tragically weak countervailing power, and his analysis offers the tools to recognize today's unnerving parallels. The flaw in his argument comes in his faith that great power inevitably creates great countervailing power—a tenet at odds with Lord Acton's famous view that absolute power creates absolute corruption, and one that blinded him and other great mid-century liberals to key parts of the American story.

The injustices of the Gilded Age, Galbraith argues, had demonstrated the danger of a society in which industrial workers were unprotected by countervailing power. America's corporations yoked workers in such brutal industries as steel, Galbraith writes, to "a twelve-hour day and seventy-two hour week. . . . Not often has the power of one man over another," he exclaims, "been used more callously than in the American labor market after the rise of the large corporation." But no such exploitive power continued as the twentieth century progressed, "for the reason that its earlier exercise stimulated the counteraction that brought it to an end."[3] Unions emerged, Galbraith argues, as one of several necessary and inevitable countervailing powers. "In the ultimate sense it was the power of the steel industry, not the organizing abilities of John L. Lewis and Philip Murray, that brought the United Steel Workers into being." Galbraith concludes that big corporations would always, by their very power, generate their own countervailing power—that uncontrolled corporate power would necessarily contain the seeds of its own demise.[4]

Inevitably, Galbraith argues, an explosive rise of countervailing powers developed in every sector of society during the twentieth century. In addition to unions, the most important countervailing power was that of the federal government. Galbraith did not see government as an intrinsic countervailing force to business, but believed that it fulfilled that role during the Depression. In the 1950s, Galbraith could write confidently that "the support of countervailing power has become in the last two decades perhaps the major peacetime function of the federal government." This was the great legacy of the New Deal: "We can now see that a large part of the state's new activity—the A.A.A., the Wagner Act, minimum-wage legislation—is associated with the development of countervailing power."[5]

The final block against corporate tyranny in an age of corporate giants was the rise of countervailing powers within the business world itself. Even when the rise of corporate empires diminished the role of an assured check on corporate power, huge companies inevitably catalyzed the rise of huge suppliers, retailers, and distributors, all of which would act to balance their power. Galbraith pointed to the rise of fast-food chains, department-store chains, and cooperative buying organizations as examples of naturally evolving, vital, countervailing powers: The rise of Sears for example, checked the power of huge oligopolistic manufacturers like Goodyear Tire, since it "was able, by exploiting its role as a large and indispensable customer, to procure tires from Goodyear . . . at a price from twenty-nine to forty per cent lower than the going market."[6]

Galbraith concluded that countervailing power was the twentieth-century antidote to Gilded Age corporate ascendancy. Adolf Berle, another of America's most influential thinkers about the corporation, shared this view. He also believed that the corporation posed a potential grave danger to both competition and democracy, and that this had been curbed in the Depression and after by the rise of countervailing power.[7]

While Galbraith was primarily interested in how corporate

market power over wages and prices could be checked by counter-vailing power, thus preventing monopolistic extortion, Berle fo-cused on the way countervailing power could check the corporate world's growing social and political power. Berle believed that corporations had accumulated so much of the economy's capital and wealth that they had become, in effect, the central planners in "a more or less" corporate planned economy. This spilled over into awesome social and political power resembling that of the Church in the Middle Ages.[8]

While such formidable power had transformed America, Berle, like Galbraith, was reassured by the rise of countervailing power that he thought inexorable. "Absolute power in any form of organi-zation," he wrote, "is commonly accompanied by the emergence of countervailing power." Berle believed that during the New Deal, not only did the state rise to balance corporate power but that a broader legal framework and public consensus was emerging to civ-ilize and tame the corporation. While it had not yet fully taken shape, he saw that "a counter force which checks . . . the absolute power of business discretion, is beginning to appear in the form of law." Ultimately, he believed that the public consensus would be sufficiently robust that it would encompass business leaders them-selves, and that they would embrace voluntarily the social responsi-bility and public interest demanded by the community.[9]

The Liberal Flaw

The notion of countervailing power is a key to understanding the development of corporate power, yesterday and today. Yet there are serious problems with the countervailing theory developed by New Deal intellectuals. The very concept of countervailing power, as used by Galbraith, Berle, and other eminent liberal theorists, is misleading. It suggests independent spheres of economic and political life which can "balance" themselves and check one form of power against another. The intertwining of corporations and government has become so extensive in this century that the notion of a democratic balancing act has become a dangerous illusion—and one of the cornerstones of the corporate mystique.

The growth of government has boosted corporate power as much as curbing it. Galbraith's and Berle's description clouds the influence that corporations exercise over government as well as the benefits they receive from it. It also tends to distract attention from the extent to which business elites, allied with political leaders, have always exercised extensive power in America.

Since the Gilded Age, public and private power have become intimately intertwined. Government and corporation, each of which wields public powers, have partially melded to create a public/private monolith. Through much of the twentieth century, this joint enterprise has served the interests of both business and political leaders rather than balancing them off against one another.

Galbraith and Berle also share a misplaced faith in the inevitability of countervailing power. Their belief that great concentrated power inexorably creates countervailing force in liberal societies—because of both spontaneous market dynamics and the general population's demand for the ultimate accountability of all forms of power—has not, unfortunately, been borne out by our national history. Countervailing power has never been fully up to the task of checking corporate power; worse, from time to time in our history it has dramatically weakened.

The robber barons' accomplishments went far deeper than a simple shift in the balance of countervailing power. Their new corporate order involved the transfer of sovereignty from the public to the corporation itself, with the state as a joint participant. Prevailing liberal notions of countervailing power suggest that resolving the problem of corporate dominance is a matter of restoring the balance. In truth, what needs to be restored is public sovereignty over the corporation and the government itself.[10]

This being said, the idea of a balance of forces can be helpful in understanding changing relations among corporations, the government, and other leading institutions. Corporation and government are not wedded in eternal bliss; historically they have gone through bruising conflict, if not outright divorce. In periods like the New Deal, as Galbraith and Berle suggest, government has asserted itself as a genuine countervailing force, helping to balance rising corporate power. Other institutions such as labor also assert themselves periodically as aggressive counterforces and change the balance. The balance shapes the spirit of the era. In times when countervailing power to the corporation declines—that is, periods of corporate ascendancy—democracy itself is put at risk.

Today, as in the Gilded Age, countervailing power to business has been severely eroded. Without the emergence of more robust countervailing power, as Galbraith and Berle rightly understood, competition on its own will not be enough to protect democratic pluralism, or, indeed, civil society itself.

The Waning of Countervailing Power

Our present era is defined by three central tendencies. The first is the rise of giant global corporate empires linking producers, retailers, distributors, and suppliers in integrated worldwide business networks. The second is the downsizing of the federal government and its increasing role as an advocate for, rather than adversary to, business. The third is the erosion of labor unions. Together, these trends mark a great decline of the forces of countervailing power that had developed through much of the twentieth century, and a return to a balance of forces reminiscent of the late 1800s.

Decline should not be confused with collapse. As mentioned, today's corporate ascendancy is taking place in the context of a regulatory regime that sets important limits on business even while buttressing its authority. Labor has been in a near freefall of power and membership, but it still wields significant influence. Moreover, new countervailing forces—including institutional investors, giant competitors, and the financial markets, as well as an array of grassroots social movements—are rising to check corporations in novel ways. Nonetheless the countervailing power of the New Deal has been decisively eroded, and no new countervailing regime—despite the abiding liberal faith in its inevitability—has securely replaced it.

The fate of labor is the most visible sign of the end of the New Deal's countervailing regime—a story that neither Galbraith nor Berle could anticipate in the halcyon days of the 1950s. While total membership began declining by the mid-fifties, the influence of unions continued to grow until at least the late sixties. But by the early seventies globalization and automation had already begun to weaken unions severely, and in the eighties corporations and the federal government moved aggressively to undercut labor's remaining power. Arguing that unions were a threat to global competitiveness, corporate leaders engaged in the most systematic antilabor campaign since the Gilded Age. GM, GE, and other trendsetters routinely broke labor contracts, and demanded wage, benefit, and other concessions. High-tech leaders joined them in creating a new industry of lawyers, personnel specialists, and consultants specializing in union-busting and prevention. Universities and hospitals fired organizers and spent millions to tie up certification in legal wrangling. Even when GM was making *concessions* a household word in Michigan, Harvard University was leading a decade-long struggle to prevent clerical unions from getting a foothold in the enlightened groves of academe.[11]

Corporations were getting aid and comfort from Ronald Reagan's Washington. Reagan's devastating assault on PATCO—the air traffic controllers' union—was one of his first presidential acts. FDR used the government to help create organized labor, but in so doing he created a movement deeply vulnerable to the whims of the state's labor bureaucracy. Reagan turned the full weight of that apparatus against the labor movement, appointing regulators to the National Labor Relations Board who sided routinely with corporations on jurisdictional and certification disputes and would make it difficult to contest even blatantly illegal corporate acts such as firing organizers. The Great Communicator also used his bully pulpit to persuade the public, already predisposed to think of unions as corrupt, to see unions as special-interest groups which corrode democracy—a view that many labor leaders contributed to by their own blatant abuse of union power or dues. In tandem with the corporate campaign that pictured unions as subverting competitiveness, Reagan helped turn most Americans into foes of unions, an especially notable achievement while massive downsizing and declining wages were the order of the day.

Combined with changes in market scale and technology, those antilabor campaigns sounded the death knell of labor as a vigorous countervailing force while also signaling the shift of government from countervailing power to corporate booster. Union membership fell precipitously—from its peak of 34 percent in 1954 to its current low of 15 percent of the nation's workforce. The influence of labor plummeted. While there are promising signs of revival in the late nineties, the labor movement has not been so weak since before its takeoff in the New Deal.[12]

The fate of government as a countervailing force is more complex. The Reagan, Bush, and Clinton administrations have all embraced a corporate agenda. Bill Clinton's conversion to corporate priorities such as the balanced budget, international free trade, and privatization is especially notable, since it marked the end of the federal government (under either party) as an aggressive counterweight to business. Nonetheless, the regulatory state remains large and powerful in its contradictory role as a force of both restraint and support for corporate ascendancy. As the two major political parties increasingly act in the interest of business, government's role as an underwriter of business increases, but this has by no means eliminated the regulatory state's countervailing role. President Clinton, who unabashedly solicited corporate contributions and sponsored corporate America's leading policy initiatives, also supported environmental regulation, medical-insurance reform, and family medical-leave programs—all of which were opposed by business. Clinton's administration illustrates mainly the dramatic erosion of government as countervailing power, but also the lingering role of the state as a friendly corporate adversary.

As unions and governments weaken, grassroots social movements are rising, that—if joined with labor and governmental activism—could help create a new countervailing regime. Since the seventies, sociologists have identified feminism, minority-rights groups, and the environmental movement as "new" social movements largely grounded in the middle class. These movements, which might seem unlikely corporate adversaries, increasingly target corporations. In the nineties, minority groups led a series of attacks on Texaco and other leading corporations for racial discrimination, while feminists lambasted the "glass ceiling," the pink-collar ghetto, and widespread sexual harassment in the suites. In 1998, Jesse Jackson went to Wall Street demanding that it was time for America's financial establishment to embrace racial and sexual diversity, and redirect its great coffers of wealth to the nation's dispossessed.

The new social movements have already helped write into law constraints that the robber barons never faced, including laws banning sexual or racial discrimination, affirmative-action mandates, and vast environmental regulation. They have shown that corporations both internalize and often promote electrically charged sexual and racial hierarchies in the larger society. Corporations have created specialized "secondary" labor markets for women and minorities, and even when seeking in good faith to implement affirmative action, reproduce and add new fire to sexual and racial stratification. In beginning to identify corporate power as both gendered and racialized, feminists and minority movements have mobilized opposition that—if linked to a revived labor and populist movement—could shake the corporation to its roots.

Nonetheless, in their current incarnation, the new social movements are an ambiguous and limited countervailing force. Feminists and racial-pride or -rights movements have been far more concerned with issues of identity than economics. Their corporate demands—centered on affirmative action and nondiscrimination—involve fair access to the system rather than systemic transformation. While such demands can change the entry and promotion rules, placing limits on explicit corporate cronyism, they can also subtly legitimate the underlying corporate order, by pitting the sexes and races against each other rather than uniting them around common concerns. Except for small subgroups, the new movements have not challenged corporate ascendancy as an inherent threat to democracy or social justice. Even should they fully realize their aspirations for diversity, affirmative action, and nondiscrimination, they will have barely disturbed a corporate system that already legitimates itself on claims of meritocracy and universalism. If the percentage of female or African-American corporate leaders were to grow dramatically, this would be a major advance. But it would scarcely erode corporate ascendancy, just as promoting more women and African-Americans to the top ranks of the Pentagon does little to subvert militarism.

Many analysts suggest that the power of corporations is today curbed mainly by the financial markets themselves, as they exercise relentless short-term financial discipline on all large companies. It's hardly the case that corporations find themselves stripped of meaningful power or choice, at the mercy of lenders, but the core financial institutions of the capitalist system have certainly become a countervailing force in the corporate world. The financial markets, while servicing corporations, have emerged as an important counterweight to corporate autonomy.

In the Gilded Age, the financial markets were not the countervailing force they are today. Financiers such as J. P. Morgan were capable in the 1890s of simultaneously dominating both the markets and the largest corporations themselves; there were limits to Morgan's power, but he could personally ensure that the financial markets and corporate sector were aligned in ways that are not possible now. Today, massive global expansion of the capital markets and the diffusion of ownership make it impossible for any one plutocrat—or even any group of business elites—to dominate the financial markets or smoothly integrate them into a coherent corporate agenda. The markets now treat individual corporations as ruthlessly as corporations themselves treat workers in the age of downsizing.[13]

There are, nonetheless, significant limits in the 1990s to the balancing power of financial markets. Their motivations, of course, are the same as those of the corporations themselves—profit and capital accumulation—rather than the social values of traditional countervailing powers such as unions and governments. They empower corporations as much as they constrain them, and advance their interests in the economy and in the larger context of American politics. While the relation between financial markets and corporations is complex and imposes powerful constraints on even the biggest corporations in the world, in truth they are interdependent and mutually reinforcing, not fundamentally antagonistic. The new markets evolved to meet the financing needs of rapidly expanding global corporations as well as the growing corporate-ownership class. As the corporations helped bring the new global markets and creative-financing instruments into being, the markets developed power the corporations did not anticipate. Nonetheless, the markets serve the needs of two masters—the corporations and their owners—tolerably well, and neither the financial markets nor the corporations could survive without each other.

America's new ownership class, which is being modestly democratized as millions of ordinary citizens become small shareholders through their retirement plans, is another unexpected countervailing force on the rise. While they hold a minority of corporate stock and share the interests of wealthy large holders in maximizing financial return, they also have social interests as employees and members of their communities. Should they ultimately decide to use their ownership holdings to advance social values, they could play an entirely unexpected countervailing role.

The rise of stockholders, or owners, as an emergent countervailing force is one of the ironic developments of our time. Much depends on whether they exercise their latent powers within the capitalist system itself to humanize it, an astonishing twist on the Marxist idea that capitalism could create the seeds of its own transformation. Marx believed that capitalism would inexorably bring workers together to oppose it, but never anticipated that it would create an oppositional ownership class. Yet such a creative exercise of ownership power may not ever take hold, for the most practical reasons: as corporations cut back pension benefits, economic insecurity of the middle classes about their retirement leads them to act not as revolutionaries but like traditional investors, narrowly, even greedily, focused on making a profit. The new owners can help impose short-term financial discipline on corporate executives, but they are not likely to become the kind of countervailing social force that challenges the fundamental power or mission of business.

Market Scale and Global Musical Chairs

Today's system of corporate ascendancy has emerged because of momentous changes in markets and technology that have weakened our systems of countervailing power. The key change—which also midwifed corporate ascendancy in the Gilded Age—was a quantum leap in market scale. When the size of markets expands as dramatically as it has in our times, corporations inevitably expand along with them—and such breathtaking expansion can severely erode countervailing power. It is the secret of the tie between the Gilded Age and our own time.

The dramatic shift in scale from local markets to a national economy helped define the Gilded Age. Rockefeller and his colleagues were visionaries who saw the opportunities opened up by radically expanded markets. The Gilded Age economy and its business leaders grew up around railroads, the new transportation grid that physically knit together local markets into regional and eventually national ones. The railroad barons literally made a cross-country market possible, and in so doing became the first corporate elite with a truly national perspective. As railroads competed furiously with one another to dominate the new national market, they also developed the national collaborative networks and strategies that would join the robber barons into a cohesive national economic and political force.[14]

Quantum leaps in the scale of the market made it virtually impossible for any one individual to capitalize a firm large enough to compete nationally. The origins of the modern corporation can be found in the needs to raise vast funds to compete in rapidly expanding markets. Corporations also mushroomed in size to capture the economies of scale that larger markets made possible.[15] While corporations had strong local and state roots in the pre–Civil War period, Gilded Age business leaders sought to liberate the corporation from geographical anchors of any form. In a struggle to free themselves from restrictive and inconsistent state regulations, American corporations became, in essence, among the leading champions of the national regulatory state. Though their leaders avidly denounced government, it was, ironically, only the national government itself that could liberate them from their roots and turn them into the footloose entities they would eventually become.

The rise of national markets created unprecedented potential for the accumulation of wealth and power. Corporations gained access to far broader pools of capital, as well as reaping the benefits of a national labor market and clientele. They also discovered the strategic benefits of mobility and the gains that could be secured by pitting one state's workers or government against another's. National mobility was the key corporate resource that Gilded Age business exploited to subvert countervailing power by both workers and state legislatures.[16]

The quantum jump in market scale was not an unmitigated blessing for business. As markets grew, so did competition. Contrary to popular mythology, Gilded Age corporations—with a few exceptions such as Rockefeller's oil monopoly—rarely succeeded in eliminating competition. Established railroads found themselves constantly challenged by upstart firms from other parts of the country, and the competition became so fierce that the railroad barons ultimately became among the first industrial champions of national regulation, in a desperate move to create price stability.[17] Moreover, as the national market grew in the Gilded Age, modern unions, too, began to take shape, their ranks swelled by the horrific treatment of workers; but they lacked the ability to coalesce into a powerful national contender to the new corporations. Labor can never be as mobile as capital, since individual members inevitably develop local roots and cannot transplant themselves from town to town without deep disruptions in their lives, making it more difficult for labor to assert itself as a countervailing power when markets are expanding geographically.

Today's shift to a global economy is a comparable epic leap, and the quantum jump from national to global trade colors our period as vividly as the shift from local to national scale a century ago. While globalization is neither completely new nor by any means fully developed, it is already more debilitating to the forces of countervailing power than the rise of national markets was in the last century.

The Information Age corporation—whether Microsoft, Disney, General Electric, or Chase Manhattan Bank—is designed to grow, communicate, operate, and consolidate on a global scale. Corporate capital's mobility, compared to the place-dependency of individual workers, unions, governments, and communities, is especially striking in the new global environment. Millions of workers in the United States and elsewhere are stranded in ghost towns while their corporate patrons waltz off to Mexico or Asia to hire the cheapest labor in the world. Unions and governments scream but can do little. While the ease of moving capital and the relative immobility of human beings and their protective associations always loomed as the great threat to countervailing power, global capital mobility poses the most serious challenge yet seen to labor, national governments, and other countervailing forces.

The business world designs and controls new information technology that permits instant worldwide communication and lightning shifts of production from one corner of the globe to another. Big business also enjoys unique access to global financial markets and the billions of dollars necessary to manage and dominate worldwide production. The multinational corporation has become less geographically anchored than ever before, prospering with diminishing loyalty to individual workers, communities, and the nation-state itself. Reebok or Nike can flourish by making every sneaker designed for American feet on foreign soil—a phenomenal display of national disaffiliation.

In contrast, the ability of unions and governments to operate on a global scale is limited not only by their inherent ties to place but by immigration laws restricting mobility, and by the existence of rival national unions and governments, all of whom jealously maintain their own territorial authority. Unions can exploit the fax and the Internet to develop new global networks that link workers in different nations, and governments can coalesce in international bodies to regulate global commerce. But neither the AFL-CIO nor the American government can ever go global in quite the way the multinational corporation can.[18]

The rise of the national economy a century ago was not as great a threat to countervailing power, because the new national corporation remained on American soil ruled by the federal government. Rockefeller's Standard Oil in the 1880s and 1890s could and did try to bribe and manipulate presidents and Congress, but could not bully them by threatening to leave the country or playing America off against the Kaiser or Britannia. In contrast, the new world economy permits an Exxon, General Electric, or Chase Bank to weaken national governments in ways that their Gilded Age corporate ancestors could not have imagined.

Globalization has enormous positive potential for increasing prosperity in poorer and richer nations alike, but corporations have gained control and created a new game of global musical chairs. By moving south and west toward union-free environments and pitting one state government against the other, the old robber barons had played musical chairs inside America, choking the growth of unions and limiting the regulatory powers of the states. The federal government, however, eventually set limits on the process. It set a floor on the concessions companies could extort and helped to level the playing field through New Deal regulatory and labor legislation that made possible national unions with real countervailing power. Today, global companies pit entire nations against each other, putting overwhelming pressure on unions around the world to agree to cuts in wages and benefits, and on governments to agree to cuts in corporate regulations and taxes. The declining ability of national governments to control the multinational corporation jeopardizes all forms of countervailing power.

Economist Paul Krugman has argued that the actual level of foreign investment and trade remains such a small fraction of the total production of advanced economies that globalization cannot be regarded as the source of the evils commonly attributed to it.[19] True, global investment and trade today, much of which consists of internal shifts of parts or money within global companies, is still in its early stages and not much greater than decades earlier. But merely the credible threat of shifting production abroad is enough to set the stage for a shift in the balance of power between corporations and countervailing institutions. Changes in technology and communications have greatly increased the credibility of capital flight. Even if the threat is rarely carried out, workers and governments recognize that the terrain has shifted, and that any refusal to make concessions on wages, benefits, and working conditions—or on regulatory standards—can be suicidal. When GM outsources a new part or supply contract to Mexico, all GM workers know that their own jobs can be sent across the border. Communities, states, and government leaders understand the same threat.[20]

The prospects of capital flight and global redeployment, then, need only be *credible* in order to make a difference. There is an economic variant of the nuclear deterrent system at work here: Nuclear aggression is deterred only by the threat of nuclear retaliation—a threat that is virtually never exercised but remains credible. Likewise, aggressive strategies by forces arrayed against the corporation are deterred by a credible threat of relocation, even though it may never be acted on.

This threat to countervailing power sets the stage for corporate ascendancy around the world. In America, where unions and government have always been weak relative to business, the purest model of the new order arises. Unions are suffering a more precipitous decline here than anywhere else, with union members now only about 15 percent of the entire national workforce compared to about 35 percent in Germany and more than 80 percent in Sweden. Pundits correctly note that labor's continuing strength has contributed to some economic problems in Europe, but it has also sustained protections for European workers which ensure that the unemployed German is less likely to be poor than many Americans who work. The countervailing role of the federal government, despite its great size and influence, is also fading especially fast here, partly because of the constitutionally sanctioned influence of corporate money on campaigns and legislation which weaves government and business into a new web of fused ideology, money, and power—and partly because of the remarkable success that Reaganites have had in villainizing and downsizing "big government."

Despite the greater historical success of countervailing forces abroad, though, today a tidal wave of rollbacks has begun to crash over much of the rest of the world, reflecting the global character of the new corporate ascendancy. In 1900, as the robber barons undermined countervailing power in America, European labor movements and national governments were building the welfare state. Today, hostility to government and labor threatens Europe as well as America, and the incessant drumbeat by European-based global corporations to roll back wages, job security, and social spending in Germany, France, and even Scandinavia evokes the specter of a European order supplanting social democracy altogether. The explosive French strike against social cutbacks by the Chirac government in 1995 that brought much of France to a crashing halt, followed by the 1997 elections that brought a socialist government under Lionel Jospin to power, is evidence that corporate dominance in Europe will encounter greater resistance because European unions and the public commitment to the welfare state remain strong. Globalization, however, continues to erode the social contract all over Europe. A new regime in Japan is also possible, as the Confucian social protections—such as lifetime employment—that have long distinguished Japanese capitalism also show signs of crumbling.

Technological revolution helps foster the global shift toward corporate ascendancy. The rise of postindustrial technology—notably the computer, the Internet, and the worldwide network of electronic production, communication, and distribution that defines the Information Age—not only fuels globalization but also radically alters the balance of power between business and labor. Commentators reflecting on the demand for labor in an electronic economy speak of the "end of work" and a "jobless future."[21]

As in the Gilded Age, labor-displacing technology has played a pivotal role in decimating countervailing power. Computer-driven automation creates high levels of unemployment and underemployment all over the world and devastates the bargaining power of unions. As the seemingly infinite labor pool in China, India, and other third-world countries massively inflates the supply of labor, Information Age technology shrinks the demand, putting the global corporation in the driver's seat. Critics of the globalization thesis, such as Krugman, acknowledge that the technological threat is real; indeed, most analysts differ only in their assessments of the relative importance of new technology and globalization as forces creating a new corporate ascendancy.

The prospect of corporate-dominated societies arising all over the world—leg by a particularly virulent form in America—hovers over our millennial crossing. If the world can look forward to a new social contract engineered by the world's leading corporations, then our future will be one of free markets, global growth, and individual responsibility; the new order will create development in many nations and benefit many executives, shareholders, and skilled employees; but it will drive down the living standards of countless millions prevented from sharing the huge profits the new system will generate. It will also widen the gap between rich and poor all over the world.

Yet nevertheless there are reasons for hope. There are signs that governments, unions, and new forms of countervailing power will resurrect themselves on the global stage, with the potential to introduce to the globalization process a new and more democratic set of rules and rule-makers. Moreover, global corporations today are increasingly driven by contradictory imperatives, including needs for new forms of partnership with employees, consumers, and other stakeholders that could explode the new regime from within.

THREE

The Mouse, Mickey Mouse, and Baby Bells

Bill Gates tells us that Microsoft exists to put "a personal computer on every desk and in every home." But Gates's unabridged motto, for company eyes only, adds a few key words: "a computer on every desk and in every home, *all running Microsoft software.*"[1] With Microsoft's operating systems running 85 percent of the world's personal computers, the company is flying toward its dream of a globe-straddling monopoly. Erich Schmidt, chief technology officer of Sun Microsystems, puts it succinctly: "Microsoft is the most powerful economic force in the United States in the second half of the twentieth century."[2]

James Gleick, a respected technology analyst, notes that Gates and other Microsoft executives used to joke about their goal of world domination. Now that Microsoft's competitors and the Justice Department's Anti-Trust Division no longer view it as a laughing matter, Gates and his colleagues are more discreet. "Microsoft's people are taught to avoid using the word *dominate* in public discussion of the company's role . . . the preferred word is *lead.*"[3]

Mitchell Kapor, the founder and former chief executive officer of Lotus Development Corporation, does not find the new terminology reassuring. "The question of what to do about Microsoft," says Kapor, "is going to be a central public policy issue for the next twenty years. Policy-makers don't understand the real character of Microsoft yet—the sheer will-to-power that Microsoft has."[4]

Microsoft is the archetypical symbol of the new corporate era. The technological wonders developed by Microsoft win it great loyalty and admiration from many in the public. Bill Gates is a business genius who has done a great deal for America. But when *Fortune* magazine suggests that Gates might have more influence than Bill Clinton, it is time to be concerned about the quiet shift of power now under way—one that could reduce democracy to a playground of global corporate oligarchs.

Controlling communication, regulating commerce, and effectively taxing many on-line transactions, Microsoft is exercising many powers traditionally reserved for government. One of the most profitable and fastest growing corporations in the world, with the eleventh largest market value in the United States in 1996 and the nineteenth largest in the world, Microsoft produces not only software but news services, magazines and books, music and films. Partnered with virtually every other leading American corporation—from GE to Chase Bank to Time Warner—Microsoft jointly runs banking systems, movie studios, cable TV networks, and telecommunication and satellite systems.

It is not the range of products, however, that distinguishes Microsoft, but its potential to lock up the world's new electronic distribution channels. Microsoft understands that we will purchase more and more goods—from news to financial services—on-line, and the corporation is consequently homing in on all forms of electronic commerce. Software analysts foresee a new world in which Microsoft "will soon be in a position to collect a charge from every airline ticket you buy, every credit card purchase you make, every fax you send, every picture you download, every Web site you visit."[5] A top executive in a software company warns: "Basically what Microsoft is trying to do is tax every bit transition in the whole world. When a bit flips, they will charge you."[6]

Steve Case, president of America Online, observes that "the operating system is to a computer what the dial tone is to a telephone:

the thing you have to use to go anywhere at all."[7] No business can communicate, produce, or sell electronically without tailoring its product to the operating system's standards, now definitively Microsoft standards built into Windows 95 and its successors. "There was a moment in history, just a few years ago," observes James Gleick, "when any number of operating systems, real and imagined, could have emerged to run the world's personal computers. That moment is past. The Microsoft architectures have established themselves so deeply in every segment of the computer business that they cannot be displaced, not even by Microsoft." Microsoft's standards are "like the 60-hertz electrical current that flows to every American household." They are the high-tech equivalent of the standard sizes for nuts, bolts, and wheels which once made mass production and the Industrial Age possible.[8]

Control over the Internet is the key, as Bill Gates now sees it, to Microsoft's road ahead. Gates-watchers said they had never seen Gates as revved up as when he talked about dominating the Internet. "The Internet," said Gates at the end of 1995, "is the primary driver of all new work we are doing. . . . We are hard core about the Internet."[9] By 1996, Microsoft had reinvented itself as an Internet company. "People aren't asking anymore if Microsoft will be killed by the Internet," says an industry analyst. "Now, they're asking whether Microsoft will dominate the Internet."[10]

Microsoft executives have not been subtle about their aspirations—whether about its PC monopoly or the domination of the Internet. In the words of senior Microsoft executive Mike Maples, in 1991: "My job is to get a fair share of the software applications market, and to me that's 100 percent."[11]

Ann K. Bingaman, former head of the Justice Department's Anti-Trust Division, acknowledged in 1994 that Microsoft was "locking up the market with practices which every computer manufacturer despised." But in 1995, when the issue of Windows 95's potential monopoly over the Internet came into view, Bingaman refused to take any action against Microsoft. Delaying the introduction of Windows 95 until the resolution of protracted litigation would have had such a disastrous impact on the American stock market and the whole world economy that the Justice Department determined that it would be irresponsible. In other words, the very size and scope of Microsoft's monopoly made prosecuting the company as a monopoly impossible.

Microsoft's relentless focus on locking up the Internet led Bingaman's successor, Joel I. Klein, to try again to tame the giant. In 1997, he and his boss, Attorney General Janet Reno, sued Microsoft for seeking to leverage its PC monopoly into an Internet monopoly by attaching its own Internet browser to its Windows operating programs, a clever move that makes it difficult for Internet rivals such as Netscape to compete. In what may emerge as one of the great antitrust cases of the century, Klein asked the court to hold Microsoft in contempt and even review future Microsoft products in advance for antitrust intent. Ironically, Klein, a man historically friendly to big business and supported by conservative Republicans, came to see one of America's great corporations as the threat to the twenty-first-century free market. But as numerous observers have commented, Microsoft's entrenched PC monopoly probably makes Klein's sally into the fray too little too late.[12]

The Top Thirty: Our Private Government

Microsoft is only one of about thirty giant global companies that sit at the center of the American economy. These companies are the top tier of the group of a few hundred corporations that dominate their respective markets and touch the lives of virtually every American.

The top thirty are among the biggest in the world, but size is not the only reason they stand out. The top thirty represent the pivotal powers in the new world of corporate ascendancy. They are creating the future, for better or worse, and they are unmatched in their ambition, technological dynamism, and global reach. While they are carriers of new ideas of freedom, economic cooperation, and even of the possibility of community on a global scale, they embody the key elements of the new corporate order: vast size, dominant market share, and a new ethic of minimal loyalty to employees, communities, and the environment.

The major corporations are larger than most governments in the world, with revenues and assets ranging up to almost $1 trillion in a single company. Of the world's hundred largest economies, fifty-one are global companies and only forty-nine are nations— and the vast majority of the global corporate Goliaths are American or Japanese. Collectively, the top thirty own assets worth several trillion dollars, perhaps a fifth of the world's total corporate wealth.[13]

Since their decisions affect the livelihood and future of millions of the world's citizens, these corporations function as private governments, a term coined by the influential political scientist Grant McConnell in the 1960s to describe corporate giants and other private-sector associations that exercise great power. This includes market power over products, wages, and prices as well as influence over political affairs and cultural images, fashions, and ideas. McConnell observed that private government melds traditional private economic power with broader quasi-political powers over workplace conduct, public policy, and public opinion traditionally exercised mainly by government itself. But unlike government, the corporation does "not have the checks upon power or the protections for individuals that have developed out of long experience in the constitutional order of the United States."[14]

The "private economic government" of the biggest corporations today, writes Yale law professor Charles Reich, "is a far more important factor in the lives of individuals than public government. Private government controls people by controlling their ability to make a living. In order to get a job, have a career, escape the abyss of being rejected or discarded, people will accept the dictates of corporate and institutional employers, even when these dictates go far beyond anything that public government could constitutionally impose."[15]

Corporations exercise political power over employees by making rules they have to live by. These can include what is permissible in terms of dress, speech, and a way of thinking consistent with corporate culture. Corporations can read employees' e-mail messages and legally instruct workers about when they are free to go to the bathroom (a problem that has led a urologist to write a book about work-related prostate conditions) and, in 1998, led President Clinton to issue an edict calling for new toilet rights). The corporation mostly writes its own internal laws—making it a nation within a nation. Such authority, when restricted to the workplace, might conceivably still be viewed as private or market power rather than public or governmental, even though it affects behavior that is not strictly economic and involves invasive control over people's lives similar to that entrusted to governments. But in addition to this inherently political side of market power, corporations are increasingly involved through trade associations, lobbyists, and campaign financing in shaping the nation's political agenda and legislation, a more explicit and transparent form of corporate public power. Through their ownership of the mass media (such as GE's ownership of NBC and Westinghouse's ownership of CBS as well as a vast radio empire) and increased corporate funding of schools, they are also helping mold the minds of American citizens.[16]

Famed management theorist Peter Drucker has noted that corporations control the access of citizens to their livelihood and thereby determine "the citizen's effectiveness, if not indeed his very citizenship." Drucker marvels at the extraordinary scope of this evidently public power—both within the marketplace and beyond it—as it is exercised by publicly unaccountable institutions. Not only do corporations determine "the lives and livelihoods" of countless citizens, but their decisions "very largely determine the character of our society."[17]

Adolf Berle, the greatest corporate theorist of this century, argued that corporations, exactly like governments, exercise profound political authority which cannot be justified by the traditional logic of private ownership. He did not see the corporation as a government per se, but a nonstatist political institution which—because of the expansive powers it exercised both in the marketplace and the public domain—needed the same checks and balances as government itself. Because he continued to believe in a meaningful separation between the private and public realm—the core American belief that has always been at the heart of faith in capitalist democracy—Berle believed that government and the larger public supporting its authority could balance corporate power and ensure its social responsibility. This liberal faith would ultimately bolster many current popular myths—integral to the corporate mystique—about the compatibility of private government and public sovereignty.[18]

Unlike those of national governments, the public powers of the leading corporations cross national boundaries—and their top officials cannot be replaced by popular vote if they violate the public trust. Corporations have succeeded in diverting the frustration generated by downsizing and stagnant wages into a furious attack on governments rather than on themselves. Terrorist "patriot militias," who bomb public facilities, are symptomatic of the millions who blame government rather than business for their economic stress and in their antigovernment zeal have no inkling of business as a kind of government itself. Only when 1996 GOP presidential aspirant Patrick Buchanan targeted corporate greed did a flash of populist anger spread to big business itself.

Populist anger toward Washington is not entirely misdirected, since public and private government have become increasingly intimate in their joint management of the economy and public life. While the post-Communist ideology of free markets is celebrated everywhere, the lines between big government and big business have ironically blurred in the most capitalist of nations. Corporate money pours into American political coffers while corporate welfare—in the form of public subsidies and tax breaks—has become central to the profitability of America's biggest firms. Public and private government remain formally distinct and continue to confront each other with hostility on occasion, as President Clinton's tussles with the big tobacco companies and with auto companies (over air pollution laws) demonstrate. But as in the Gilded Age, our public leaders have increasingly accepted their new role as advocates for our private corporate government.[19]

In the Gilded Age, populists had seen the dangers of the private government that had developed at the hands of the robber barons. While the populist movement sought to build countervailing forces, the size and power of corporations continued to grow in the twentieth century, dwarfing the companies of the Gilded Age. John Kenneth Galbraith and Adolf Berle showed by the 1950s that a few hundred corporations dominated much of the nation's economic life.[20] Since then, public governments have been downsized and more closely aligned with business, unions have declined, and global corporate leaders have lost much of their sense of responsibility for the well-being of the nation. Private government has become larger and more narrowly profit-oriented, while intruding more deeply both into our public affairs and private lives.

The Three Myths of Corporate Disempowerment

Our private government has created a striking set of myths about power. These have such magical authority in today's culture that they need explicit attention before we get down to the business of showing how America's most powerful corporations help rule the economy and much else.

Americans have been schooled to deny the existence of overwhelming corporate power, or to see nothing wrong with it. One college student in a class of mine, for example, announced that he could not imagine Disney and Microsoft, in his view purveyors of everything good about America, becoming too powerful. America's leading companies cast a spell over many Americans, who are charmed by their technological wizardry, mesmerized by their advertising, and often understandably grateful for the products they serve up. Americans have been persuaded that the main threat to the nation is not the growth of American corporate power, but its potential collapse in the wake of relentless global competition.

Three overlapping myths help cloud Americans' understandings of their new private government. One is the view that big businesses are dinosaurs unable to compete with more nimble and entrepreneurial small firms. Influential business theorists and pundits tell us that small businesses are inevitably replacing big corporations as creators of jobs and profits. Big businesses, so the myth goes, are collapsing under their own weight—a remarkable notion in an era of massive mergers and unprecedented concentration of capital.[21] Yet business magazines such as *Fortune* and *Fast Company* routinely tell us that only the small corporation is nimble and flexible enough to prosper in the new economy.

It is true that large corporations are decentralizing their operations, spinning off divisions in many industries, and downsizing employees, leading to a decline in the percentage of the national workforce they directly employ. But the percentage of national profits and sales directly accounted for by the nation's largest companies has not declined, but rather continues to grow. Manufacturing firms with assets over $1 billion, for example, increased their share of the nation's industrial profits from about 50 percent in 1971 to about 67 percent in 1991.[22] The combined assets of the top one hundred American industrial corporations grew from 22 percent of the nation's total manufacturing assets in 1962 to 30 percent in 1993.[23] The number of nominally independent small firms that are effectively under the control of larger firms has also grown, significantly increasing the indirect economic power of the largest corporations in today's networked capitalism.

Economist Bennett Harrison has definitively demolished the

myth of small business resurgence. Reviewing national employment data, Harrison concludes "that the proportion of Americans
working for small companies and for individual establish-
ments (particular factories, stores, warehouses, or offices) has barely
changed at all, since at least the early 1960s."[24] While the largest
firms—those with over 500 employees—are only 1 percent of all
companies, they still employ close to two-fifths of all workers—
and nearly 70 percent within the realm of manufacturing.[25]

Instead of becoming dinosaurs, many of America's biggest companies are getting bigger through growth and mergers, while also
creating global networks of smaller contractor firms under their
control. The dramatic rise of "vertical networks"—the clusters of
companies under the control of a single giant firm like GE, IBM,
or GM—helps explain the paradox of growing big-business power
in an age of downsizing and vertical dis-integration. "Production
may be decentralized into a wider and more geographically far-
flung number of work sites," writes Harrison, "but *power, finance
and control* remain concentrated in the hands of the managers of the
largest companies in the global economy." In other words, vertical networks actually increase the power of giant companies that
are decentralizing and appear to be vertically dis-integrating.
Such networks, which in another form were also a well-known
characteristic of nineteenth-century robber-baron corporate
organization, create what Harrison calls "concentration without
centralization," the illusion of small-firm proliferation within a
reality of power concentrated among the largest corporations.[26]

The unprecedented size of the largest firms is not necessarily a
problem. Growth through expansion, merger, or network affilia-
tion can create economies of scale that reduce prices. In many
cases, growth is necessary to reach global markets and contend
with giant foreign competitors. Large corporations historically
also have had a better track record with employees on wages and
job security and can offer consumers greater conveniences and variety, as the millions of eager customers flocking to Wal-Mart or
Home Depot suggests. But huge companies with sales larger than

the revenue of most countries also can dominate markets and the political lives of nations themselves. Before concluding whether the trend toward bigness is good or bad, we need first to acknowledge that it is taking place so that we can then assess its consequences on workers, consumers, and the public.

A second myth is that new competition is so fierce and technological change so rapid that there is no reason to worry about big-business monopolies and oligopolies. Paul Samuelson suggested in 1996 that "to a remarkable degree by now our Fortune 500 companies have lost their absolute-monarch status within their niches." Not only global competitors, but new upstart domestic competitors spawned by deregulation and technological innovation, are undermining the power to set prices and dominate markets that big companies such as GM or U.S. Steel had only a few decades ago.[27]

Antitrust officials of the federal government have also taken a more relaxed view about competition and the threat of market concentration. The Supreme Court has not heard a merger case in two decades, and—despite a few high-profile antitrust suits such as the one against Microsoft—the chances of government in the mid-1990s stopping a merger are less than one in a thousand, reflecting the new belief that the positive effects of economies of scale and dynamic global markets outweigh the adverse anticompetitive effects traditionally ascribed to monopolies or oligopolies. In his influential book on antitrust, Supreme Court nominee Robert Bork wrote that "Business efficiency necessarily benefits consumers by lowering the costs of goods and services . . . whether the business unit is a competitor or a monopolist."[28] This reflects a new consensus among leading economists and judges that competition may not be necessary if efficiencies are being realized, and that the new global environment will ensure that adequate competition will almost certainly prevail even in markets dominated by two or three rivals. The presumed market efficiency of giant merged firms trumps fears of diminished competition. The new perspective focuses more exclusively on the purely economic effects of mergers and monopolies, without considering the political and social consequences of giant firms with giant market shares. Even Joel Klein, prosecuting the Justice Department's antitrust case against Microsoft, says, "I really view our mission as market driven," meaning that he is not concerned about monopoly per se but about preserving whatever market arrangement sustains "innovation" and "economic efficiencies."[29]

True, technology is racing beyond the capacity of any firm to predict, and competition among global giants threatens the orderly, predictable world that managerial capitalism created in the fifties and sixties. Even a Microsoft cannot anticipate the technological changes bred by the Internet or do away with all of its Internet rivals at home and abroad. Moreover, Japanese competition has undeniably undermined the capacity of GM to set and pass along price increases, while the new Asian and American minimills have eliminated Big Steel's traditional market dominance.

Foreign penetration has clearly changed the dynamics of competition and reduced the market power of even the largest American firms. Moreover, the speed of technological change is blurring markets and constantly redefining who may emerge as a competitor—as when supermarkets begin dispensing stamps and cash, thereby becoming new competitors of the postal service and banks. Even as firms grow larger the level of competition in many sectors remains intense, and corporations are increasingly turning, as they did in the Gilded Age, to collaboration with rivals or to government itself to find relief.

To equate such changes with the collapse or weakening of monopoly power—or to conclude that such power no longer carries danger to the consumer or the citizen—is, however, deeply misleading. While the *global* market share of *American-based* firms has declined in some industries such as auto and steel, oligopolistic dominance—as reflected in the percentage of market share controlled by the largest American, European, and Asian firms—has remained extraordinarily high. In many cases, market share by the top firms has actually increased in both global and American market sectors. By the early 1990s, five firms controlled more than 50 percent of global market share in the consumer durables, steel, aerospace, electronic components, airline, and auto industries. In oil, personal computers, and media, five firms controlled more than 40 percent of the market. In American markets ranging from commercial airlines and aerospace to computer hardware and software to household appliances, three or four firms control up to 90 percent of the market, and market share concentration continues to increase through mergers and targeted growth strategies.[30]

GE's CEO Jack Welch's dictum is that "if any of his far-flung divisions was not No. 1, 2, or 3 in their markets he would sell them." According to Harvard Business School's Michael Porter, the new economy may be making even Welch's version obsolete: "Even No. 3 in any market segment can no longer be assured of survival." Information Age industries require enormous capital for front-end fixed cost investment, as well as for global production and marketing. With their deep pockets, the leading corporations have moved aggressively to specialize in market segments they can dominate, shaping a global economy of virtually monopolized market niches, from microscopic semiconductors to wide-body jet engines. Each of the top thirty companies is a mosaic of hundreds of specialized monopolies or duopolies knit together in a single corporate game plan.[31]

Chemical Bank chairman Walter V. Shipley says his bank, one of the biggest in the world, needed to merge with Chase Manhattan because it didn't dominate enough of its various markets. "When I look back at the old Chemical . . . I shudder to think how vulnerable we were because we weren't a leader in enough of our businesses. But what the Chemical Chase merger gives us is to position us in market leadership across the businesses." His old Chemical Bank was among the top five in America. To become a player in the new economy, you need to be among the biggest in the world.[32]

Oligopoly, as just discussed, does not necessarily imply price control or a lack of competition; we live in a world simultaneously characterized by giant oligopolies and fierce competition—conditions that also prevailed during the Gilded Age. But as one of the nation's most authoritative studies on oligopolistic competition found almost fifty years ago, the "greater the number of sellers, the more likely they are to behave like genuine competitors." Commissioned by the 20th Century Fund, the study's first recommendation to ensure effective competition was to "see to it that the number of producers, industry by industry, is as large as possible" and to see that "they act independently."[33]

Unfortunately, neither condition has been achieved over recent decades, with a smaller number of dominant giant competitors acting less and less independently of one another. The new system of corporate networks is a critical factor. At the same time that they compete, the world's biggest firms are building a dense set of both vertical and horizontal partnerships, alliances, and joint ventures through which they manage the competition in their joint interests. While some of these alliances take the form of outright mergers, many are short- or long-term alliances (sometimes with cross-linking ownerships as in the telecom and media industry) or partnerships (such as the new ten-year partnership between Disney and McDonald's announced in 1996) which allow companies to jointly plan research and development, marketing, and other shared concerns.

In many cases, the leading oligopolistic competitors merge, as in the case of Boeing and McDonnell Douglas, or partially meld, as in the case of GM and Toyota, who are among each other's leading partners and coproducers. Their joint ventures gave Toyota greater access to U.S. markets, while giving GM exposure to Toyota's fabled lean production techniques, an example of how network capitalism can offer benefits for both companies and for consumers. But when the world's two leading producers not only increasingly meld their own operations, but engage in intimate collaboration with the four or five other globally dominant firms, the imperfect competition of all oligopolistic markets can easily become collusion. GM and Toyota still compete, but they share so many common assets and interests that the competition between them is less and less distinguishable from the competition between the various units of GM itself. Even if fierce, this is hardly a form of competition that robustly protects the interests of consumers, suppliers, and the general public.

While the new networks do not typically function like classic cartels engaged in illegal collusion, they serve as a new system of legal price coordination, as when partners United Airlines and Lufthansa are permitted to set fares jointly on the routes they dominate. Delta and United—whose new proposed alliance will control one of every three seats on U.S. flights—and Northwest and Continental are teaming up to control even larger market shares. In combination with traditional oligopolistic practices, including "price leadership," trade-association collaboration, and government lobbying and intervention, the new network capitalism generates a kind of competition entirely compatible with oligopolistic dominance. The new corporate web brings economies of scale and productive synergies but also hidden concentrations of market and political power. Many experts view the disproportionately high profits in industries marked by very high market share concentration as an indicator of collusion and unfair pricing among networked giant oligopolies.[34] Business itself has been even blunter. In 1997, MCI charged that the Baby Bells were outright monopolies using their market choke hold over local lines to tax long-distance companies and consumers with exploitative access fees. The long-distance companies claim that the Baby Bells, by virtue of both their monopolies and their collective political influence over regulatory changes, have been averaging a 30 percent return on investment, virtually double the corporate national average.

The new pattern of oligopolistic networking and cooperation is a type of private central planning carried out by our largest firms. It does not succeed in eliminating competition, nor is it a sinister conspiracy that permits large companies to control their markets unchecked. But the new planning is on a vast global scale, involves new forms of interfirm alliances, and provides a generally unseen strategy of big-firm collaboration—and sometimes collusion—in the wake of new competitive threats. Orchestrated by business leaders who have lost their sense of loyalty to workers and the nation itself, it has become newly threatening to employees, consumers, and communities who remain uninformed about its existence and purposes.[35]

Corporate private planning is part of a broader long-standing system of administered markets in which governments aid corporations in the management of unruly competition. Railroad barons in the Gilded Age turned to the Interstate Commerce Commission when they were unable to quash upstart competitors through private self-policing "pools." While the public thought the ICC was curbing monopolies, it was actually put in place partly by railroad magnates who recognized that only national public regulation could stabilize their industries, set minimum rates, and disqualify dishonest, cutthroat, or otherwise unwelcome new competitors.[36] Today, America's biggest and most powerful companies, such as Exxon or the Baby Bells, continue to use their disproportionate power over politicians and federal regulatory commissions as a vehicle to manage global competition and protect established oligarchic power against both domestic and global competition.[37]

Such private and public planning is largely invisible, while the global competition it seeks to manage is the subject of endless discussion. This helps explain the third and most important myth: that of corporate disempowerment. Millions of Americans believe that globalization threatens the very survival of many large businesses based in the United States. They view them as besieged by global competition and technological change racing out of control—as well as increasingly burdened by government regulation. As a result, we are disinclined to fault them for new corporate practices that seriously hurt workers, such as downsizing and the shift toward temporary work. Rather than worrying about big-business power and its harmful effects, we worry about the very survival of American business.

Corporate disempowerment is not a total distortion. The tides of change sweeping the world now rock even the biggest companies, such as GM, IBM, and AT&T, all of which have come close to crashing on the shoals of swirling markets and new technology in the last decade. Even the top thirty must cope not only with giant domestic and foreign competitors, but with regulation from governments and resistance by employees. In the new international order, corporations have great power relative to countervailing institutions, but they do not enjoy anything like absolute power.

Corporate ascendancy in no way implies corporate omnipotence; nor do the parallels to the Gilded Age suggest a demonic conspiracy among greedy corporate executives with insatiable power-lust and the ability to control everything. Corporations and their top executives are constrained not only by state regulation and public opinion, but by new limits dictated by the financial markets, institutional shareholders, and giant competitors. These new countervailing players, however, while they limit the ways in which corporations are able to exercise their power, in no way challenge basic corporate values or priorities.

The regulatory power of the federal government, meanwhile, limits corporate power, but also preserves and extends it in ways that the public has not understood. These go beyond the management of competition just discussed. In the Gilded Age and Progressive Era, as Gabriel Kolko has shown, big business relied on government regulation to stabilize competition, increase demand, and promote other corporate agendas they could never fulfill on their own.[38] The same is true today.

The subtlest corporate myth may be about the threat of "big government" to corporate power. Government remains the most important potential countervailing threat to corporate power, and business has historically resisted uninvited regulation. But despite all the sound and fury by business today about its burdens, and its genuine opposition to much regulation, corporate leaders in many key sectors continue in private to champion government intervention. The magnitude of "corporate welfare"—involving 300 billion dollars yearly in subsidies and tax breaks—makes clear that the federal government has committed itself irrevocably to the survival and profitability of the largest firms—and that such support has become essential to big business. More generally, the federal government's trade, fiscal, and tax policies are increasingly oriented, now as in the Gilded Age, toward ensuring corporate profitability. This is the defining feature of Bill Clinton's Democratic administration, as well as all recent Republican regimes.[39]

The reigning corporate myths have seriously diverted attention from the reality of corporate dominance and the durability and growing reach of America's largest corporations. The top thirty include some new companies, but many were founded by the original robber barons, and have been around for a century. While globalization and technological change have destabilized the economy, the largest corporations have been able to weather turbulent conditions far better than small companies or the American worker. With their deep pockets, global networks, and political influence, the large corporations have collectively mushroomed in size and strength. The truly disempowered players in the new global theater are small businesses, workers, and their unions.

Getting Wired: Robber Barons of the Information Highway

The top thirty corporations consist of both American and foreign multinational companies in four key sectors. A key sector in the Information Age is the one Microsoft inhabits, encompassing the densely intertwined corporate worlds of computers and high technology, telecommunications, and media. Because these are the companies that wire the world and increasingly control content or "programming," they are the masters of the world's information highway. As such, they occupy a power position comparable to that of the old railway barons, whose control of miles of track gave them a monopoly choke hold on the key distribution channels of the Industrial Age. Information Age wiring allows the new corporate baronies to move minds as well as freight, giving them enormous power over how we think, work, and consume.

Joshua Shenk points out that "common carriage"—or access to all comers—as well as "open architecture," or the ability of any party in a network to access the other—are the keys to an information highway that can truly serve the public. The robber barons turned the railways into proprietary networks by controlling and limiting access until populists and government trust-busters forced them to charge nondiscriminatory rates and take into account the public interest. The weakening of countervailing power has allowed companies today to follow the model of their rail-baron predecessors. While the myth of the information highway as an open architecture and common-carriage system prevails, the reality is that giant corporations in computers, telecommunications, and media are rapidly moving to take proprietary ownership of all electronic communication. They already monopolize huge stretches of the highway and the information that flows through it—with Uncle Sam bending over backwards to help the process along. James Boyle writes that governments are "granting monopolies over information and information products that make the monopolies of the nineteenth century robber barons look like penny-ante operations."[40]

Intel is to computer-chip hardware what Microsoft is to software. With its chips running an astonishing 90 percent of the world's personal computers, Intel's monopoly—which exceeds even that of Standard Oil in the Gilded Age—is projected to make it the most profitable company in America by the year 2000. Such dominance—which led federal regulators in 1998 to prepare a major antitrust suit against Intel—makes laughable the notion of anarchic competitiveness in the information industry. "So great is Intel's market power," writes the *Washington Post's* Steve Pearlstein, "that it is able to strong-arm reluctant computer companies to adopt its new, more expensive and more powerful microprocessors just as its competitors are coming out with a lower-cost version of the old chips." As a former Intel senior manager explains, Intel "has built so many technical walls around its business, and accumulated such a treasure chest of profits, and developed such leverage over the computer makers, that it is really impossible for any competitor to come along and dislodge it."[41]

IBM, while often viewed as a dinosaur, remains the 800-pound gorilla of most sectors of the computer industry, dominating with 22 percent of American computer sales and a 56.5 percent share of the CD-ROM hardware platform market. A huge player in hardware, software, and services, IBM is moving from manufacturing mainframes toward monopolizing cyberspace with its new IBM Global Network. When IBM took over Lotus Development Corporation, CEO Louis Gerstner crowed the world is "coming back our way."[42] Big Blue's new ethos was highlighted by its massive increase in top executive salaries, while shedding a stunning 200,000 workers between 1985 and 1995—a remarkable renunciation of its tradition of lifetime employment, a symbol of America's old social contract.

In late 1995, IBM announced a partnership with Ameritech, one of the Baby Bells. The joint venture reflected the new intertwining of computers and telephones, and the unsung importance of phone wires as prize electronic distribution channels. Because of their special monopolies of connectivity, giant telecommunications corporations sit close to the seat of power in the Information Age. AT&T, the fifth largest company in the world in 1995 and second largest in the United States, rules a 100-billion-dollar long-distance market. It is now poised to dominate global markets worth $3 trillion, even as the passage of the Telecommunications Deregulation Act of 1996 greases the way for it to move aggressively into local service again and cherry-pick up to 30 percent of the local market. AT&T's proposed acquisition of TCI, the nation's largest cable company, in 1998, creates a one-stop communications empire. Bell Atlantic executive Ivan Seidenberg called it the merger of "King Kong and Godzilla."

Ironically, Seidenburg was planning his own Godzilla, proposing to merge Bell Atlantic—which swallowed Nynex in 1997—with GTE, the largest local phone company in the United States. His new Baby Bell would be a telecommunications empire second in size only to AT&T. Even before the new wave of telecommunications mergers, the Baby Bells were among the most powerful corporations in America. In the landmark Telecommunications Deregulation Act, they helped rewrite deregulation on their own terms, steamrolling Washington's most powerful politicians. "Baby Bells," indeed, is an astonishing misnomer for a group of companies that rank among the top fifty of the world's corporations. The new Bell Atlantic will be larger in market value than General Motors. The acquisition by SBC Communications of Ameritech and PacTel creates a company rivaling Bell Atlantic in size, with worldwide phone, wireless, and broadcast capacities. Bell Atlantic, SBC, and Bell South are trolling for foreign partners and acquisitions that will turn them into multinationals with unprecedented global reach, even as they invade new markets at home.

The Baby Bells control 98 percent of the phone revenue in their regions—about $100 billion annually—and jealously guard their monopoly over the millions of lines into homes and offices with the help of their ubiquitous Washington lobbyists, whom the *Washington Post* calls "the Kings of Capitol Hill." The Baby Bells' golden infrastructure, encompassing cable and cellular wireless connections as well as phone lines, is undoubtedly the closest parallel to the railway infrastructure of the robber-baron era; no new product or communication in the next century is likely to go in or out of a business or home without passing in some way across Baby Bell connections.

Deregulation will free the Baby Bells to plunge full tilt into long-distance, cable, and satellite ventures, with US WEST swallowing Continental Cablevision, the nation's third largest cable company, and Bell Atlantic and others projecting full-scale TV and cable programming networks by the late nineties. After congressional passage of the 1996 Telecommunications Act, Ivan G. Seidenberg, chief executive officer of NYNEX, speculated on the global future of his company and the coming merger with Bell Atlantic: "I don't look at NYNEX as being one-seventh of the United States. I look at us as being the center of the whole planet."[43] Seidenberg was overly grandiose, but *Business Week* projects that deregulation may, in fact, "be the signal for some of the biggest mergers of all time," with a smaller number of monster companies—controlling both wired and wireless connectivity—growing out of the current Baby Bells and fusing technology, telecommunications, and global media empires.

The world's leading media companies are increasingly also telecommunications and computer empires, frantically merging and partnering with the Baby Bells, AT&T, and Microsoft as well as with giant cable TV empires to lock up the electronic distribution channels for their news and entertainment programming. Time Warner and Disney—along with GE and Westinghouse, the nation's most powerful media firms—have made fools of the pundits who dismiss giant vertically integrated companies as relics of the Gilded Age. The Time Warner acquisition of Turner Broadcasting in 1996 created the world's biggest vertically integrated media company, one with astonishing influence over both the programming and distribution channels of American mass culture. This new conglomerate subsumes *Time, People, Sports Illustrated, Fortune,* Book-of-the-Month Club, Warner Books, Atlantic and Elektra Recordings, Warner Bros. Films, HBO, Cinemax, the TBS superstation, Turner Network Television, and CNN. The Disney merger with CAP Cities/ABC—like Time Warner's gambit for Turner's global cable empire—was a transparent move to snap up national and worldwide distribution channels. Disney lusted after ESPN for its instant access to over a hundred countries, and gobbled up ABC so that it would never have to worry about whether a network would carry its films or cartoons.

Disney's most alarming power now is over the minds of children. Its influence demonstrates the astonishing cultural power that giant corporations exercise, and the special function of the media baronies in manufacturing dreams. As in the Gilded Age, corporations are not simply economic but social and spiritual powers, notable now for helping form the character and political and cultural sensibilities of our children. *The Lion King, Pocahontas,* and *Toy Story* not only generated some of the most astonishing profits in the history of film, but burned into the brains of the young their most seductive images, fantasies, and morality tales. Toys, coloring books, dolls, and other kids' products featuring Pocahontas, Mr. Potato Head, and Buzz Lightyear fuel whole retail industries—filling the shelves of Toys-Я-Us and magnetically drawing families to fast-food chains like Burger King and McDonald's. The ten-year cross-licensing partnership between Disney and McDonald's, which will expose millions of kids to Disney ads every time their parents take them for a Big Mac, works to hook the kids to both the films and the burgers, much as tobacco companies have used nicotine and savvy ads to hook them on smoking. Says Jamie O'Boyle, who has devoted his career to analyzing Disney's influence, "Kids can keep their play based around Disney's version of American values for most of their childhood," hinting at the ideological as well as commercial power wielded by business.[44]

Rupert Murdoch's News Corporation and Sony join the six leading American-based corporations in dominating both American and worldwide communications. Murdoch's Australian-based News Corporation, which has aggressively exploited its satellite edge to dominate much of Asia, Africa, and Europe, is now also a leading power in American newspapers, publishing, television, and even politics—as the public became aware after the exposure of Murdoch's 4.5-million-dollar book advance to Speaker Newt

Gingrich just as Gingrich was shepherding the Telecommunications Act through Congress. Among the hundreds of famous American institutions owned by the swashbuckling Murdoch—who personifies the will-to-power of the old robber barons perhaps more than any other current tycoon—are HarperCollins, the publisher of the Gingrich book, and such tabloids as the *New York Post,* notable for helping to drag American journalism to a new low.

Sony, paradoxically, is as American as apple pie, the foreign corporate empire on the most intimate footing with the American public. Scarcely any American citizen has not turned on a Sony Walkman, CD player, tape deck, VCR, or TV—and soon many of us will play video games or listen to alternative rock on our Sony personal computers. Sony helped invent the 3.5-inch floppy disk and the CD-ROM, but the company is now launching its own personal-computer empire, leading a new industry trend toward melding electronic consumer appliances and computers. Sony is also moving from hardware deep into the American "software" and entertainment market. Swallowing up Columbia Pictures as well as Columbia, Epic, and CBS Records, Sony owns America's greatest pop culture icons: Michael Jackson, Bruce Springsteen, Michael Bolton, Mariah Carey, and Pearl Jam. It also owns *Forrest Gump, Seinfeld,* and hundreds of other American films, sitcoms, and other programming. Even with big losses in Hollywood, Sony is pioneering huge new American ventures not only in personal computers but in retail and direct marketing, theme parks, movie theaters, and satellites.

The divisions between technology/media companies and companies in other sectors like banking and manufacturing are fading. GE and Westinghouse are vast conglomerates that own major media networks and are among the world's most powerful media and technology companies. Microsoft and AT&T are major players in banking, as are GE and GM. The power of the new market players reaches across the whole economy.

FOUR

Companies That Run America

While Microsoft, AT&T, Time Warner, Disney, and other high-profile technology companies get the most public attention, they are only one sector of America's new private government. Three other sectors round out the new corporate establishment. Each has a few dominant players who set the rules and moral tone not only for their industries but the nation as a whole.

The defining trend in all these sectors is the concentration of capital. Whether achieved through growth, merger, or acquisition, such concentration yields a new scale of corporate power. Prevailing myths mask the realities of the financial, retail and service, and industrial sectors as starkly as they do the high-tech world. Yet even as power concentrates, countervailing powers are rising unexpectedly within financial markets and the new ownership class, presenting a balancing force that—if harnessed by populist forces outside business—could help transform capitalism from within the bowels of the system itself.

Superbanks and Finance Capitalism

As in the late nineteenth century, a dynamic, colorful, and uninhibited financial sector has become the dominant force in the nation's economy. Financial consolidation, which helped define the
Gilded Age, has become a tidal force in our own times. In both periods, mergers among financial institutions have been driven by
revolutionary shifts in economic scale and technology, allowing
the leading banks not only to dominate larger markets but also to
ally with the shrinking number of powerful competitors whose cooperation was necessary to ensure profitability of the larger corporate system. In the Gilded Age, this was achieved by the merger
of the Morgan and Rockefeller financial empires. Today, the leading American-based financial institutions descended from that
original marriage are knitting themselves into tightly integrated
global financial alliances and serving as coordinators of the corporate community as a whole. The financiers at the top are far
removed from the economic and social concerns of ordinary Americans, and are the architects of an overall business strategy that
creates stunning technological growth and record profits in a context of growing economic insecurity and poverty.

The new Chase-Chemical bank—a merger of two historic
Rockefeller family banks—is, at this writing, the biggest American superbank, and the fourth largest in the world. Its growth
through merger typifies both the unprecedented pace of merger
activity that is revolutionizing the entire industry, and the new
cost-cutting strategies that often hurt employees and other stakeholders. The merged superbank immediately laid off 12,000
workers in 1996 and shut down branches in many communities.
The merged Chase-Chemical is one of the world's new financial
powerhouses: number one in the world in loan syndication, trading, and custody.

When Chase and Chemical merged, a financial analyst proclaimed "Today will go down as the greatest day in the history of

banking."[1] But the Chase-Chemical marriage was only one of many in 1995, which went down in the record books as the biggest year of bank mergers in the history of the republic. Since then, the record pace of incessant mergers among the biggest players, symbolized by the mergers between the Bank of America and Nationsbank, Citicorp and Travelers (Citigroup), and the 1997 marriage of Wall Street giants Dean Witter Discover and Morgan Stanley, has threatened to break down barriers that traditionally prevented the development of a single financial monolith. Some analysts forecast that, in the foreseeable future, as few as twelve superbanks will dominate all sectors of American finance. The new Citigroup will be the world's largest financial services conglomerate, with total assets approaching one *trillion* dollars. It could dominate globally virtually every area of consumer finance—including credit cards, retail banking, mutual funds, retirement plans, mortgages, and insurance—and become an instant power in investment banking and trading. A melding of such global supergiants as ING, AmEx, Morgan Stanley Dean Witter, and Merrill Lynch would not match Citigroup's market. Even before the merger with Travelers, Citicorp was expecting to reach a billion customers in the coming decade, and the range of financial services integrated under the Citigroup umbrella defies the legal barriers separating commercial banking, investment banking, and insurance that have protected consumers and defined American banking for half a century.

The financial historian Ron Chernow, a chronicler of the robber barons, writes that Citigroup "alters our sense of scale and boundaries." Even Wall Street executives were said to be "flabbergasted," and famed banker John Gutfreund said "There would be lots of copycats," with enormous pressure on the other biggest players—Chase, J. P. Morgan, and Merrill Lynch—to merge with each other to stay in the game. The idea that the new superbanks violate current law and are viewed by many consumer groups as monstrous oligarchs—Ralph Nader called for congressional intervention to halt this "massive and dangerous concentration of power"—

seemed almost a footnote; the New York Stock Exchange hit its highest level ever in reaction to the Citigroup deal, recognizing that Congress would bend to the will of America's largest financial powers and that profitability would likely explode even beyond current levels on Wall Street.[2]

While consumer groups focused on the prospects of higher prices, the real issues that the new global superbanks pose are much more far-reaching. Not only will they force unprecedented financial consolidation and a rewriting of America's regulatory laws, but they concentrate a level of financial power that can tilt the economy ever more toward what David Korten and other contemporary analysts describe as "finance capitalism." Finance capitalism is dominated by financial rather than nonfinancial corporations and reifies the pursuit of money gains over the making of useful products. Capital becomes a paper commodity increasingly unrelated to production, and the profitability of stock markets and financial corporations becomes increasingly disconnected from the real economy. In finance capitalism, money markets become the dominant economic institution, financial assets grow far more rapidly than nonfinancial assets, and speculative finance, involving currency trading, hedge funds, and derivatives, tend to overwhelm productive investment serving the real needs of people.[3]

The new superbanks help shape a worldwide financial capitalism in which global money markets and short-term speculative cross-border transactions overshadow all other economic activity. Trillions of dollars managed by the superbanks swirl around the world daily in the currency and money markets, seeking quick leveraged financial returns while dwarfing the amounts of direct foreign productive investment by nonfinancial corporations. "For every $1 now circulating in the productive world economy of real goods and services," writes Korten, "it is estimated that there is $20 to $50 circulating in the world of pure finance—'investment' funds completely delinked from the creation of real value."[4] The high-flying world of derivatives, currency speculation, and commodity gambling which brought down Barings Bank and led to the bankruptcy of Orange County is a key link to the Gilded Age legacy. Kevin Phillips notes that if J. P. Morgan could be reincarnated today, he would "want to come back as head trader at Goldman Sachs or CS First Boston."[5]

In markets dominated by long-term investment, stock prices may closely mirror underlying real value. But as trading patterns become "hotter" and turn over nearly the market's whole value in a matter of weeks or months, the money markets look more like a Las Vegas gambling operation than an efficient market. Isolated speculators can do little damage, but when very short-term turnover becomes the norm, investors have little time or incentive to consider long-term value, and the markets evolve into what John Maynard Keynes called "a whirlpool of speculation," or what some call today's "bubble economy."

When stock prices soar, the public imagines that corporations are becoming more efficient and productive. But since corporations increasingly raise money for investment through retained profits, the rise in their share prices on the markets does more to increase CEO compensation by sending stock options sky-high than it does to increase the productive capacity of the company. A corporation's credit rating with the superbanks—and thus its ability to borrow—may rise along with its share value, but manic buying or rapid trading of its stocks does not change the company's underlying economic health, any more than speculative purchase of a nation's currency changes its economic productivity. While the markets and superbanks do provide new flexible financing instruments for the general population and for nonfinancial companies, their larger impact is to increase the stake and influence of those—the wealthy and superbanks themselves—who make money mainly by trading on money itself.

The new financial markets and the superbanks have evolved together as part of a radical deregulation of the nation's financial system. In the New Deal, the Glass-Steagall Act and other linchpins of a new highly regulated banking order protected consumer bank deposits from some of the speculative losses that had ruined millions of Americans in the Great Depression. Over the last fifty years, memories of the great crash have faded, and a new era of deregulation has emerged that puts many more millions of Americans at risk. The money markets exploded in the last decade through the vehicles of mutual funds and brokerage houses that were not subject to the same tight regulatory controls as commercial banks—and their new array of exotic global speculative instruments resisted close federal monitoring. As commercial banks sought to capture the high-flying action in the money markets, they had to innovate, merge with, or acquire far more risky operations, creating the prototypes of the superbanks that today unify all financial services under one roof. The superbanks are the institutional embodiment of the deregulated global markets, shifting banking from the stable regulated regime of the post-Depression era to the realm of go-go finance seeking instant bang for the buck.

As in the Gilded Age, that earlier era of national financial capitalism, the largest financial institutions have become architects of a new order. Money mediates virtually all social relationships, both within and outside of the economy, and becomes the triumphal, corrupting symbol of the age. The worship of money—symbolized by the hypnotic focus of the nation on the stock market—becomes the new religion. Finance capital, today and in the Gilded Age, creates a surreal obsession with money and money markets. The value of patient production in early America yields to an ethos of pursuing money without any regard to making something useful. Personal identity shifts from the sense of self as life-long worker to that of short-term investor.

As financial assets become the major form of capital, the superbanks' ability to determine the allocation of credit increases their power to shape the entire system of social stratification, concentrating their resources and creative financing products to serve predominantly those already wealthy. Ultimately, the problem with the superbanks is not just their size, but their legitimation of a cultural ethos of greed, and their concentration of power allowing them to dictate increasingly not only to governments and communities but to nonfinancial corporations as well. As we will explore shortly, they become along with the financial markets an ambivalent countervailing force to the rest of the corporate world, simultaneously turning the entire corporate system toward short-term profits while, contradictorily, bringing into the arena new and more diffuse owners with the potential to introduce social values into the calculus of the market itself.

Wall Street investment banks, led by J. P. Morgan, were the dominant force in finance a century ago. Today, while the line between commercial and investment banking has blurred with the emergence of the new superbanks, the leading investment banks—epitomized by Merrill Lynch and Goldman Sachs—are central to three aspects of contemporary finance. They arrange, and profit hugely from, the mergers and acquisitions frenzy; they play a leading role in managing the domestic and international money markets; and they house the small community of leading financial analysts who define the norms of money management that imperil the health of society.

Merrill Lynch and Goldman Sachs, at this writing expected to merge with J. P. Morgan or another giant, increasingly compete with other superbanks as full-service one-shop financial supermarkets, retailing mutual funds, and increasingly becoming traders and speculative investors. Merrill Lynch is the largest investment bank, with about 20 percent of the American market in 1993. It is the leading underwriter in corporate stock offerings and in virtually every debt market, the third largest mutual funds manager behind Fidelity and Vanguard, and a huge player in domestic and international speculative trading. Goldman Sachs, one of the most profitable firms on Wall Street, follows Merrill as the second largest investment bank and, like Merrill, is moving toward full-line brokerage services for both the general public and high rollers.

The financial analysts employed on Wall Street personalize the immense power and partially countervailing force exercised by the investment banks. As the high priests of the economy, the analysts are increasingly in a position to dictate standards of corporate performance, and they provide the assessments which can mean life or death for big companies. A new, upstart elite on which leading executives have become frustratingly dependent, they act as a force of severe discipline on corporate behavior, and helped create the restructuring revolution of the 1990s. Harvard Business School's Joel Kurtzman points out that under their mathematical formulae and quantitative market models lies a stark new ethos: "American corporations exist for their shareholders. Period." The analysts are helping transform banks into institutional investors enforcing the crystalline new logic of shareholder value. The interests of workers and communities are not part of their equation.

Wined and dined by the giant corporations who curry their favor, compensated in the millions for their reputations and special brand of expertise, the leading Wall Street analysts live in a rarefied ghetto of the world's business elite. Their sheltered lives and intimate connections to the world of top corporate executives may explain both their fundamental affinity with corporate values and their indifference to the plight of the most vulnerable Americans. Their computer models keep telling highly profitable banks and blue-chip corporations to cut jobs during an era of unemployment and declining wages. A former Goldman Sachs analyst, quoted after Xerox announced 10,000 layoffs leading to a 7 percent increase in its stock prices, admitted that the analysts saw the white-collar workers "in the kill zone" for the 1990s. "The Street is convinced there's 15–20 percent more fat that can be cut off of the Fortune 500, and they see all of it in those white-collar jobs."[6]

Other People's Money

Other novel superbanks such as Fidelity, in essence, have become the principal shareholders of the American economy. These new entities sit at the intersection of corporate America and a greatly expanded ownership class. They are both the agents of share owners, and huge corporations in their own right. They are part of the corporate establishment, but also serve as an ambiguous countervailing force in their capacity as managers of other people's money.

In the Gilded Age, the shareholders and corporate elites were more or less melded into the same group of robber-baron owners. Today, the diffusion of ownership has separated financial ownership and corporate management, creating the possibility of countervailing tensions between them. The institutional investors speak for both groups, occupying a vital institutional niche that did not exist a century ago. They mediate between owners and corporations, and between owners and the financial markets. They symbolize the pure financial interests of the markets, but can speak also for nonmarket values reflecting the new social base of the ownership class.

Institutional investors manage the money of a rapidly expanding ownership community, which represents a far larger base in the general population than in the Gilded Age. While the great majority of corporate shares is still held by the wealthiest 20 percent of the population, a growing number of white-, pink-, and blue-collar workers have become small owners through their 401K plans, stock bonuses, and employee ownership plans. As such, the new ownership class represents a major departure from the Gilded Age model and, as noted in Chapter 2, is a potentially profound new countervailing force within the corporate system.

While institutional investors such as Fidelity and Vanguard now are the principal designated hitters for the new owners, the owners could nevertheless choose to act through different agents less closely connected to the corporate world, as some churches and unions who control pension funds have already demonstrated. We are witnessing the rise of small movements of institutional shareholder activists—including churches, unions, and public-employee pension funds in such states as California and New York—that are beginning to introduce a social logic into the money markets and the larger corporate system. This stirring of nontraditional market players—who have immense financial clout and speak not just for financial gain but for the community concerns of ordinary workers and citizens—could grow and transform market morality and the nation itself.

For now, however, the new owners are putting their money mainly in the hands of institutional investors such as Fidelity and Vanguard, who speak for the conventional morality of the market. Fidelity and most other institutional investors are unabashed creatures of the market, driven both by the new owners' hunger to maximize their returns and by their own corporate interests in profit maximization. Instead of advancing new social interests, they have ratcheted up pressure on corporations to deliver short-term profits at the expense of long-term financial or social health. As a result, while many middle- and working-class Americans now have some stake in the stock market, this has done little to restructure the markets in their own job or community interests. The most powerful institutional owners—the giant mutual fund companies such as Fidelity as well as the largest pension funds such as TIAA-CREF—have helped fuel the corporate impetus toward downsizing, temporary labor, and capital flight, in the name of responsibility to the very same workers whose jobs are being axed or sent to China and Mexico.

Mutual funds in 1996 controlled more than $4 trillion in total, and more than $1 trillion in corporate equity (about 20 percent of the $4.8 trillion stock total in 1996), as Americans have shifted more savings into mutual funds than any other form of wealth—including their homes. The invasion of Merrill Lynch and Goldman Sachs into the mutual-funds industry catapulted them to the highest profits on Wall Street in 1995, reflecting the new importance of the funds. By virtue of their vast holdings in hundreds of America's biggest companies, mutual funds wield enormous influence. The mutual funds are increasing their clout by engaging in their own merger mania and diversifying their dizzy array of financial services. They now enjoy a growing role in 401K and other huge pension-fund management, and they bankroll much of the world's speculative markets for the world's wealthiest high rollers.

Fidelity is the elephant of the mutual-funds industry, with a 20 percent market share. FMR—Fidelity's parent corporation—is worth in 1998 more than $500 billion. More than twice as big as Vanguard, the second largest mutual-fund company, and accounting for about 7 percent of all business on the New York Stock Exchange, Fidelity is a prime enforcer of short-term profit maximization. Fidelity's ownership share is so large that even the most powerful corporations cannot ignore its demands.

Fidelity has the biggest ownership share in hundreds of companies—shares so vast that it can trigger a collapse in the market value of a stock simply by signaling a desire to sell it. This means Fidelity must act circumspectly when it abandons a company, but it doesn't stop the firm from treating companies as the companies themselves treat disposable workers. Fidelity will disinvest—precipitously or over weeks and months—if its analysts sense stock-price weakness, a pattern which tends to reward short-term return at the expense of long-term growth and tends to drive whole industries toward narrow definitions of corporate success.

The current logic of institutional ownership increasingly makes for profit maximization, as noted above, at the expense of downsized employees or abandoned communities. One of the great surprises of the present era is that a kind of robber-baron spirit has appeared in our more democratized ownership class, enacted by the new institutional investors who manage its money. Giants such as Fidelity and Vanguard, in their capacities as the principal owners of the economy and new partners of commercial and investment banks, loom as the financial powers of the coming century.

The New Robber Baron Retail Railways

In addition to financial services, the fastest-growing services of the post–Industrial Age are the retail, food and drug, and health-care sectors. Once the domain of the mom-and-pop store and the family doctor, production of personal goods and services is now increasingly dominated by global corporations that integrate manufacturing, retail, and service. Delivering intimate products for hearth and heart, they are increasingly remote from their consumers. Their only connection to the communities they serve is cold cash.

Wal-Mart is the emblematic retailer of the new age, controlling the flow of personal products we put into our homes and bodies. Now the fourth largest company in America, with 2,100 stores and sales of almost $100 billion in 1995, Wal-Mart offers interesting parallels with Microsoft. Bill Gates is the world's richest individual, and Sam Walton's family is among the world's wealthiest. Both companies single-mindedly seek market domination on a global scale. Both use the same strategy: Lock up the distribution channels with a heavy reliance on Information Age electronics.

Wal-Mart has transformed retail through its famous discounting practices, exploiting state-of-the-art technologies to connect stores to headquarters, creating just-in-time inventory management, dominating suppliers, and squeezing competitors with tiny profit margins on huge volumes of goods. Wal-Mart has become the role model for the chain discounters sprouting everywhere—from Home Depot and Kmart to McDonald's. But beyond redefining retail, Wal-Mart's real contribution has been in showing how the control of distribution is the key to accumulating power in today's economy. With its control over the freight moving on America's shelves, Wal-Mart evokes the memory of the railway barons and their masterful control of the distribution channels of the American economy a hundred years ago.

One analyst notes that "more and more of the consumer's dollar is ending up in the hands of the company that controls the sales channel . . ."[7] Like control of the Internet, control of the shelf has become a new strategy for consolidation of power. Wal-Mart uses shelf power to exert power backwards over its suppliers and forward over its consumers. Dominating shelf space by its sheer size and its success in squeezing out small retailers, it determines what the consumer will buy and the manufacturer will make. Cultivating long-term alliances with producers and suppliers, Wal-Mart makes them dependent on its own designs and orders. The Wal-Mart model creates retail dynasties that collapse the traditional divisions between manufacturer and retailer into a single vertically integrated power bloc, the ultimate triumph of marketing over both production and consumption. Discounting the same product in Mexico City, Chicago, or Moscow, Wal-Mart epitomizes the homogenizing function and price-regulating capacity of the new global retailer.[8]

Expanding from its traditional traffic in home products, Wal-Mart is adding supermarkets and pharmacies to its cavernous stores. Food and drugs are a 3-trillion-dollar market increasingly dominated by global corporate giants with their own retail empires. Like Wal-Mart, the paradigmatic food and drug corporate leaders—Philip Morris, Coca-Cola, and Merck—are pioneering a new form of vertical integration, uniting in one great chain of corporate being everything from the growing and processing of food and the manufacturing of drugs to the packaging and delivery of pizzas and soft drinks and the delivery of health care.

If there was ever any doubt that food and beverage production—at one time entirely local and need-based—could be restructured as global corporate empires, Philip Morris and Coca-Cola have put it to rest. Coca-Cola is the sixth largest company in the world, Philip Morris the fifteenth (fourth and seventh in America). Philip Morris is the world's largest food company, as well as the globe's biggest tobacco firm. Coca-Cola is the world's fifth largest food company and the overwhelmingly dominant beverage producer and bottler, selling 45 percent of the world's carbonated soft drinks. Both companies exploit new variants of classic Gilded Age strategies on a global scale, including massive mergers to achieve worldwide sales, vertical integration of production and distribution, and disregard of consumers and workers in the service of global profits.

Philip Morris led the new merger and acquisitions parade in the 1980s, gobbling up some of the world's biggest companies to dominate the global food business as it already did tobacco. In 1985 Philip Morris swallowed up General Foods for a hefty $5.7 billion; in 1987 it digested Kraft Foods for $13.1 billion; in 1990 it spent $4.1 billion to gorge itself with Jacobs Suchard, the Swiss chocolate and coffee giant. Philip Morris didn't fatten itself into master of the world's food business; it simply bought itself a new corporate identity, leveraging the superprofits of one of the world's most deadly drugs: tobacco.

The tobacco strategy spotlights the morality of today's largest corporations—and the profusion of new evidence sets the stage for a confrontation between the industry and the public that could help propel the question of corporate responsibility into one of the nation's great moral debates at the turn of the millennium. Documents unearthed by the Food and Drug Administration in 1995 and another set turned over to the government by the Liggett Group, the maker of Chesterfield cigarettes, in 1997 as part of a legal settlement, revealed that the cigarette companies have chemically manipulated their product to increase its addictive powers, while fully recognizing that cigarettes caused cancer and other lethal diseases. Liggett acknowledged systematic marketing to hook children under fourteen, a strategy reminiscent of the most ruthless Gilded Age predators. This led President Clinton to direct the FDA to regulate cigarettes as a drug and launch a high-profile campaign against marketing tobacco to children, leading eventually to the national settlement between cigarette companies and the states' attorney generals in 1997, which Congress scuttled in 1998.

Philip Morris recognized as early as the 1970s that health concerns would eventually lead the American government to move against it. To protect itself, the company simultaneously pursued two strategies that reveal the weakness of national governments in regulating global corporations. First, Philip Morris moved most of its tobacco business overseas where federal law—including the new controls proposed in the 1997 settlement—could not regulate it. Global marketing greased Philip Morris's second strategy: leveraging its fantastic cash reserves to buy up much of the food industry and legitimate itself as the purveyor of all-American Maxwell House coffee, Kraft cheese, Miracle Whip, Oscar Meyer franks, and Jell-O. By selling cigarettes abroad, Philip Morris could finance a less controversial business at home, thus taking control of two of the world's most profitable industries simultaneously while making more difficult any challenge to its increasing monopoly as the country's leading grocer.

Pharmaceutical and health-care companies are joining the elite roster of the nation's most powerful corporations. Pharmaceutical companies have long been among America's most profitable giants, and the very biggest players are now merging frantically to dominate global markets and vertically integrate health care from the drug factory to the doctor's office. Concentration in the drug industry is unprecedented, leading one analyst to marvel that "Everybody in this industry is going to merge. Ain't anyone not going to."[9]

Merck and Co., the world's second largest drug company, is the paradigmatic corporate empire in health care. Merck is America's sixth largest company and the thirteenth largest in the world, with $3 billion in profits in 1994. Second in global market share in 1997 only to the newly merged Glaxo Wellcome British giant, Merck has the top prescription-drug market share in the United States. Merck's most important innovation is its increasing integration of health-care delivery into the pharmaceutical business. Merck ran into trouble with the Federal Trade Commission in 1995 after it bought Medco, one of the largest managed care and discount prescription-management chains in the country. Merck-Medco Managed Care covered 47 million people in 1995, with 170 million prescriptions ordered by physicians within the Medco plans. The FTC and GAO are investigating whether Medco gave preference to Merck products and committed antitrust offenses, including dropping the drugs of competing companies from the preferred lists offered physicians in Medco's care plans. Columbia/HCA Healthcare Corp.—which some analysts dub the Wal-Mart of health care—and other giant for-profit hospital chains have already turned patient care into a corporate strategy, but if Medco portends the giant pharmaceuticals' takeover of the doctor's office, managed care will take on a whole new meaning, with the nation's largest corporations doing both the managing and the caring according to their own bottom-line prescriptions.[10]

Blue Chip Robber Barons

While often viewed as dinosaurs of the Gilded Age, some of the most powerful industrial corporations created around the time of John D. Rockefeller and J. P. Morgan have emerged as leaders in the post-Industrial Age. These companies—including GE, Exxon, GM, Ford, and Boeing in the United States and Shell, Toyota, and Siemens abroad—have been household names for decades. Now global and high-tech, they are increasingly financial, media, and service dynasties as well as industrial giants. As they have redistributed their factories around the world, they have pioneered the new social contract that increases growth and diffuses jobs and products globally while threatening living standards of many of the poor in advanced and developing nations alike.

The leading blue-chip industrial companies have enormous sales and assets. GM, with about $200 billion in annual sales, remained in 1997 the world's largest company, followed by Ford,

Shell, and Exxon. Ranked according to assets, GE led America with $250 billion in 1994, followed by Ford, GM, and Exxon. According to market value, Shell is the world's second largest company (topped only by Japan's telephone monopoly, NTT, which is breaking up) followed by GE and Exxon, with Toyota the seventh largest. These are the biggest concentrations of capital in the world.

In automotive, aerospace, airline, energy, electronic components, electrical, and steel industries, the top five firms control more than 50 percent of the global market and an even higher percent of the American market. The shares in America's specialized markets are far higher: Exxon controls 36 percent of the oil and gas market (and about 16 percent of the world market, second behind Shell's 18 percent in 1993); Boeing controls about 60 percent of commercial jet-plane production (prior to its merger with McDonnell Douglas); GE controls 35 percent of the jet-engine market and 40 percent of the wide-body engine market; GM and Ford together dominate the U.S. auto market with over a 50 percent share and enjoy a global dominance with Toyota, the foreign auto company with the biggest share of the American market that spurred both Ford and GM to mimic its "lean production" system. Most of the blue-chip leaders also dominate businesses outside their own core areas; Ford, for example, is the fifth largest financial services company in the United States, bigger than J. P. Morgan Bank.[11]

As they skyrocket in sales, assets, profits, and market share, the blue-chip companies are shedding workers at an astonishing rate. From 1980 to 1993, the Fortune 500 eliminated about 4.5 million jobs. About 50 percent of all major corporations during each year in the nineties reported significant downsizing, with the industrial blue-chip baronies leading the way. GE dumped over 100,000 workers from the early 1980s to the early 1990s, and GM and Ford together during the same period permanently eliminated several hundred thousand jobs. Every one of the blue-chip leading corporations has eliminated massive numbers of both blue- and white-collar positions and converted thousands of other jobs from permanent to temporary as a core strategy for growth. While profitable for the corporation and its shareholders, it has been devastating for unrepresented stakeholders, including both employees and their communities.[12]

The Top 30 and the Top 200

While the Top thirty are the leading companies, they are important mainly as symbols of the vast concentration of power in America's largest corporations. The top thirty are merely the leaders of the 200 firms that collectively rule the economy. While the top thirty are the showstoppers, the top 200 own the theater.

The top 200 control the lion's share of the America's economy, both directly and indirectly through their new corporate web of contractors and partners. Each of them has either assets or sales above $1 billion a year—and they account for a remarkable percentage of sales and profits in America. In 1970, manufacturing corporations with over $1 billion in assets accounted for about half of all manufacturing assets and half of all profits. By 1991, the billion-dollar giants accounted for more than two-thirds of all assets and profits.[13]

Even though the top 200 are shedding workers as fast as they can, they still employ—directly or indirectly—a high percentage of American workers. While downsizing and outsourcing will continue to shrink their formal employment rolls, they continue to employ millions of workers directly and to control the fates of millions more through contracting or other contingent arrangements. The myth of small business as the backbone of the American economy has not been true for fifty years—and becomes increasingly fictional as mom-and-pop stores give way to the Wal-Marts of the world. In 1987, the top 1 percent of industrial firms—those with over 500 workers—employed 40 percent of all manufacturing employees, and created a higher percentage of America's new jobs than they did ten years earlier.[14] The corporate giants and the contractors in their networks—not independent small businesses—continue to create the most new jobs and employ the plurality of Americans, even though these jobs are increasingly temporary, part-time, leased, or contract jobs.

As the top 200 spread their tentacles across America and the world, their new vast size and influence is a reflection of their unanticipated dynamism and success. Institutions which many regarded as bureaucratic dinosaurs in 1990 have resurrected themselves as the world's most productive and inventive organizations. They have earned much of the admiration that Americans shower upon them. But as their influence grows, unions and governments continue to shrink. The total budget of the AFL-CIO (and all the unions within it) is less than any one of the corporate super-baronies. Meanwhile, the new countervailing forces within the ownership class have yet to crystallize as an authentic voice for employees and communities. Similarly, governments themselves continue to downsize, devoting an increasing percentage of their declining resources to subsidizing corporate growth and profitability. As public governments decline, the top 200 corporations—which make up our new private government—are increasingly becoming the government that matters.

FIVE

Bye, Bye, American Pie

In the early 1990s, IBM hired a management consultant—call him Bill Phillips—to work on a high-level global project based in Geneva, Switzerland. He was thrilled until he actually got to his job, where he found unexpected tension and distrust among his coworkers. Phillips couldn't understand it until he learned that they all were former IBM engineers and programmers who had been laid off—many after thirty years—and then rehired on a contract basis to do the same work.[1]

They all lived in something like a state of panic. Most were uncertain of whether IBM would keep them on for the duration of this project or hire them for another. Phillips said they reminded him of survivors on a lifeboat jostling to see who would stay on board. Their insecurity and dark mood undermined their ability to cooperate on the team. And these were the winners among the nearly 200,000 IBM employees who had gotten pink slips in recent years. What must the others be like? thought the new man on the job.

All of them, says former labor secretary Robert Reich, are on the same wobbly lifeboat—members of America's new anxious class. The anxious class consists of the millions of Americans, in his words, "who no longer can count on having their jobs next year, or next month, and whose wages have stagnated or lost ground to inflation." Since 50 percent of Americans now say they worry about losing their job, and up to 70 percent of Americans have been seeing stagnant or declining real wages for twenty years, the anxious class is not only anxious but big. It encompasses a huge chunk of the middle class, the entire underclass, at least ten million working poor, and even many professionals such as IBM's dispossessed computer engineers.

The anxious class is making America nervous—keeping an entire industry of analysts in the pink. It is being measured by pollsters, profiled by the media, and addressed by politicians. But despite the deluge of attention, Americans have not learned the real meaning of the cataclysm. Drenched in a dizzying fog of business babble about reengineering, self-reliance, and the new entrepreneurship, the anxious class has been profoundly misled about the causes of its anxiety, blaming itself for its faintness of heart while accepting the rollback of its social protections as the inevitable cost of global competitiveness.

The torrent of analysis about the anxious class has, nonetheless, established two new realities about America. One is that a level of economic insecurity that has not been seen since the Great Depression now permeates the nation—a particularly vexing phenomenon in an economy which is enjoying growth, renewed productivity, and high profits. "For the first time in fifty years," says Richard T. Curtin, director of the University of Michigan's Consumer Surveys, "we are recording a decline in people's expectations. And their uncertainty and anxiety grow the farther you ask them to look into the future." Polls in the mid-1990s, including 1997 surveys carried out at the peak of a remarkable market expansion and economic boom, showed that about two-thirds of Americans saw job security as lower than it was a few years ago, and more than half said they expected this greater insecurity to last for many years.[2]

Louis Uchitelle does not mince words: The anxious class is "the losing class." Caught in America's long-term downsizing blitzkrieg, they are losing their jobs with no assurance of another.

Trapped in a quarter-century of wage standstill, they are losing their prosperity.[3] Millions of Americans, former New Jersey senator Bill Bradley agrees, "are adrift on a gigantic river of economic transformation that carries away everything."[4] Bradley hints that Americans are losing more than job security and middle-class wages. Global corporations are bulldozing the economic foundation stones that made a middle class possible.

The most remarkable thing about the anxious class is its empathy with management. Public opinion polls show that most Americans, despite their persistent sense of insecurity, do not blame their employers. Instead, they see business itself as a victim, disempowered by the global tide of competition and technological change. Sociologist Joel Rogers says workers tell him: "'My boss is trying hard, but there is nothing he can do either'. . . . They say he does not have the ability to protect them, which is much different than saying 'He could protect me if he wanted to but he chooses not to.'"

If it sees any enemies, the anxious class has been persuaded to point to politicians and big government rather than the corporate system. Pollster Florence Skelly marvels at the degree of disorientation: "You would think that in a free enterprise system, there would be more criticism of its warts. Instead, we say that government should be run more like a business. And we deal with the boss by ousting the Congressman."[5]

The Anxious Class and the Robber Barons: The Social Contract as Social Darwinism

Most Americans were part of another anxious class a hundred years ago. Made up mainly of farmers, immigrant workers, and an aspiring middle class who lived close to the brink, its economic insecurity gave rise to the violent labor uprisings and the prairie populist movement that exploded against the robber barons in the 1880s and 1890s. The rebirth of the anxious class today marks the rise of a new era of corporate ascendancy. The new power of the corporate community liberates it from the burden of long-term social obligations to employees and their communities. The anxiety of the anxious class reflects its visceral understanding that the social contract that brought it into being is unraveling.

A social contract is the set of laws and social norms that establishes long-term responsibilities and protective moral covenants among employers, employees, and communities. While it seems the foundation of any society, a social contract is not to be taken for granted in market societies. Again the Gilded Age model is instructive: The robber barons purged social covenants by crushing nonmarket forces and enshrining the amoral ideology of the market as the ultimate morality.

In the Gilded Age, business leaders, politicians, and intellectuals preached the gospel of social Darwinism—a variant of market fundamentalism that has resurfaced today. Herbert Spencer, one of England's leading Darwinist thinkers a century ago, summed up the Gilded Age view of safety nets and social contracts: "The whole effort of nature is to get rid of such [the poor], to clear the world of them, and make room for better . . . it is best that they die." William Graham Sumner, another of the period's most influential writers, saw the rich as nature's elect—and any effort to distribute wealth to help workers or the poor as contrary to the natural order: "The millionaires are a product of natural selection . . . if we do not like the survival of the fittest, we have only one possible alternative, and that is the survival of the unfittest. The former is the law of civilization; the latter is the law of anti-civilization." He argued that poor workers were nature's losers and should be treated as such.[6]

Unlike today's business leaders, the robber barons did not have to roll back a social contract so much as ensure that none arose. This meant aborting the rise of unions and activist government, the embryonic countervailing forces at the end of the nineteenth century that sought to limit exploitation of workers and infuse Gilded Age companies and markets with social responsibility. The robber barons rose to the challenge with their customary enthusiasm. Jim Fisk's response to a strike of the Erie railway brakemen was to "send a gang of toughs from New York under orders to shoot down any man who offered resistance." Fisk's stated view of unions as an unacceptable "special interest" resonated among all the robber barons. George F. Baer, a leading industrialist who headed the Philadelphia and Reading Co., said that "the rights and interests of the laboring man will be protected and cared for" not by unions or intrusive legislators but "by the Christian men to whom God has given control of the property rights of the country."[7]

The lack of any Gilded Age social contract beyond social Darwinism created America's first anxious class. Ordinary Americans in the Gilded Age were unprotected by law, self-organization, or the prevailing God. They would be anxious until countervailing forces became powerful enough to create a genuine social contract for twentieth-century Americans.

The Death of the Anxious Class and the Rise of the Middle Class: The New Deal Social Contract

It took the Great Depression to end the agony of America's first anxious class. Desperate circumstances propelled ordinary Americans to take their fate in their own hands. They launched the most powerful challenge to corporate rule ever seen in American history—shutting down factories, marching in the streets, and voting en masse for a new type of political leader. The Depression led to the creation of America's most powerful labor movement and the election of the activist Democratic government of Franklin Delano Roosevelt.

Roosevelt preserved capitalism, but he was a revolutionary

nonetheless, and he created a new American social contract. The New Deal was a genuine alternative to Gilded Age capitalism, and the nation's most decisive repudiation of social Darwinism. It established the protections of the welfare state, giving the anxious class its first dose of guaranteed social security. It also gave legal protection to unions—a dagger in the heart of Gilded Age economics, since it returned some basic rights to workers and institutionalized a modicum of countervailing power among unions. A bold new labor movement and a series of riots among the poor and homeless during the Depression helped force Roosevelt to accept and enact major changes.

For fifty years, the new social contract liberated a majority of ordinary Americans from economic insecurity. The New Deal, to be sure, did not eliminate poverty or create a paradise for the new vast middle class it brought into being. Nor did it dismantle the giant corporations that arose during the Gilded Age. To the contrary, Roosevelt's National Recovery Act institutionalized a close relation between business and government that greatly expanded the public power and character of corporations. Corporate empires built by Rockefeller and J. P. Morgan grew even bigger after the New Deal. But while the New Deal did not shrink the size or influence of the nation's largest corporations, it ended monolithic corporate control of America, giving labor and government itself a seat at the table.[8]

Another decisive shift came after World War II, symbolized by the accommodation made by the big auto companies to a long-term relation with the United Auto Workers. UAW leader Walter Reuther and Charles Wilson, the head of GM in the 1940s, wrote a corporate marriage contract that changed America. While still bureaucratic and authoritarian, the new GM accepted long-term responsibilities to employees and to the nation as the condition of doing business. GM endorsed multiyear agreements, building a corporate safety net that catapulted GM workers out of the anxious class. Guaranteeing annual pay increases and cost-of-living adjustments, as well as an expanding package of benefits, the new GM delivered 3 percent yearly wage increases above in-flation for a quarter of a century. The steadily expanding job-security, health-care, vacation, pension and unemployment benefits it offered rivaled those that the European welfare state was delivering to its own new middle class.[9]

Protected by its own dominant position in the auto market, GM committed to a primitive version of corporate communitarianism. The company treated employees and their unions as members of the GM family. Both partners acknowledged the legitimate adversarial interests of the other, but also accepted a set of mutual moral obligations. The specific wage, benefit, and seniority arrangements, while balm to the soul of an anxious class, were ultimately less important than the simple affirmation that the company owes its workers a share of prosperity and the dignity due a member of the family.[10]

GM found that nonmarket values had long-term market payoffs. Beyond generating an abiding loyalty among its workers, which helped increase productivity, it put money into the American worker's wallet—which helped, in turn, to boost the demand for GM cars.

The GM initiative became a catalyst for national change. America's giant corporations—from AT&T to U.S. Steel—wrote their own new social contracts. These took two forms: an industrial model, which followed the GM blueprint, and a salaried model typified by IBM. Both were based on internal labor markets—instead of hiring from outside, companies would promote from within, institutionalizing the expectation of a long-term marriage between worker and company.[11] In the GM model, workers increased their security by hewing to union-enforced narrow job classifications and rigid rules that decreased the arbitrary power of management to reassign workers and decide whom to hire, promote, or demote.[12] In the IBM model, management resisted narrow work rules and had a freer hand to redeploy workers flexibly, but made a firmer commitment to job security. With its famous

11:00 P.M.   UC-CONNAN   CHF

1-6ft out w/sign @9:30a. left:L-shape a
ft;center front: podium w/ stationary &
le:3rows; 3-6ft=1st row, 4-6ft=2/3rd

10:00 A.M. - 12:00 P.M.   UC-MCCONOMY   ADM
    event time is 10:30a-? NEED TRIPOD FRO

11:00 A.M. - 04:00 P.M.   UC-DOWD   CHE

11:00 A.M. - 04:00 P.M.   UC-PAKE   CHE
    NOTHING

11:00 A.M. - 11:00 P.M.   UC-C '87   GAM
    nothing

12:00 P.M. - 05:00 P.M.   UC-MCCONOMY   MAY
    event time 12-5pm.

01:00 P.M. - 05:00 P.M.   UC-POOL   ATH

02:30 P.M. - 05:30 P.M.   UC-ACTIVITIES LUN
    event time 2:30-5:30pm

05:30 P.M. - 11:59 P.M.   UC-MCCONOMY   Stud
    american pie

Please have all rooms cleaned and opened befo

lifetime employment policy, Big Blue promised the ultimate antidote to the anxieties of the anxious class.[13]

The new social contract gave birth to a middle class free of the debilitating economic insecurity that is today revisiting their children. This triumph of countervailing forces was made possible both by the political mobilization of the New Deal and by the postwar prosperity and dominance of American corporations. After World War II destroyed the European and Japanese economies, the American century came into full flower. The absence of significant global competition made it far easier for American corporations to treat their unionized employees generously, since higher wages could be passed along to the consumer in higher prices without jeopardizing corporate profitability. But such generosity, which increased employee loyalty and productivity, came into being only through the power of the labor movement and of their liberal allies in postwar governments. Corporations resisted unions and long-term contracts, finally embracing them only because the balance of political forces gave them little alternative.[14]

The limits of the postwar contract should not be forgotten. For one thing, business remained the business of America: Giant corporations still ran the economy. Unions won a foothold in industry and the public sector, but never got a welcome mat in the new high-tech, service-oriented economy. Even in the union sector, New Deal workers won security but not the right to help run the company.

Only one part of the business world, moreover, made a gesture toward a social contract—the biggest corporations such as GM and IBM that couldn't afford not to. Smaller companies—under less pressure from unions and government—continued to treat workers as they always had. The New Deal contract also left out millions of African Americans and women. Three of the New Deal legal linchpins—the National Industrial Recovery Act (1933), the Social Security Act (1935) and the Fair Labor Standards Act (1937)—explicitly excluded agricultural laborers and domestic servants, instantly writing the majority of African Americans out of the New Deal. The New Deal also inherited and perpetuated a dual sexual standard based on the notion of a full-time male worker and a female worker marginally attached to the labor force. Men (and a small number of full-time working women) would gain a form of labor rights and social insurance—including bargained wages and working conditions, unemployment compensation, disability payments and pensions—designed to promote independence and self-reliance. Women (and a tiny fraction of permanently unemployable men) would receive welfare designed to promote dependency.

While the New Deal thus excluded and disenfranchised many Americans, its accomplishments should not be diminished. It forced business to share power with labor and government and civilize its attitudes toward workers. It weaned a nation from its faith in social Darwinism. And it led America's most powerful corporations to recognize, finally, that good business is more than just a commercial enterprise.

The Contract on America: The End of the Job and the Rebirth of the Anxious Class

In 1993, sociologist Russ Eckel went to an innovative truck-assembly plant in Indiana to study the new GM. Expecting to find a model cooperative plant sparked by hopeful, empowered employees, he planned to interview hundreds of workers and learn what made worker participation work. Instead, he found himself running de facto therapy sessions for workers so shellshocked they could hardly tell their stories without breaking down.[15]

Virtually all the workers were migrants from other plants that had downsized or shut their gates. Most had been displaced several times, and were undergoing divorce, alcoholism, and depression. Calling them "industrial gypsies," Eckel found in the GM workers a group that had dropped from the middle class into the anxious class.

In this, General Motors has once again become a trendsetter. As it relocated south of the border and across the Pacific, GM laid off tens of thousands of workers, annihilating job security. It tore up the contracts Reuther and Wilson had written, voiding multiyear agreements long before they were due to expire. Three percent wage hikes were replaced by 10 percent cuts; workers who once got two more vacation days each year now got two fewer. As Newt Gingrich was leading the charge against the entitlements of the welfare state, GM was scrapping the entitlements it had promised its own workers for fifty years.

GM is spearheading a rollback that defines the present era and has precipitated the anxiety of the anxious class. While corporate elites claim that rollbacks have been forced on them by the harsh pressures of global competition, the real story is more complex. The revival of Japan and Europe created intense new competition in sectors such as auto and steel. But the termination of the New Deal social contract represented an economy-wide initiative by leading corporations—some exposed to new competitive pressures and some protected from it—who no longer found themselves compelled to make a deal with unions or communities. The abandonment of the social contract has had a mixed effect on competitiveness, cutting costs in the short term but threatening loyalty and productivity over the long haul.

Sensing a historic window of opportunity, big companies are rushing, nonetheless, to consolidate their new regime. This corporate revolution is twofold: It is rolling back fifty years of employee protections and social regulation, while at the same time writing a new contract that shifts risks and responsibilities from the corporation (who bore them in the New Deal model) back to workers. The new contract, which is being sold as a system of empowerment through entrepreneurship, is more precisely distinguished by the willingness of leading corporations, as Bruce Butterfield writes bluntly, "to treat long-term workers as the enemy."[16]

The new contract voices the rhetoric of employee involvement, but jeopardizes the very idea of employment as currently understood. At its heart is the decision to end the job as currently understood and replace it with contract labor. The most significant change currently afoot in the American economy, it is the rickety structural foundation of a permanent anxious class.

Job Genocide, the Virtual Corporation, and the Virtual Worker

Nike, the company known by its motto "Just Do It," is living up to its name. A 5-billion-dollar company making almost half a billion dollars in profits, Nike rules the lucrative world of sneakers. But Nike doesn't employ a single worker who makes shoes.

A new class of global contract workers produces Nike's sneakers. While it announced a new policy in 1998, Nike, in the early and mid-1990s, contracted mainly with Indonesian and Vietnamese suppliers, who pay young girls and women about one to two dollars a day to make its footwear—not enough, according to government sources, to keep them adequately fed. In 1992 Nike paid Michael Jordan more for helping market the shoes than the total it paid all 75,000 of its Indonesian contractors. The workers are forced to work overtime; they have no right to strike and no union to represent them. In 1997, Thuyen Nguyen, founder of Vietnam Labor Watch, reported that "Supervisors humiliate women, force them to kneel, to stand in the hot sun, treating them like recruits to boot camp."[17]

Nike is a model of the new virtual corporation that solves the old problem of labor in a new way. While it does have a few thousand employees—all in management, design, and sales—Nike has contracted out all employment in its core line of business. The virtual company is a jobless company. As such, it is practicing job genocide, a strategy for cutting costs and ending long-term corporate obligations to employees by getting rid of jobs as we know them.

While downsizing and automation have brought a great deal of attention to job displacement, these are only symptoms of a far more profound change. "What is disappearing," writes the organizational theorist William Bridges, "is not just a certain number of jobs—or jobs in certain industries or jobs in some part of the country or even jobs in America as a whole. What is disappearing, is the very thing itself: the job. That much sought after, much maligned social entity, a job, is vanishing like a species that has outlived its evolutionary time."[18]

The end of the job is not, however, a product of natural evolution, but part of an evolving corporate strategy that has more ambitious aims than global competitiveness. The full-time permanent job became the focal point in the New Deal for building a labor movement, regulating the company, and vesting workers with legal rights and economic and moral claims on the company. The labor legislation passed in the New Deal created a framework for ensuring employee representation and legal rights tied to full-time work. This approach to the social contract, based on the assumption that most families would be supported by one full-time wage earner, continued to guide labor law until the present day. Conventional full-time employment remains today the key institution protected by the social contract, with virtually all legal rights and labor representation written to apply to full-time conventional employees.

As long as conventional jobs prevailed, it was difficult for corporations to free themselves from the constraints imposed by both unions and government. The shift toward contract labor is a brilliant maneuver designed to evade the social contract. Without an employment structure based on conventional jobs, workers lose their rights, unions lose their organizing power, and government's ability to protect workers goes into limbo. Contract or "virtual" workers have little meaningful protection under most federal laws governing unionization, collective bargaining, wages and working conditions, discrimination, occupational safety, family and medical leave, or pension and health benefits.[19]

Critics tend to assume that companies shifting toward contract labor are just out to save a buck, mainly on health care and other fringe-benefit costs.[20] The underlying corporate benefits and motives are more far-reaching. Contract labor is a systemic assault on America's Magna Carta of worker rights: the 1935 Wagner Act, which guaranteed the right to unionize and bargain collectively, and the Fair Labor Standards Act of 1937, which governs wages and working conditions. Both these acts remain on the books, but the shift toward contract labor will make them irrelevant for millions of twenty-first-century workers.

Temporary and leased workers are in name still protected, since they can claim their temping or leasing agencies are legally designated employers who must respect their rights to unionization, the minimum wage, and nondiscrimination. But since the agencies do not determine their actual conditions of work and the constantly changing corporations in which they work bear no legal liability for violating their rights, such protections are almost meaningless in practice. Temp workers are so widely dispersed, and turn over so rapidly, that it would be nearly impossible to determine who would qualify to vote in a certification election for a union at Manpower, much as it would be an impossible task for union organizers even to identify and locate the temps themselves. Similarly, compliance with overtime or antidiscrimination laws could be theoretically facilitated by the temporary or leasing agency, but the transience of the workforce and the inability of the agencies to determine workplace conditions makes both monitoring and enforcement a prospect that is increasingly remote.[21]

Although the shift to contract labor effectively ends the New Deal social contract for millions of workers, the change cannot be read as purely a matter of conspiratorial strategic planning by heartless corporations. Several studies have suggested that such contingent arrangements have evolved in a far more ad hoc fashion in many companies, driven by unanticipated budgetary pressures or scheduling problems. In an early 1980s study, Richard Belous found that lower-level managers in supermarkets, factories, and department stores frequently experimented with temp labor or contract workers to resolve such problems, without any guidance from senior managers, many of whom had no idea how many of their workers were contingent—nor any theory of how many should be. Only in the nineties, as the radical expansion of their numbers made contingent workers a public issue, did most corporations begin to think systematically about how to restructure their labor markets and consciously design a new model of work organization. Today, as many corporations have moved opportunistically and with greater formal planning to consolidate contingent arrangements in their own interests, corporate motivations cannot be reduced to a simple formula. Nonetheless, the effect has been a radical transformation of New Deal employee social protections, and a systemic shift in risks from companies to workers.[22]

Nike's approach to job genocide—the replacement of workers with contractors—is becoming commonplace. While a relatively small number of corporations—such as Bugle Boy, which makes almost none of its clothes, and Mattel, Inc., which manufactures few of its toys—have joined Nike among the fully virtual corporations, it is hard to find a major corporation in America that is not contracting out jobs in big numbers. Many airlines contract out their cleaning and repair work, computer companies make only a fraction of their electrical components, and auto companies contract out from 30 to 50 percent of their subassembly supply production. Some major corporations, such as Volkswagen, are taking genuinely remarkable steps, creating the first fully virtual auto manufacturing plant in the world. Located in Brazil, it is a VW plant completely operated by contractors, without a single

VW employee. All functions in the plant, from sweeping the floor to line assembly to management itself, are carried out by other companies who bring in their own help.

Almost all workers in some occupations, such as security guards and janitors, have been turned into contractors. Millions of secretaries, data-entry clerks, cashiers, salespeople, and other employees have suffered the same fate. Editors, engineers, and even doctors are joining the ranks, and Microsoft is moving along with other high-tech companies to contract out thousands of highly skilled computer-software jobs. In 1995 there were more than 225 American companies specializing in professional and high-tech contract services for corporate giants like Microsoft and IBM. Nationally, about one in every ten workers is outsourced—the new corporate lingo for contract employment.[23]

"The reason business executives outsource," says economist Lester Thurow, "is because they can't look a janitor who's been with them for 15 years in the eye and explain why he'll earn $6 and get no medical benefits going forward, rather than $12 he now gets with the same medical benefits as the company vice president."[24] By going virtual, however, the company gains more than just saving the cost of health care. It gains access to a full spectrum of new labor strategies that the New Deal had outlawed. It can refuse to pay benefits, disregard the rights of workers to organize, and in some cases opt for sweatshop labor at home or child labor abroad. The Internal Revenue Service recognizes that corporations are reclassifying millions of domestic employees as independent contractors to avoid paying Social Security, Medicare, unemployment, and disability taxes, and is now going after some of these companies as tax dodgers. The government is also showing broader concerns about the use of foreign contractors who may be convict labor in China or toddlers in Guatemala.

Contractors constitute only one category of the virtual workers who make up America's new contingent labor force. The others include roughly three million temps; a million leased workers, who—like temps—are rented by the hour, day, week or month;

and nearly 25 million part-time workers. Collectively, contingent workers now make up between one-fourth and one-third of all American workers. "If there was a national fear index," says economist Richard Belous about these new charter members of the anxious class, "it would be directly related to the growth of contingent work."[25]

Not all these workers are paid badly; the most skilled can get substantially higher wages than their conventional counterparts. And the proliferation of part-timers reflects a growing demand by employees—including many women seeking to balance work and family—for nontraditional jobs. Corporations have argued that contingent labor is driven by the needs of the new workforce as much as corporate profit. While the percentage of involuntary part-timers is growing dramatically, suggesting that many contingent workers seek conventional employment, the social need for flexible schedules and nontraditional employment is real.[26] But the new jobs strip workers of traditional benefits and substitute flexibility without commitment. They are off the corporate map, and the company is free to treat them as disposable. One scholar describes contingent work as "the workforce equivalent of the one-night stand."[27] Few contingent workers enjoy the rights and protections which fifty years of labor law and collective bargaining secured for America's corporate employees through much of this century.

Companies like NYNEX—at this writing being merged with Bell Atlantic into one of the biggest telecom companies in the world—are half-virtual, typical of corporate profiles in America today. Full-time NYNEX employees are paid $19 an hour with good benefits, but they work shoulder to shoulder with temps and contractors who get $8 an hour and no benefits. NYNEX denies it is exploiting its new virtual workers, saying they are getting a competitive rate in the current market. Replacing 16,000 additional full-time jobs in 1996 with temps or contractors, NYNEX is testing how far it can push a contract-labor strategy without destroying the morale of its remaining permanent employees.[28]

United Parcel Service (UPS) is going even further, massively re-placing its full-timers with second-tier part-timers who loom as the great army of the new millennial workforce. The huge national strike against UPS in 1997 symbolized the national anxiety about the elimination of middle-class jobs and the shift of highly prof-itable major corporations toward contract and part-time work. Over 60 percent of all UPS jobs are now part-time, including 80 percent of the new UPS jobs created in the last four years. Kate Bronfenbrenner, a labor scholar at Cornell University, says that "The situation at UPS represents the dark side of job creation. Jobs where you work fewer than 20 hours a week, that have com-pletely irregular hours and that disappear after three months. . . ." Many of these "part-time" jobs involve more than 35 hours a week but are paid at about $9.00 an hour, compared to $19.95 for full-timers doing the same work. Said one union organizer, "UPS wants throwaway jobs that no one can live on."[29]

One of the UPS part-timers, Leatha Hendricks, 36, expressed the general mood of both full- and part-timers: UPS doesn't "even look at workers as human beings anymore. My name is Leatha, but to them, I'm just a machine. All they care is that you've got some strength in your back. And when your back goes out of whack it's over. You're gone." Most are gone soon. Of the 180,000 part-timers hired in 1996, only 40,000 remained in 1997, the rest too transient to qualify for benefits. Part-timers may seem less new and exotic than leased or contract workers, but they are no less dis-posable.[30]

Industrial relations expert Harley Shaiken notes that UPS, an industry leader with over $1 billion in profits in 1996, is pioneer-ing one of the new models of work: "Over the last five years, part-time work has shifted from being an occasional strategy to being a way of life at UPS. That's why there is the anger right now. For UPS workers it represents, in effect, a hidden downsizing." Econ-omist John Schmitt comments that "You have a company that is a textbook example of the new economy, a service sector industry that's highly computerized, that's based on information, organization and smarts. If this kind of company cannot offer workers middle class wages, that's a bad omen for the future." UPS gives the country a glimpse of how the new virtual corporation will work.[31]

Even for the millions of Americans—particularly women with young children—who desire part-time work, the UPS-style mass conversion to a part-time workforce is devastating, since it allows the company legally to wipe out the economic and social protections in the old social contract. As Chris Tilly, an expert on contingent labor, observes: "It is against the law to discriminate against women or people of color," who are the majority of contingent workers. But once they are contingent, such corporate discrimination magically becomes legal. "It is *not* against the law to pay part-timers half the hourly wage of full-time workers or to deny them standard fringe benefits that are available to other workers, or to bar them from opportunities for promotion." The task at UPS, as in the nation, is both to add many more full-time jobs and to create a new legal framework to ensure that all employees are protected equally under a fair social contract. This hardly requires the elimination of all part-time jobs, but means aborting the emerging two-tier system of rights and benefits that threatens the solidarity and organizing power of labor and the well-being of all working Americans.[32]

The UPS full-timers protected under the old contract are almost as traumatized as the part-timers and contractors, since they know they could be next. Veteran full-time driver Gary Clark of Pontiac, Michigan, says that full-timers have to support the part-timers: "The more you surround yourself with people working at eight bucks an hour," Clark observes, "you're cutting your own throat. It gives the company an incentive to get rid of you."[33]

Nobody in any company can say what will be the next department slated for job genocide. Economist Audrey Freeman says that corporations have committed themselves to permanent downsizing, which turns even the full-time regular employee into a type of virtual worker: the "temporary permanent." Downsizing—which is the second pillar of the strategy to deconstruct the job as we know it—led in the last ten years to a million workers laid off in just four companies that used to be paragons of the old social contract: IBM, AT&T, Sears, and GE. One-fourth of the jobs in America's Fortune 500 companies have been eliminated over the last decade.[34]

AT&T illustrates the intimate relation between downsizing, contingent work, and the virtual corporation. In 1996, when it was flush with profits, the company announced it was laying off 40,000 employees. James Meadows, a vice president for Human Resources, explained that this was part of a process of turning all AT&T employees into contingent workers: "In AT&T we have to promote the whole concept of the workforce being contingent, though most of the contingent workers are inside our walls. . . . People need to recognize we are all contingent workers in one form or another. We are all victims of time and place." Meadows told employees that they were no longer AT&T workers: "People need to look at themselves as self-employed, as vendors who come to this company to sell their skills." This reflects the transformation of AT&T into a virtual corporation: "Jobs are being replaced," he explained, by "projects" and "fields of work." AT&T is proudly leading the path, he claimed, to the new jobless America.[35]

Corporations portray the end of the job as the dawn of a better world. "Bid farewell to unconditional lifetime employment," says Kevin Becraft, director of employee relations at IBM, but say hello to "shared responsibility. Employers have an obligation to provide opportunity for self-improvement; employees have to take charge of their own careers."[36] Losing job security is "rich in opportunities," writes William Bridges, and actually a form of personal growth, writes another enthusiast: "Employees become far more responsible for their work and careers: No more parent-child relationships, but adult to adult. . . ."[37]

Flexibility, according to management enthusiasts, makes the new employment inevitable. "In a fast-moving economy, jobs are rigid solutions to an elastic problem. We can rewrite a person's job description occasionally, but not every week. When the work that needs doing changes constantly, we cannot afford the inflexibility that the job brings with it. . . . Jobs are no longer socially adaptive. That is why they are going the way of the dinosaur."[38]

Flexibility helps keep companies competitive, or so goes the master thesis espoused by corporate leaders to legitimize contingency. The relationship between contingent labor and competitiveness, as noted earlier, is complex. It can be a source of dramatic short-term cost savings, and for some companies helps generate long-term efficiencies and growth. Downsizing and outsourcing may be a necessary last resort for firms that have been managed so poorly that they face extinction without emergency surgery.

But there is another side to the story. Annual American Management Association surveys show that downsizing and outsourcing do not tend to increase profitability. The AMA surveys show that only one-third of companies who downsized between 1990 and 1995 reported increased operating profits after the first year of layoffs or outsourcings, and even fewer firms report such gains in following years. A Harvard Business School scholar, after studying downsizing at one hundred major American corporations, concluded that "on average, downsizing doesn't pay." Companies may thus be cutting short-term costs and shifting long-term risks to workers, but without necessarily increasing profitability or competitiveness.[39]

Reengineering guru Michael Hammer now laments that many corporations have used his own prescriptions as an excuse to work cheaper but not better. By hacking permanent jobs off the organization chart and replacing them with virtual ones, companies frequently undermine rather than improve their long-term competitiveness. One analyst dubs it "dumbsizing," pointing out that hundreds of companies are living to regret downsizing and outsourcing decisions. "Despite warnings about downsizing becoming dumbsizing," companies greedy for short-term savings "continue to make flawed decisions . . . that come back to haunt them, on the bottom line, in public relations, in strained relationships with customers and suppliers, and in demoralized employees." When Digital contracted out hundreds of sales and marketing jobs in its health-industries group, it "disrupted long-standing ties between its veteran salespeople and major customers." Contract workers are usually clueless about inside knowledge specific to the firm, and lack key social ties in and out of the company necessary to close deals and maintain relations to customers. Digital, Kodak, Planters, and other firms have found that the decision to save money up front by going virtual comes back to haunt the companies, plaguing long-term competitiveness.[40]

Harvard economist James Medoff argues that competitiveness was never the real issue in the first place for many firms: "At first, the firms that were permanently laying off full-time workers were really over a barrel. But now, a lot of firms aren't over a barrel at all. But they say, 'Hey, we can get away with it. So we'll do it.'"[41]

Corporate virtual reality is more than just opportunism. It systematically shifts risks borne by the New Deal social corporation to contract workers, who now bear all the brunt of business cycles and shifting markets. It also radically redistributes income from the new class of contract workers—the majority of whom make lower wages and receive a fraction of the health, pension, and other benefits of conventional workers—into the already flush corporate coffers of the nineties—a period in which corporations experienced their highest profit rates in decades. Most important, it frees the corporation to disregard its legal and social responsibilities to employees, established through fifty years of struggle by workers, unions, and legislative reformers.

The undermining of the Wagner Act, the Fair Labor Standards Act, and other foundations of labor law is the story that has not yet caught the public eye. Contingent workers stand naked before the law. They have no rights in practice to collective bargaining or equal pay for equal work. They have no enforceable claim on wages or negotiated benefits of the kind that are extended to conventional employees. Their protection under antidiscrimination laws is severely compromised. Since corporations bear no legal liability for discrimination, harassment, or other injuries incurred by contractors, they have reduced incentives to ensure that such abuse does not occur.

Even during the postwar years of the social contract, the rights of American workers were limited and less developed than their counterparts in Germany and other European nations. The shift toward contract labor is a giant step back toward the Darwinian workplace of the Gilded Age. It will take an entirely new legal framework to protect the twenty-first-century contingent work-force.[42] But since contingency undermines the protection to unionize, the prospects for the new workforce are dim. Contract labor is a kind of coup de grâce for the labor movement as we know it, undermining the countervailing power that is essential to bring disposable workers the security and dignity they deserve.

High Road versus Low Road: The New Contradictions of Capitalism

The corporation's constant expression of fear about declining competitiveness is an alluring excuse. The relentless pressure to remain competitive is a harsh reality for even America's biggest and most powerful corporations. But management itself—which relies on the rhetoric of competitiveness to justify downsizing, deep cuts in labor costs, and the broader assault on workers' rights and protections—is deeply conflicted about the merits of these practices as competitive strategies.

Corporations have become schizophrenic about how to compete. Influenced by Japanese successes, American business is embracing the notion that educating, empowering, and partnering with workers is a key to competitiveness. The corporate rhetoric on this matter has never been clearer. Paul Fireman, the CEO of Reebok, says, "For hundreds of years they whipped people to build the pyramids. It seems to me that it would have taken a lot less time if these people were enthralled with the idea of building pyramids and excited and felt more like they were partners in the relationship."[43] Levi Strauss's Mission Statement proclaims: "We all want a Company that our people are proud of and committed to, where all employees have an opportunity to contribute, learn, grow and advance based on merit, not politics or background." FedEx says their competitive strategy can be boiled down to two words: "People first."[44]

Corporations have not been entirely hypocritical about such aspirations. As with GM, virtually all the Fortune 500 have put in place employee-involvement programs designed to build competitiveness through participation and commitment. But GM exemplifies the new corporate schizophrenia: even as it inaugurates its new Japanese-style involvement at plants from Saturn to Nummi, it massively downsizes and outsources its workers. GM has seemingly embraced two contradictory logics of competitiveness, one based on building loyalty and the other on destroying it.

AT&T policy embodies the same contradictions. On the one hand, it has sought to build a new partnership with its workers and unions, cooperating with the Communications Workers of America to create one of the nation's most sophisticated employee-involvement programs. But when former CEO Robert Allen laid off 40,000 employees in 1996, only the most recent of huge AT&T downsizings in the nineties, he destroyed the trust and loyalty that his worker-participation programs had tried to nurture.

This schizophrenia can be viewed as a conflict between "high road" and "low road" approaches to competitiveness. The high road seeks to enhance competitiveness by investing in workers' skills and empowering them as loyal partners. The low road looks to compete by shifting costs and risks on to workers. Downsizing, outsourcing, and the shift toward contingent labor are the hallmarks of the low-road strategy.

The schizophrenia is ultimately suicidal, and most corporations, while embracing the rhetoric of a high-road strategy, appear in practice to be choosing the low road. A recent study shows that among the thousands of firms that have embraced participation plans, only about 5 percent have genuinely empowered employees.[45] Virtually all of them, however, are moving rapidly toward one or another variant of the virtual corporation. The disloyalty endemic to such models sabotages even the most earnest employee involvement plans and threatens long-term productivity.

Why, then, have corporations taken the potentially suicidal low road? The short-term gains—for CEOs' pocketbooks and corporations' quarterly reports—are immensely seductive. It's difficult to reject an expedient path with tangible, immediate returns in favor of uncertain long-term economic outcomes.

Even more compelling is the prospect of power consolidation over the long term. The low road, as we've seen, promises the kind of unfettered dominance that corporations have not enjoyed since before the New Deal. The low road may have uncertain long-run effects on competitiveness, but it takes corporations toward an irresistible new union-free and deregulated corporate environment. After the Civil War, corporations used courts and legislatures to defang countervailing forces and create just such a permissive environment. Now, after a half-century of regulatory legislation and union-building, corporations have settled on the contingent-labor strategy as an escape from the constraints of the New Deal social contract.

While power is the heart of the matter, executives have offered a simpler defense that deserves attention: the rise of the shareholder movement. The huge new financial institutions that have become dominant among shareholders have enslaved companies, management cries, in perpetual service of shareholder value. Downsizing, going virtual, and the other components of the low-road strategy are being forced on corporations by newly assertive shareholder blocs—especially mutual and pension funds—that want only maximum and immediate return.[46]

"Look, we're not back in the fifties and sixties. The pressures on me to maximize profits are immense now," one executive told then–labor secretary Robert Reich when he asked why corporations have abandoned their commitments to workers and communities. "The old gentlemanly days of investment capitalism, those are gone," another executive reported to Reich. "We are now competing, brutally competing. We have got to maximize those shareholder returns."[47]

This complaint deserves at least as much consideration as the tale about competitiveness. The rise of giant institutional shareholders is an unexpected new countervailing force, which has eroded the degree of freedom once enjoyed by corporate top brass. Huge mutual funds and pension funds have ironically played a major role in pushing corporations into decimating payrolls—and have even begun robbing managers themselves of the security they once enjoyed.

As the influence of workers and communities has faded, shareholder influence has risen. CEOs exaggerate the degree of bullying they experience from mutual and pension funds—the executives are still in charge, even if they must now listen more attentively to the major concerns of their biggest shareholders. But the executives hint at two legitimate points. First, maximizing shareholder value is not necessarily the same thing as increasing competitiveness—and may, in fact, seriously erode it. Second, the institutional giants who manage shareholder money are responding only to the narrow interests of their investors, which frequently violate their long-term broader interests in good jobs and healthy communities.

Job genocide, downsizing, and the collapse of corporate responsibility are likely to continue as long as shareholders are the principal countervailing forces to the corporation. Corporations and their shareholders have their differences, but as contenders for power they tend to share priorities—each as likely as the other to favor corporate profit over social responsibility. The only groups with different priorities are those who are neither managers nor big owners but stakeholders: Workers, consumers, and others who have their own stake in the corporation and, more important, in

America itself. These stakeholders, who collectively constitute the larger American public, are our best hope for the future; the people themselves have the capacity to shift sovereignty back from the corporation to the public, but to do so will require clearing our vision of the confusing new myths that seem to cast corporate dominance in a surprisingly benevolent light.

SIX

The Making of the Corporate Mystique

I sometimes ask my students if they believe in the democratic idea of one person, one vote. They all say yes. Then I ask whether they would extend the same principle to the corporation: one worker, one vote. Most say they have never thought about it, and are surprised by the question. They cannot easily explain why we don't apply the same democratic logic to the world of business that we do in town meetings, but they often object that business is different from government and should not be held to the egalitarian standard of public life. One student commented that to give each worker a vote would suggest that the workers who'd built his house deserved a say in how he himself should live in it—and he didn't like that idea at all.

Americans are steeped from childhood in the ideals of democracy and the notion of popular sovereignty. But the rise of corporations in our culture is rooted in a way of thinking that endorses our very undemocratic business culture as vital to American democracy itself. This triumph of ideology—the corporate mystique—is the intellectual and legal foundation of our new corporate order. Without the powerful corporate mystique so deeply imbued in our culture, the tensions between corporate autocracy and civic democracy would quickly surface as the paramount issue in American political life.

All forms of power are ultimately rooted in a way of thinking, a set of shared beliefs and values. The corporate mystique is a symbolic universe of ideas and laws that has become almost universally accepted in American life—a way of thinking that both venerates and disguises corporate ascendancy. It is flexible enough to allow for the discovery of specific abuses of corporate power—but not enough to betray the underlying system that gives rise to them.

Understanding the phenomenon of corporate ascendancy requires cutting through the filmy veils of the corporate mystique, a task that involves challenging the most basic assumptions in American culture and business. At the heart of the mystique is the view of the corporation as private enterprise: An article of faith that is shared by virtually all Americans, this is the central illusion underlying our corporate system.

Einstein said memorably that everything about the world has changed except the way we think about it. This is a fair way of describing the grip of the corporate mystique on the American mind and in American law. We live in an era when business and government are growing ever more intimate, corporations are growing more dependent on public subsidy, politicians are becoming ever more dependent on corporate funding, and corporations are taking over more and more schools, welfare, and other formerly public services, amassing almost unimaginable public powers in the process. Yet the mystique of the corporation as a private enterprise remains deeply embedded in both American law and the popular imagination—where it has resided for a century or more.

A basic faith in the separation of public and private arenas plays a central role in American thought. This faith enables us to believe that it is possible to have great concentrations of power and wealth in the "private" sphere while still practicing true democracy in the public. It is a notion that masks the melding of government and business that is one of the defining features of our times. It is the premise that allows my students to maintain their belief in democracy while never thinking to challenge the undemocratic structure of the corporation and the larger economy.

These beliefs are not mere figments of my students' imaginations, or those of Americans at large; they are inscribed into our constitutional system and our most basic laws of property and contract. In discussing the corporate mystique, we must train a microscope on the legal ideas that are integral to the corporate mystique and ultimately undergird corporate power in our society. The American Constitution defends the sanctity of private contracts, and melds our concept of freedom with the freedom of property. It links the protection of personal property with corporate protection from government intrusion or other democratic assault—the kind of threat my student demonstrated in his fear about his house. The idea of corporate privatism is today being written more deeply into the Constitution, and the distinction between what is public and what is private is embodied in (and enforced with) the sure hand of the law itself.

Yet it wasn't always this way. The American concepts of private and public have undergone many historical transformations, and the view of the corporation as private has periodically yielded to a very different understanding. The most profound challenge to the corporate mystique comes from American history itself, which demonstrates that the question of whether corporations are public or private entities is far more complex and provocative than most Americans might expect.

The two chapters that follow this one look at the role of the corporate mystique in America today. But to understand that role we must first take an excursion into legal and intellectual history, back to the Gilded Age and even earlier—to the founding of the Republic. For at America's dawning the corporation was a much different animal: conceived in both the law and popular imagination as a *public* rather than private enterprise. And as we revisit the Gilded Age, focusing this time on the sometimes surreal world of business ideology and law, we will see how the corporate mystique was first constructed—and how it has come back to haunt us.

Before the Corporate Mystique

Within the story of early America, before the rise of the corporate mystique, there is a subplot concerning the corporation—what Richard Grossman calls a hidden history. Few Americans are aware of it, though if this story were better known it might change the way we run our lives. Behind this tale there is a basic, surprising, empowering idea: that the corporation, in its original formulation, was a public rather than a private institution—and one that owed accountability to the American people. The general reader may view this kind of historical and legal background as better left to specialists. But they are part of our national history about which all Americans should be better informed—and, in this case, they may hold the key to our future.[1]

The corporate mystique today tells us with legal and moral certitude that the corporation is a private enterprise. But many decades before the mystique took root, the American corporation was developed as a public institution, in at least three senses. It was the creation of the government, and understood by the public as such. It was obliged to serve the public interest. And, through the state charters that brought corporations into existence, legislatures and ordinary Americans kept corporations on a relatively short leash through most of the period until the Civil War—exercising a degree of public control that would be considered subversive to suggest today.

The notion of a private corporation—so central to the contemporary corporate mystique—would have made little sense to Americans in the early years of our nation. The colonists had inherited their understanding of the nature of the corporation from England, which since the Tudors in the sixteenth century had seen it as a creation and servant of the reigning sovereign. The Tudor and Stuart monarchs chartered joint-stock companies to advance their mercantile, colonial, and state-building objectives. They chartered the East India Company, the Massachusetts Bay Company, and Hudson's Bay Company to build their empire and control colonial trade and property. While the companies colonizing America were given unusual freedom, agents of the king or queen typically controlled the joint-stock companies, directed their activities according to state dicta, and ensured that state authorities pocketed a good portion of the profits. Since royal charters created each corporation and dictated the terms under which it could do business, the corporation was a pure creature of the state—very much a political and public institution.[2]

Of course, being chartered by a monarch hardly made early British corporations accountable to the people. Yet with the American Revolution that is exactly what emerged, to a surprising degree. Early American corporations could only be created through special charters of incorporation granted by state legislatures. The charters in most states put rigid strictures on how long a corporation could exist, what it could do, and how many assets it could accumulate: They also outlined specific ways in which corporations were obliged to serve the public interest. State charters assured, at least in theory, that each corporation would serve the people—and gave them the authority to revoke the charter if it failed to do so.

At the nation's inception and for nearly a century thereafter, the law was unambiguous about the "publicness" of the corporation. In the legal theory of the early 1800s, corporations were classified as "concessions" or grants from the government. The corporation was deemed a legal fiction with no claim to a natural place in the order of things or in the spontaneous associations or contracts of private parties. In striking contrast to Americans under the spell of the corporate mystique today, early nineteenth-century Americans understood that the corporation was a political creation, made by a government for its own ends, as in the forthright language of the Pennsylvania legislature in 1834: "A corporation in law is just what the incorporating act makes it. It is the creature of the law and may be moulded to any shape or for any purpose that the Legislature may deem most conducive for the general good."[3]

This premystique legal language, similar to that of most early state incorporation charters, made clear that the *primary* function of the corporation was to further the public interest. In serving such ends, whether building canals, turnpikes, or colleges, private parties were free to gain wealth and profit. But as the Virginia Supreme Court argued in 1809, if the intention of the corporators is "merely private or selfish; if it is detrimental to, nor not promotive of, the public good, they have no adequate claim upon the legislature for the privileges."[4]

The logic of this system held that the only way to ensure that such a company would remain faithful to its public mission was to make it directly accountable to the people, and so a unique system of public control emerged in the form of state constitutional language, state charters, and other laws. In the eyes of Jacksonians and others who fought to preserve and expand it, only direct control of corporations by the people, through their elected representatives or their own direct initiatives, could keep democracy alive.

And the state-imposed control of corporate business was more than merely theoretical. Spurred on by an abiding distrust of corporations among ordinary farmers, artisans, and workers, early legislatures were reluctant to grant charters at all—and did so only after much deliberation and if local communities had no objection. Moreover, while British joint-stock companies were chartered in perpetuity, early American ones were strictly time-limited. Pennsylvania limited manufacturing charters to twenty years; Delaware voted a constitutional amendment in 1831 that limited *all* corporations to a twenty-year life span. Banks, which were especially feared, were often limited to three years.[5]

As businesses created for specific public ends, such as building a canal or a college, early American corporations had no right to venture into other arenas. Legislatures reserved for themselves all powers and goals not explicitly granted to corporations, thereby ensuring that the people retained sovereign authority over the corporation rather than the reverse. Early state legislatures were not shy about asserting public authority over the internal affairs of their corporations. They dictated rules for "issuing stock, for shareholder voting, for obtaining corporate information, for paying dividends and keeping records. They limited capitalization, debts, landholdings and sometimes profits." Many states refused to grant limited liability to corporate directors, seeing the new liability clauses as shields that unfairly protected the wealthy. Moreover, scaled voting balanced the power of large and small investors, laws prohibited directors serving on more than one corporate board, and directors could be removed at will by shareholders.[6]

When President Jackson in 1832 vetoed the extension of the charter of the Second Bank of the United States, a private national corporation, he was asserting the ultimate public control. The right to revoke corporate charters had been established in Pennsylvania in 1784 and was commonplace in states before the Civil War. What the state giveth, it can take away, as Justice Story ruled in *Terrett v. Taylor* in 1815: "A private corporation created by the legislature may lose its franchises by a misuser or nonuser of them . . . This is the common law of the land, and is a tacit condition annexed to the creation of every such corporation."[7]

As late as the 1840s and 1850s, states from Ohio to Mississippi routinely revoked charters when corporations were seen as violating the public trust or exceeding the limited authority they had been expressly delegated. Well before the emergence of the robber barons, corporations were seen as a threat to ordinary people. In 1791, James Madison and Thomas Jefferson opposed the chartering of a national bank, expressing the nation's earliest fears about corporations as monopolies that threatened democracy. Madison told Congress that corporations "are powerful machines which have always been found competent to effect objects or principles in a great measure independent of the people." They believed corporations endangered the Republic itself, lacing their republicanism with populist sentiments that marked much of the population in the nation's first several decades. As a New Jersey editorial expressed in the 1830s, the "Legislature ought cautiously to refrain from increasing the irresponsible power of any existing corporations or chartering new ones," lest people become "mere hewers of wood and drawers of water to jobbers, banks and stockbrokers."[8]

No image of the early charters should obscure the reality of the pre–Civil War corporation as a monopoly privilege reserved largely for the wealthy. Since legislatures and politicians tended to represent the propertied classes, and since the special charters essentially created a form of public/private monopoly, the chartering system was hardly a guarantee of genuine public accountability. The kind of state regulation we have today did not exist. Huge abuses took place, giving rise to smoldering anticorporate sentiment in the Jacksonian Era and beyond.

Early Americans, unblinded by the corporate mystique, understood the tension between property rights and democracy that the rising corporation symbolized. Their efforts to fashion a corporation compatible with the common good offer an illuminating counterpoint to notions of corporate responsibility or government regulation current today. Nineteenth-century Americans did not trust corporate directors to define social responsibility themselves. Nor did they expect bureaucrats or judges to be regulators defending the public interest, insisting that control must rest with the people or their elected representatives. Recognizing that corporations posed a profound challenge to popular sovereignty, they insisted that the authority of the corporation derived from ordinary citizens and could never be taken from them. As late as 1855 the Supreme Court agreed, declaring in *Dodge v. Woolsey* that people of the states have not "released their powers over the artificial bodies which originate under the legislation of their representatives . . . Combinations of classes in society . . . united by the bond of a corporate spirit . . . unquestionably desire limitations upon the sovereignty of the people. But the framers of the Constitution were imbued with no desire to call into existence such combinations."9

The Corporate Mystique Is Born

When it came to reimagining the corporation, the businessmen who became known as the robber barons were radicals. Using their vast economic and political clout, they chopped away at all the elements of public accountability in the old system, and created a sovereign corporation. In the name of property rights and individual freedom, they privatized the corporation in law and ideology, even as they expanded its public powers and their own. Thus was the corporate mystique born—a view of the world so compelling that generations of Americans thereafter would accept without question the myth of the corporation as a private enterprise.

The Gilded Age, like our own, was a great era of privatization. Most contemporary Americans, who assume that corporations were always private, today debate the merits of privatizing everything else, from public schools to prisons and welfare services. But the privatization of the corporation was the great drama of the Gilded Age, involving a revolutionary remaking of the pre–Civil War corporation and the emergence of the corporate mystique as the dominant ideology of the era. Then as now privatization was mainly an act of legal fiction, designed to appeal to the public imagination and strip away the legal and cultural justifications for corporate accountability to the people. As the Gilded Age philosophy of laissez-faire private enterprise took root, the corporation's public character and dependence on government became ever more pronounced. The illusion of privatism under such conditions is another of the striking parallels with our own times, integral to the corporate mystique both then and now.

Privatization of the corporation and the development of the corporate mystique were the preoccupation of intellectuals, lawyers, judges, politicians, and even theologians in the Gilded Age. It was through privatization that corporate rule of America was institutionalized, as Gilded Age business was freed from the inconvenient constraints of legislative control and popular sovereignty. But different sectors of the elite approached the new ideas of private enterprise, laissez-faire economics, and social Darwinism—all part of the broader ideological context of corporate privatization—from their own interested perspectives. And while populists, workers, and even some sectors of the elite sought to hold on to or re-create elements of public accountability, they were buried by the constellation of interests that, as today, were making privatization a tidal force.

Privatization was a matter, first, of reimagining the corporation, and here legal theorists took the lead. As long as the British legacy of the corporation as a creature of the state prevailed, the corporation could not be considered private enterprise in any true sense. In a momentous step toward the manufacture of the corporate mystique, Gilded Age legal thinkers radically broke with the state-grant theory, and replaced it with the idea of a voluntary contract among private persons, a "natural entity" that was part of nature.

Harvard legal historian Morton Horwitz views this as a paradigm shift in the law that was not fully consolidated until the Progressive Era. The traditional paradigm of the corporation as an artificial creation of the state began giving way during the middle of the nineteenth century to the notion that incorporation was a natural way to do business; yet as late as the 1880s and 1890s, the new paradigm had not fully jelled and had two variants. One school painted a picture of the corporation as the product of spontaneous contracts among individual shareholders; another group of thinkers began to interpret the corporation as a natural entity separate from both state and shareholders, with rights roughly akin to those of individuals, and substantially autonomous even from its owners.

What was radical about both notions was that they rejected the earlier view of the corporation as an artificial creation, portraying it instead as a natural manifestation of free exchange among individuals. This redefinition was at the heart of privatization and the new corporate mystique since it branded the corporation as private rather than public. "Over and over again," writes Horwitz, "legal theorists attempted to find a vocabulary that would enable them to describe the corporation as a real or natural entity whose existence is prior to and separate from the state."[10] Famous legal theorists at the University of Chicago such as Ernst Freund and Arthur W. Machen kept hammering at the idea that the corporation existed before the law did. Wrote Machen, "All that the law can do is to recognize, or refuse to recognize, the existence of this entity. The law can no more create such an entity than it can create a house out of loose bricks."[11]

The implications of this change are not hard to fathom. On one hand, the corporation was legitimized as a natural evolution within civil society. Even Progressives contesting the robber barons would come to acknowledge the right of the corporation to exist as a natural economic entity. Moreover, corporate accountability to the state and the public suddenly seemed problematic as a political and legal concept. "The collapse of the grant theory," observes Horwitz, "eventually produced the best of all possible worlds for the expansion of corporate power. By rendering the corporate form normal and regular, late nineteenth-century corporate theory shifted the presumption of corporate regulation against the state. Since corporations could no longer be treated as special creatures of the state, they were entitled to the same privileges as all other individuals and groups."[12]

This was the next step in the making of the corporate mystique: corporate personification, which would both vest new constitutional powers in the corporation and equate such powers in the popular mind with the freedom of ordinary citizens. If the corporation was not an artificial entity created by the state, it was easier to identify it as the extension of a person, whether the individual entrepreneur or the shareholders. But it took explicit court action in the Gilded Age to move from the idea of the corporation as a natural entity to the view that it was a legal person with constitutionally protected rights. The pivotal decision was the Supreme Court's 1886 Santa Clara case, which declared that the corporation should be considered a person entitled to the due process rights guaranteed to all persons by the Fourteenth Amendment. For the first time, individuals were being unambiguously instructed by the Court that their own liberties were intertwined with those of corporations—and that taking away corporate rights was equivalent to challenging their own constitutionally guaranteed rights.[13]

While the Santa Clara case is an epochal symbol, it was only one of the all-encompassing shifts in power, ideology, and legal thought that set the stage for corporate ascendancy. Social Darwinists and laissez-faire theorists during these years redefined the pursuit of happiness and other inalienable rights guaranteed by the Constitution to include the right to acquire, possess, and enjoy property—including the intangible rights of corporate ownership. The only role of government, and of public sovereignty more broadly, as Judge Beck of the Iowa Supreme Court declared about 1870, is to protect such rights against other government interference.[14]

Ironically, it was the Fourteenth Amendment, created to protect the dignity and equal rights of freed slaves, that would become the chief legal instrument for protecting the corporation. When the Supreme Court in the Santa Clara case decided that the corporation was a legal person with all the citizen rights guaranteed by the amendment, it was only one of a chain of remarkable decisions that made its relevance and benefits to the corporation at least as significant as those to the slave. A key clause of the amendment holds that no state "shall deprive any person of life, liberty, or property, without due process of law." Thomas M. Cooley, the most influential constitutional scholar of the Gilded Age and a militant proponent of the philosophy that the best government is the least government, persuaded an entire generation of corporate lawyers and jurists to view the due-process clause—and the entire amendment—as a protection of intangible property such as corporate shares, making the Fourteenth Amendment a legal pillar of the corporate mystique.[15]

In three important cases between 1887 and 1897, the Supreme Court declared for the first time that liberty of contract was guaranteed by the Fourteenth Amendment, that the due-process clause restricted the police and regulatory powers of the state, and that the term "person" in the due-process clause applied to artificial persons, i.e. corporations, as well as individuals. By 1900, the corporation had the blessing of the Court as a new citizen of the Republic. Like all other private citizens, it was constitutionally protected, endowed with inalienable property rights and the liberty of contract that neither government nor the broader community could take away or limit. This turned the old notion of public control over the corporation into a violation of the same set of constitutional privileges enjoyed by the public itself. In the name of the people's own rights and liberty, a new conception of corporate sovereignty was emerging that put democracy—the power of the people themselves—at risk.

And so the old tenets, one by one, were discarded. The pre–Civil War chartering restrictions and state legislation that had kept corporations subject to some public accountability fell by the wayside. Gilded Age courts interpreted such laws as violations of the due-process clause, radical overextensions of the police power of the state, or fundamental subversions of the liberty of contract. In 1905, in *Lochner v. New York,* the Supreme Court struck down New York State legislation that kept employers from requiring bakers to work more than sixty hours a week, arguing that voiding the right of the workers to work longer, or the right of the corporations to make them do so, violated their rights of contract as protected under the due-process clause of the Constitution.[16]

Meanwhile, other forces were at work blowing apart the public-accountability features of the old state chartering system. As the robber barons' business expanded, they felt constrained not just by regulation per se, but also by the archaic state-by-state regulatory machinery that fettered their ability to operate freely across state borders. Most of all, they were seeking to build great national corporations serving the huge new integrated market created by cross-country railroads; but before they could do so, Gilded Age courts had to step in again to help. As Scott Bowman observes, they paved the way for corporate expansion by severely limiting state regulations through an expansive new interpretation of the national commerce power. The right of state legislatures to regulate corporations engaged in interstate commerce was nearly eliminated, and the freedom of corporations to operate in national markets, rather than just the state in which they were incorporated, became constitutionally protected.[17]

Larger political and economic forces, finally, were dealing the final blow to the old system. State legislatures, while forced to yield much of their sovereignty by higher federal authority, still competed among themselves to draw business by scrapping their restrictive charters. They rushed madly to transfer sovereignty to the corporations they could entice to stay, and in the process crafted an entirely new world in which business could expand unfettered.

The Corporate Mystique and the End of Democracy

As these cornerstones of the corporate mystique were laid, the public-charter system—and the democracy it represented—collapsed quickly. The new legal order, which transferred sovereignty from the states to the corporations, replaced it. The fact of the change was crucial, but so are some of the individual steps taken along the way—which illuminate the intimate relation between the legal consolidation of corporate rule, and the creation of the corporate mystique.

The collapse of state sovereignty took place in the late 1880s and 1890s, ironically in the wake of popular attacks on the robber barons' monopolies in oil, sugar, and other industries. Corporate concentration was becoming the most explosive political issue of the day, and populists were targeting the trusts—the ingenious corporate devices designed by Rockefeller to maintain control over legions of seemingly independent companies, thereby evading state limits on corporate size. By the late 1880s, six different states had brought suit to revoke the charters of corporations associated with famous trusts like Rockefeller's Standard Oil and the Sugar Trust.

In defense, the corporate lawyers took a new approach. Rather than fighting to defend the trusts, they decided to seek changes in incorporation laws that would make them unnecessary. In 1889 New Jersey obliged, revising its incorporation law to permit one corporation to own equity in others. Rapidly, Delaware and other states followed suit. The trusts were dismantled, but not before they had become unnecessary as newly legal mergers and acquisitions created even more formidable corporate Goliaths.

The real significance of New Jersey's action was to trigger a race by states all over the country to gut their own charters and shamelessly turn sovereignty over to corporations. In effect, the states were agreeing to disavow the "publicness" of the corporation and legally affirm its "privateness." And their motives weren't complex: After passing its new incorporation act, New Jersey found that so many corporations shifted their headquarters to the state that it was able to fund its entire budget out of corporate filing fees. So many big corporations "were paying tribute to the State of New Jersey," observed corporate lawyer Charles F. Bostwick, "that the authorities had become greatly perplexed as to what should be done with its surplus revenue."[18]

Bostwick, who practiced in New York, noted "the sudden exodus of hundreds upon hundreds of millions of dollars, controlled by corporate interests and financiers from New York into the State of New Jersey." Although New York had declared it would not get into a bidding war with New Jersey, in 1892 the Empire State quickly made its rules on corporate acquisitions even more inviting and permissive than New Jersey's to seduce the companies back. The Gilded Age race to the bottom had begun.

Foreshadowing today's competition among nations for corporate revenue, the New York–New Jersey match became a bidding war to see which state would move faster to tear up its own chartering restrictions and hurtle toward corporate privatism. Retaliating against New York's bid, New Jersey passed a revolutionary General Revision Act in 1896 that permitted unlimited corporate size and market share, removed all time limits on corporate charters, permitted incorporation for any lawful reason, legalized radically permissive mergers, acquisitions, and corporate purchases of other corporate equity, and substantially reduced shareholder powers in favor of corporate directors. New Jersey was not shy about its giveaways, setting up an official bureau to let corporations know about its splendid enticements. By 1900, 95 percent of the country's biggest corporations had moved to New Jersey.[19]

The state's governor could boast in 1905 that "of the entire income of the government, not a penny was contributed directly by the people."[20] But Lincoln Steffens was not fooled, calling New Jersey the "traitor state." In fact, New Jersey had delivered the coup de grâce to meaningful charters and started the devastating game of musical chairs that allowed corporations to liberate themselves from accountability.

As corporations sharpened their skills at playing one state against another, other states, beginning with West Virginia, Maine, Delaware, Maryland, and Kentucky, sought to outdo New Jersey and each other. "For a state to be conscientious," wrote one law-review commentator, "would be synonymous with cutting its own throat."[21] The ultimate winner of this suicidal competition would be Delaware. With a long probusiness history, the little state, as another astute law-review cynic put it, "is determined to get her little, tiny, sweet, round baby hand into the grab-bag of sweet things before it is too late."[22] In 1899, it passed its General Incorporation Law which it accurately touted as "the most favorable of existing general incorporation laws . . . far beyond New Jersey."[23]

Delaware's new law stated that "the certification of incorporation may also contain any provision which the incorporators may choose to insert . . . creating, defining, limiting and regulating the powers of the corporation, the directors and stockholders; provided such provisions are not contrary to the laws of this state." As Ralph Nader has noted, "These sanguine little words literally turned corporate law inside out."[24] The early chartering system had reserved for the state all powers not expressly granted to the corporation. Delaware blew away this fundamental tenet of state sovereignty by allowing corporations to define their own powers and make their own laws as long as they didn't contravene explicit state prohibitions. This new Delaware Act was the Magna Carta of modern corporate sovereignty, ratifying in law the view of the corporation as a private enterprise.

The Gilded Age race to the bottom is far from running its course. It is happening now on a global scale, as corporations play nations off against each other as they did individual states a century ago. But by 1900, it had served its purpose, having by and large consummated the Gilded Age dream of liberating the corporation from popular control.

Lessons for Today

The image of the corporation as private property that privatization theorists created was as much illusion as reality, conjured up by Gilded Age business leaders, jurists, and intellectuals as a centerpiece of the corporate mystique. But its phantom quality in no way diminished its importance in reshaping the power structure of the nation.

The lawyers and judges who created the law of the private corporation were scarcely the prime movers behind the rise of the robber barons. But they helped make the legal fiction of the private corporation a collective necessary illusion, and in so doing became principal architects of the corporate mystique. Their intellectual handiwork propped up the authority of Gilded Age business and made possible its perpetuation well after the robber barons passed from the scene.

An alarming contradiction emerged at the founding of the corporate mystique. As Gilded Age Americans were learning to see the corporation as purely private, it was becoming a quasi-governmental institution—the kind of "private government" discussed in Chapter 3—which exercises vast powers over the lives of workers, citizens, and communities. At the very time that the corporation was dismantling the charter system of accountability, it was developing the public powers that those systems of public accountability were initially developed to restrain. The purpose of corporate privatization, both in the Gilded Age and in its new form today, is to liberate business from the burden of public accountability that would seem logically to be demanded by its public powers and growing public dependency.

Gilded Age corporations came of age by conflating in the law their own rights with those of ordinary citizens. Building on the historic American view that liberty depended on the constraint of government, they linked the political fate of artificial persons— that is, corporations—with those of real ones. The legal fiction of the corporation as private person did, in fact, create a certain community of interests between artificial and natural persons, but it set up a straw man of government tyranny against which corporations supposedly needed protection—and masked the conflict between corporate and public sovereignty which is the real story of the Gilded Age and our own times.

The corporate mystique that reigned a century ago has reappeared in new language and full force. It constitutes another exquisite mix of fact and fantasy that sustains today's corporate power arrangements. It is to this new corporate mystique that we now turn.

SEVEN

Reinventing the Mystique

Today, one hundred years after the era of the robber barons, a kind of romantic faith in the idea of private enterprise has once again captured the imagination of the country. Much like their counterparts a century ago, business leaders, politicians, intellectuals, and jurists are purveying a new seductive image of the privatized corporation, one intended to strip away the rationales for public regulation. The construction of a new corporate mystique is fully under way. If successful, this new ideology will once again seriously erode democracy. As in the Gilded Age, it will shift constitutional powers toward the corporation in the name—and at the expense—of the people's own rights.

Privatism Undone

The corporate ascendancy of the Gilded Age didn't last forever. By the 1930s the corporate order was no longer working for millions of forgotten Americans, who were unemployed, poor, or homeless. This desperate failure helped spark a profound questioning of America's core values. It also mobilized the kind of countervailing force that helped put new ideas into political practice.

One of the great accomplishments of the New Deal was to challenge the reigning corporate mystique of the Gilded Age. FDR's "kitchen cabinet"—the inner circle of intellectuals, lawyers, and political leaders who helped shape the president's philosophy and policy—did not question capitalism per se, but they did insist that the corporation had an essential public dimension. They championed, and succeeded in having implemented, public regulation designed to restore some power to the people.

Adolf Berle, the most influential of New Deal thinkers, is famous for perceiving how the corporation had unwittingly undermined the American idea of private property and ownership. The corporation's "dissolution of the atom of property," wrote Berle, "destroys the very foundation on which the economic order of the past three centuries has rested." The revolutionary impact of corporations was to separate ownership from control—the two things which the idea of private property is supposed to join like Siamese twins at the hip. As thousands of dispersed shareholders became owners, with no real knowledge about or active involvement in the company, corporate control shifted to managers. When owners no longer exercise effective control and the executives in control are not necessarily owners, the corporation is no longer property, or even private, in the traditional sense of these terms. This was Berle's first chink in the armor of the Gilded Age corporate mystique.[1]

Berle went further. Passive shareholders, "by surrendering control and responsibility over the active property, have surrendered the right that the corporation should be operated in their sole interest—they have released the community from the obligation to protect them to the full extent implied in the doctrine of strict property rights. At the same time, the controlling groups," or managers, Berle proclaimed, "have in their own interest broken the bars of tradition which require that the corporation be operated solely for the benefit of the owners of passive property."[2]

Suddenly, the fiction of the private corporation was laid bare. It was hallucinatory to see such an entity as run by its private owners; in fact, in the classic sense, shareholders weren't owners at all.

But then to what ends was the vast power of the corporation to be directed? To whom should it be accountable? And if it were not private, what was it?

Berle's answers, carefully watched by New Deal–era judges and politicians as they sought answers to the crises of the time, sounded the death knell of the Gilded Age corporate mystique. While shareholders and managers still had a legitimate claim on the corporation, traditional property rights claimed by the corporation "must yield before the larger interest of society." The community was now "in a position to demand that the modern corporation serve not alone the owners or the control(lers) but all society."[3]

Berle and other New Deal liberals were not remotely communists or socialists. They did not completely reject the private character of the corporation, nor the fundamental separation between the corporation as a private institution and the government as a public one. Their quasi-public character, these thinkers argued, meant that corporations owed some responsibility to the people. But Berle did not seek to strip away the constitutionally protected rights corporations had won in the Gilded Age.

As Berle and other liberals hammered away at the fiction of the private corporation, their ideas began being taken up by politicians and judges who were in a position to change things. New Deal courts did not fully embrace Berle's theories, but they began to hint that corporations owe allegiance to the public. In the 1934 case *Home Bldg. & Loan Assn. v. Blaisdell,* the Supreme Court upheld a Minnesota statute that gave relief to Depression homeowners having trouble paying off their mortgages.[4] This constituted blatant interference with a corporate contract, but the court argued that "The State . . . continues to possess authority to safeguard the vital interests of its people." The court was reasserting that powers reserved by the state on the public's behalf can supersede even the most basic private-property rights.[5]

This signaled a major change of heart on the part of the Court. For several decades following the Blaisdell case, the Court rarely favored the Constitution's clause about the sanctity of contracts over a perceived need to regulate the corporation. In contrast to Gilded Age Courts, the New Deal jurists reasserted the government's imperative to "safeguard the vital interests of its people." It relied frequently on language about the reserved sovereign powers of the state to permit corporate regulation that would have been viewed as treasonous by Gilded Age jurists. Faced with an economy that had nearly been undone by unchecked financial speculation and corporate expansion, the courts were implicitly returning to the pre–Civil War idea that the corporation is a subject of the state and not its master.

William T. Allen, currently chancellor of the state of Delaware, argues that America has alternated between a property-based conception of the corporation, as sanctified in the Gilded Age, and the view of the corporation as a public or social entity that was revived in the New Deal. As a social entity, the corporation is understood as a creation of the state to serve all of society. It must respect the claims of shareholders and creditors, he writes, but there are "other purposes of perhaps equal dignity: the satisfaction of consumer wants, the provision of meaningful employment opportunities and the making of a contribution to the public life of its communities."[6]

The notion that the corporation must serve the community echoes the New Deal vision of corporate social responsibility. As this view gained increasing public acceptance in the decades following the Depression, it helped point the way toward affirmative action, environmental laws, and other regulatory reform that defined the activist spirit of the 1960s and 1970s. It also appeared to put to rest the fiction of the private corporation, thereby burying the corporate mystique as it had taken hold of America's imagination during the Gilded Age.

Resurrection

In a famous public statement, Nobel Prize–winning economist Milton Friedman wrote in 1970 that "the one and only social responsibility of business" is to increase its profits. In retrospect this might be viewed as an intellectual shot heard round the world, for it signaled the birth of a new American myth that has become sacred not only in the United States business community but—in the wake of the end of the Cold War—among elites across the planet.[7]

Friedman foreshadowed the rise of the contractarians, a new school of theorists who have dictated much contemporary thinking about the corporation and the free market. The contractarians are a group of eminent economists, political theorists, lawyers, and other policy analysts who have a home at the University of Chicago and other leading universities around the country. Contractarians populate influential Washington institutes such as the American Enterprise Institute, and fill the columns of national journals of public opinion. They are sponsored by generously endowed corporate foundations such as the Olin Foundation, which fund their research and disseminate their writing and speeches to intellectuals, politicians, and the general public at home and abroad.

The contractarians have resurrected Gilded Age faith in a new private enterprise religion for the twenty-first century. The high priests include Daniel Fischel of the University of Chicago Law and Business Schools and Frank Easterbrook, a U.S. circuit court judge. Their 1991 book, *The Economic Structure of Corporate Law,* is the contractarian Bible on the corporation. While not well-known to the public, it offers the most influential intellectual foundation for the corporate mystique that has taken hold in America today.[8]

Fischel and Easterbrook define the corporation as a private "nexus of contracts," a phrase repeated so often that it is the virtual mantra of the contractarians. It paints a picture of the corporation as a purely voluntary affair among many different private individuals coming together to contract among themselves for their own purposes. Contractarians endlessly emphasize that the agreements are private and freely chosen, thus anchoring the corporation in the cherished liberty of each individual citizen.

The corporation in this unsentimental view is nothing but a micromarket in which self-interested individuals are seeking to make as much money as possible. There are no social or moral obligations binding the parties, nor any ties of loyalty. Any notion of the corporation as a social organization, a human shelter from the market, or a distinctive entity of any kind melts away. There are only individuals passing in the night. This captures the increasing individualism, self-interest, and burgeoning profit motive of today's corporation. But there are deeper truths it grossly obscures: The corporation has become a vast entity unto itself, with powers and rights threatening not only the larger public but the individuals within the nexus itself.

The contractarians acknowledge that employees, customers, and suppliers are part of the corporate nexus as well as shareholders and managers. While there is nothing in contractarian theory that inherently privileges either shareholders or managers, employees and other contracting parties tend to disappear in contractarian discussions. Shareholders are kings of the corporation, and managers their agents.

Contractarians argue that employees have contracts that fix their compensation in advance and minimize their risk, while shareholders are last in line to get their take. Using this technical argument, they have added to the traditional notion of the God-given rights of property an economic notion of residual risk to justify the fact that shareholders alone get the vote. Yet a few contractarian heretics have recently blown the whistle on this sophisticated fiction, demonstrating that workers and others have their own kinds of social or human capital invested in the firm, bear residual risks of their own, and are just as tied to the contingent fate of the firm as shareholders. Working within the contractarians' own assumptions, they have exploded the argument for shareholders as kings of the corporate castle.[9]

Yet the contractarians press on. In the measured language of legal scholars, they blithely dispose of nearly a century of Progressive and New Deal thinking about the corporation—sending us back toward a future of Gilded Age privatism and individualism. Their corporation is, first and foremost, a purely private creature. Fischel states the main contractarian article of faith: "Because the corporation is a particular type of firm formed by individuals acting voluntarily and for their mutual benefits, it can far more reasonably be viewed as the product of private contract than as a creature of the state."[10] Contractarians Henry Butler and Larry Ribstein make the circular argument that since today's permissive incorporation laws allow virtually anyone to form a corporation on his own terms for his own purposes, the notion that the corporation is a public entity created by the state is patently absurd. "The fact that corporations are brought into existence by a perfunctory state filing does not justify a 'state creation' view any more than does the role of obtaining a birth certificate indicate state creation of a child."[11] The fact that such a perfunctory system of state supervision is the legacy of a century-old era of discredited robber-baron capitalism goes unanswered in their argument.

While contractarians are not given to the language of natural rights, their viewpoint is largely consistent with conservative property-rights theorists who root the corporation in the God-given rights of the individual. Richard Epstein, another University of Chicago Law School professor, cites John Locke, who "was emphatic in his emphasis that individual natural rights, including rights to obtain and hold property, are not derived from the sovereign. . . . The sovereign has no absolute power to generate rights," since they precede the state itself and the main purpose of the state is to protect them. The most important of such sacred rights are property and contract rights, he argues, as embodied in the modern corporation. The corporation is thus protected by the laws of nature against the meddling of the laws of men.[12]

The political implications of contractarian philosophy are not subtle. The arrangements by which corporations are governed are their own business, the logic goes, not the public's. Any attempts by the government or community to shape the constitution of the corporation violates the constitutional rights of its individual shareholders and executives.

Contractarians haven't attempted to question the right of the state to regulate corporations in regard to pollution or other issues that obviously affect society. But they have privatized the corporation in the key sense intended by Gilded Age leaders—conceiving the corporation as a sovereign world of its own making, with built-in immunity from citizen control in the name of every individual citizen's inalienable rights. As legal scholar Kent Greenfield puts it, contractarians are remaking our legal system with an eye toward ensuring that "corporate law is outside of politics." Since in their eyes corporations are purely private contracts among freely contracting parties, "statutes having to do with corporate governance are illegitimate because they invade the private law sphere—they 'disrupt voluntary relationships.'" The relationships struck among shareholders, managers, and other contracting parties are, as Greenfield puts it, "shielded from public debate and impermeable to the concerns of the public, who are, after all, not parties to the contract." What's private is private, period.[13]

But Greenfield points out that to speak of the corporation as merely a web of contracts is to depoliticize corporate law—and render ordinary Americans impotent. As he characterizes their argument: "The government is encroaching on the rights of individuals when it imposes a corporate governance regime that is different from that derived by the agreements of the parties themselves. To change this contract is coercion. Contractual relationships maintain a pre-legal, pre-political, and perhaps super-constitutional status. Corporate law—because it is contract law—is private, and is not, and should not be, subject to the political and legal processes."[14]

To depoliticize the corporation, based on the same set of illusions about the distinction between private and public life that dominated the Gilded Age, is to render it an unaccountable body, answering to nobody but itself. To a remarkable degree, this is already a reality, bolstered by Reagan-era politics and a generation of judges and lawyers schooled in the contractarian faith.

The CEO as King George III: Corpocracy

Robert Monks is a patrician Republican long known for his scholarship on the corporation and advocacy for shareholder rights. Monks believes deeply in capitalism and in the view that the purpose of the corporation is to maximize wealth for its shareholders. He is not a New Deal liberal, or indeed a liberal at all. But from his conservative position he is sounding the alarm that the corporation is gaining the kind of absolute sovereignty that the American Revolution was fought to overthrow.

Monks argues that corporations and their executives today are not even answerable to the shareholder contract held so dear by many contractarians. "The conventional wisdom," Monks writes, "is that corporate management is accountable to ownership, that the directors and officers work for the shareholders and that this accountability sufficiently limits corporate power so as to make it tolerable in a free society." He notes that this view is perpetuated by corporate management "because of the convenience of actually being accountable to no one while having an absolute defense against charges of excessive power . . . There should be no doubt, however, that accountability to ownership in the United States is only a polite fiction."[15]

The corporation, in other words, has privatized itself even more radically than implied in most contractarian discourse. It is beyond the will of even its own shareholders. The CEOs as described by Monks, are more like England's George III than the robber barons—who at least were major shareholders in their companies.

Unaccountable CEOs have become symbols of the consummately privatized, sovereign corporation. Monks calls this "corpocracy."[16]

The rise of huge institutional shareholders, such as giant mutual-fund companies like Fidelity and pension funds like TIAA-CREF, has begun to turn the tide. Monks sees them as the hope for the twenty-first century. The financial clout of the biggest institutional shareholders—who control pension and mutual funds worth trillions of holders—has the potential to cut King George down to size and give some real voice to the owners. Institutional shareholders have clearly gained ground in the mid-1990s, bringing "shareholder value" to the lips of every executive and helping to make corporate boards more independent and sensitive to the demands of big shareholders. But corporations remain, in Monks's view, essentially free agents, empowered by the law, public opinion, and their own political resources to do as they see fit.

The relation of corporations to their shareholders is the subject of endless current debate in business, financial, and intellectual circles. Many contractarians, in contrast to Monks, are not in the least disturbed about managerial oligarchy, believing that the discipline of the financial markets ensures that shareholders are getting what they contracted for. What gets ignored in the debate between executives and shareholders is the continuing powerlessness of workers and communities. They are at the mercy of corporate downsizing, outsourcing, and other current trends, which dish out rewards to both shareholders and top management at the expense of the larger society. Corpocracy threatens shareholders, but it is the larger public who really suffers.

Monks's anguish about the plight of shareholders has led him to protest "corpocratic" legal changes which insulate the corporation from both shareholders and the public. The contractarians view CEOs as designated hitters for the shareholders, but the law now gives them the power of team captain, umpire, and league commissioner. And their first strategic defense is the business-judgment rule, a common law development that is the equivalent of the Magna Carta for the CEO.

The rule offers corporate executives the legally protected right to make virtually any business decision they please, as long as it is not patently illegal and can be reasonably understood as sound business judgment. It has provided CEOs increasing discretionary power over matters of great importance to shareholders, including takeovers, executive pay, valuation and pricing of stock, dividend declaration, and the like. Moreover, it serves to insulate a growing range of corporate decisions from review by the courts, making the rule increasingly the flagship doctrine of corpocracy.

Judges use the role to immunize corporations against shareholder or public suits on both criminal and civil matters. District Court Judge Robert L. Carter, in a case that concerned Exxon's stated policy of not initiating suits against directors even if they were found to be involved in illegal activities, illustrates the rule as judicial protection policy. Should the court get involved in Exxon's internal business, he wrote, "it would necessarily involve itself in the business decisions of every corporation, and be required to mediate between the judgment of the directors and the judgment of the shareholders with regard to particular corporate actions." The corporation's—and Judge Carter's—message to the courts: *Stay out of our business.*[17]

As Scott Bowman writes, Judge Carter's deference to the sound business judgment of the corporation reflects "the judiciary's long-standing trepidation about unraveling the veil of privacy that shrouds corporate affairs and from its presumed incompetence to judge matters of internal policy—a familiar refrain in the law of corporations."[18] The contractarians' privatism doctrine has given judges the ammunition to fight off public demands to bring corporations to the bar. The "exercise of corporate power, however public in its consequences, may be relegated to the private sphere, where oligarchy will presumably be tolerated. In this sense, private enterprise is private government."[19]

Takeover disputes involving Time Warner and other huge corporations, mostly in the corporate-friendly jurisdiction of Delaware courts, suggest a judicial buy-in to corpocracy. Monks maintains that the Delaware courts reinterpret words to mean whatever corporate officials want them to. "The courts and legislatures have bent so far backwards to defer to the 'business judgment' of directors—some have even gone so far as to eliminate liability not just for acts committed in good faith but for negligent acts as well." Since not even the shareholders have recourse, Monks argues that this "repudiates the entire basis for corporate legitimacy." By shielding corporate officers from political and judicial review, judges are elevating the CEO to the status of "philosopher king."[20]

The rise of corpocracy reveals the gross inadequacy of the contractarian story as a picture of the real-world corporation. Contractarians see in the corporation nothing but the ghostly traces of the free exchange of contracting individuals. They speak little of corporate entities, recognize no such thing as corporate personality, and worry not at all about the power of an institution that presumably has no life of its own. But the corporation is undeniably a formidable entity unto itself, whether conceived as natural or a political creation. It can enter into its own contracts, sue or be sued, and live forever.[21]

The realities of corpocracy belie the new fashion of reducing corporations to contracting individuals. The business-judgment rule and the growing set of constitutional rights vested in the corporation have created an unaccountable entity with sovereign powers far greater than natural entity theorists of the Gilded Age could ever have imagined.

Regulating the Corpocracy

While the business-judgment rule gives vast discretionary power to corporations, they are still required to abide by the law and work within the regulatory framework established by the government. This includes a huge body of legislation that has grown up since the Gilded Age: child-labor laws, clean air and water legislation, antidiscrimination and affirmative-action laws, and laws protecting unions. The very fact of such regulation can be seen as evidence that corporations, despite all their new power, remain subject to public control. But regulation has profound limits as a curb on corporate power—and, ironically, has served only to buttress America's faith in the corporate system.

For liberals and conservatives alike—and members of each group have misled the public and themselves about the issue—the debate over regulation carries a powerful electric charge. Liberals since the Progressive Era have put their faith in regulation as the public's defense against the sovereign corporation. Conservatives see the vast new regulatory system as a public assault on private enterprise. In the end, though, both of these views are somewhat myopic. Regulation has been one of the most important public counterweights to corporations—and, at the same time, has become a cornerstone of corporate ascendancy.

In an age of privatization like ours, it is hardly surprising that deregulation is becoming a tidal force. Virtually every major industry, from airlines to banking to telecommunications, is being deregulated. Deregulation has been touted as the answer to nearly every problem in the economy, and as a way to revitalize American democracy.

Regulation is, in fact, one of the great vehicles by which the public can exercise some measure of power over the corporation. Implementing the radical deregulatory agenda sponsored by Speaker Gingrich in the 1994 Contract for America—which would require a cost-benefit analysis that would essentially overturn much of our existing environmental and social regulation—would be the final stage in consolidating corporate sovereignty. Its failure, as of this writing, suggests that neither the corporation nor its contractarian religion have totally won the day.

But while regulation can be seen as the people's bulwark against corpocracy—and while a regimen of radical deregulation could prove catastrophic for civil rights, the environment, employee well-being, and other vital necessities—regulation is more complex than both liberals and conservatives assume. Regulation may threaten some corporate interests, but it can also serve corporations in hidden ways. As the next chapter shows, regulatory legislation, intended as a purely public benefit, often carries vital advantages for the private sector as well. The regulatory system is a terrain of conflict between government and corporation, but also joins them in common interest. It reinforces the image of private enterprise that helps keep the corporation safe from public accountability, while ironically propping up public faith in the private-enterprise system—hardly the threat to corpocracy that both liberals and conservatives have implied.

In 1995 a New York Republican congressman, James Walsh, tried to eliminate legislation regulating certain genetically engineered plants. But Monsanto and other chemical giants actually lobbied *against* the change, with success. A journalist covering the story explained that, "contrary to conventional wisdom, Monsanto and other industry giants love EPA regulation. It adds another stamp of approval to their products, and it squeezes out smaller companies that can't afford the time and money the regulatory process demands. The big firms will spend whatever it takes to topple the competition, and Monsanto's lobbying is so masterful that once regulation is in place, manipulating the process is a breeze."[22]

While corporations routinely denounce regulation, they have historically helped sponsor and shape much of the current regulatory system. Historian Gabriel Kolko, as noted in earlier chapters, has shown that corporations have desperately sought regulation throughout our history, at moments when problems of competition and other economic crises left them otherwise vulnerable. The Sherman Act and Interstate Commerce Act both gained support from railway barons because federal regulation and rate-setting turned out to be the only way for the established companies to wipe out complex state-to-state inconsistencies and replace them with a set of uniform national standards. Not coincidentally, by setting up barriers to entry and minimum standards, such regulation also provided the established railroad giants with a foolproof way to shoulder out leaner, younger bargain competitors—the Valu-Jets of their era.[23]

Similarly, in the Progressive Era, meatpackers ended up supporting regulation because it was the only way to deal with unscrupulous competitors whose contaminated meat was leading European governments to ban American imports. Wall Street turned to Washington as the only way to create a coherent national financial system, with J. P. Morgan's partner Henry P. Davison telling Congress flatly in 1912: "I would rather have regulation and control than free competition."[24] Regulation, as Kolko describes it, has often arisen out of corporations' perpetual need to turn to the political system for problems they cannot solve on their own. "National regulation," concludes Kolko, represented corporate efforts "to find political means to resolve the economic problems which economic decentralization, competition, and a whole panoply of new challenges made endemic to American capitalism."[25]

Kolko fails to mention that leading manufacturers from Henry Ford onward, as well as utilities, mining companies, and many other energy industries, have never embraced the regulatory state. Business has always been conflicted about regulation, and while leading sectors have championed national regulation, other sectors have fought it tooth and nail. The corporate turn to regulation has been a more complex and selective affair than Kolko suggests, and even business enthusiasts understand that the regulatory apparatus could become a far more powerful tool of public control than it now is. But Kolko's view is a vital corrective to current myths, making clear that, as early as the founding of modern regulation in the Progressive Era, business has played a leading role in creating regulation and has helped turn it into a cornerstone of corporate ascendancy. The difference between now and the Gilded Age is that corporations a century ago achieved dominance without relying on a vast regulatory regime, but have since learned to use that system as a major buttress of their own authority.

While regulation in theory makes corporations ultimately accountable to the people, there are clear reasons that it does not fundamentally threaten the corporation, but in fact adds to both its power and its legitimacy. Historically, regulation developed as an alternative to the more radical populist proposals for direct popular control of the corporation—whether through a revival of tough state charters or through a change to direct governmental ownership. The Progressives accepted not only the Gilded Age view that corporations should be private, but also the notion that regulation's purpose was both to protect the public *and* to maximize a company's efficiency and profitability. Justice Louis Brandeis and other Progressive champions of regulation argued that corporate responsibility involved "maintaining the highest possible rate of profit; in other words, the elevation of profit to not merely one goal but the preeminent raison d'être of the corporate entity."[26]

The Progressives' obsession with scientific management, efficiency, and profitability led them to create a form of regulation that offered modest social protections without fundamentally upsetting corporate priorities or authority. Instead of calling for a system of direct public initiatives to create or revoke charters—a return to the genuinely democratic side of the early chartering system—the Progressives created regulatory bureaucracies, dominated by experts who were often drawn from the industries themselves. The bureaucracies were almost as removed from public accountability as the corporations themselves. They saw their goals as maximizing efficiency as well as providing a modicum of public safety—a fair description of the regulatory system today.

Attorney Howard Schweber has described the evolution of regulation from the early chartering system through the Gilded Age, the Progressive Era, and up to today. Corporations evolved, he writes, from "publicly created entities devoted to a public purpose, to private entities bound by restrictive public charters, to 'natural' business entities bound by broadly applicable private duties, to combinations bound by strictly delimited private duties in the name of public goals, and finally to private business entities regulated by public authority solely in the interest of promoting efficiency and profit."[27]

The early charter system was intended to preserve popular control over the corporation and ensure that it served the purposes of the public. In contrast, today's regulatory system is built on the premise that the corporation is a purely private entity serving private ends. Its goal in regulating the corporation is not to reshape it to serve public purposes but to try to see that in the pursuit of private or selfish ends it does not do undue harm to the larger community.

Even while imposing limits upon it, regulation has paradoxically supported the agenda of corporate privatization. By offering the image of a protective system in which the public can put its faith, it has distracted public concern from the growing concentration of corporate power and the legal changes that increasingly shield corporations from interference in their internal affairs. As Scott Bowman writes, "As corporate power over society has been subject to increasing regulation through public law, the powers of the corporate hierarchy have been increasingly fortified through the law of corporations." Legislators and judges treat corporate law as the proprietary domain of corporations, since regulatory law presumably is where the public gets its say.[28]

Regulation, in other words, has become a real but exaggerated and somewhat illusory counterweight to a body of corporate law that defends "sound business judgment" against public scrutiny. Since corporations have to abide by regulations, we can allow them to govern themselves internally according to their own business interests. Since the regulatory system accepts the legal fiction of the corporation as a private legal citizen endowed with the constitutional rights of all citizens, it subtly promotes the notion of the corporation as an actor who can be trusted to act responsibly. Companies that can't will be subject to regulation by experts and bureaucrats; the debate never gets taken to the next level—to the extent of calling for a change in the system of corporate governance. Regulation has become a kind of panacea, a gentle substitute for a populist movement that would seek to return corporate control to the people.

The ultimate insurance corporations have about regulation is their mounting political power. If ordinary Americans were sufficiently incensed about downsizing or other corporate depredations, they could create a political climate that might transform the regulatory apparatus into a genuine instrument of public sovereignty. A populist movement could make regulation in practice the decisive restraint on corporate power that deregulation advocates claim it already has become. But since global economic and political forces favor corporations, they will continue to have the clout to ensure that the regulatory apparatus serves their own interests as much as those of the public. Small businesses may be different, but our most powerful corporations are happy with regulation just the way it is.

EIGHT

The Dependent Corporation

Abraham Lincoln is famous for saying "You can fool some of the people all of the time and all of the people some of the time, but you can't fool all of the people all of the time." He also said "Never underestimate the stupidity of the American people." In promoting the fiction of the private corporation, big business may be proving him wrong on his first statement and right on the second. Few Americans now view the corporation as anything but private property. It is time to get explicit about how this illusion at the heart of the corporate mystique flies in the face of reality.

Although the corporation obviously serves private interests, it is in fact a quasi-public institution with a political side that continues to mushroom. To describe the corporation as public does more than just recognize it as a creation of the state, "a mere creature of the law," as Chief Justice Marshall put it. Corporate welfare—the current label for the billions of dollars of public subsidies and tax breaks awarded to big business—is one of the extravagantly costly ways in which corporations draw on the public till to keep private enterprise afloat. Corporate welfare does more than pad corporate profits. As we will see, it is institutionalized life support for chronically dependent corporations.

Modern corporations have found innumerable ways to suckle at the breast of government, making them more and more public creatures. As business leaders and politicians rhapsodize about the virtues of privatization, corporations have grown so dependent on public provision that the whole corporate system would collapse without it. Such public dependency is a potentially explosive issue, since it blurs the distinction between government and business, and throws doubt on the American religion of private enterprise.

As corporate welfare has exploded into public attention, so has the issue of money in politics. Exactly a century after the elections of 1896, when the huge corporate funding of President McKinley's campaign created a national scandal, the money raised by Congressional Republicans and by President Clinton to bankroll his own campaign has again made the influence of corporate money on politics one of the nation's leading concerns. Billions of dollars in corporate welfare are regularly recycled back into the pockets of politicians running for office. Corporate contributions buy huge influence over public policy, a transparent kind of public power now exercised by corporations.

Corporations have now amassed vast public and quasi-public powers, both by privatizing large parts of government and by buying influence over what is left of it. By exercising such expansive authority—over national economic policy, the condition of our environment, public opinion, and the quality of everyday life for the entire citizenry—corporations threaten democracy itself. This exercise of wholesale public powers ought to give long pause to those who see the corporation as private enterprise. It also dramatizes the need for corporate responsibility and accountability to the public.

Corporate Welfare

Ralph Nader notes that "corporations collect more government handouts than all of the nation's poor people combined."[1] If the new attack on corporate welfare were confined to liberals such as Nader and Reich, it would hardly be news. But libertarian right-wing groups like the Cato Institute as well as conservative "new Democrats" like the Progressive Policy Institute are waging their own crusade against corporate welfare. Leading Republicans like House Budget Committee Chair John Kasich have said that as we reform welfare for the poor, "the time has also come to reform welfare for the people who have power."[2]

"The term welfare is not accurate," responds Johanna Schneider, speaking for the Business Roundtable, the most powerful association of Fortune 500 corporation executives. "Nobody's subsidizing companies to do nothing. These programs generate revenue and business and jobs."[3] Many Americans, nonetheless, see a glaring contradiction in pulling the plug on welfare for millions of mothers and their children while continuing to keep an open pipeline for multibillion-dollar corporations.

Nader has recently pointed out that when mining corporations find gold beneath public land, they can buy it for no more than five dollars an acre; as he quips, this is "taking inflation fighting too far."[4] The Cato Institute notes that the gold giveaway is just par for the course. "Over the past 20 years, the Forest Service has built 340,000 miles of roads—more than eight times the length of the interstate highway system—primarily for the benefit of the logging companies." The Cato analysts also describe the ways in which Uncle Sam pays for corporate advertisement of products abroad: "In 1991 American taxpayers spent $2.9 million advertising Pillsbury muffins and pies, $10 million promoting Sunkist oranges, $465,000 advertising McDonald's Chicken McNuggets, $1.2 million boosting the international sales of American Legend mink coats, and $2.5 million extolling the virtues of Dole pineapples, nuts, and prunes."[5]

Common Cause has pointed out that $50 million of taxpayer money has gone to help market California wines abroad. Two hundred fifty million dollars in public subsidies over the last five years has gone to Getty Oil, Pacific Power, and other private oil com-

panies through below-market fees for using public lands. The tobacco industry gets millions for its price support system, and defense contractors such as Martin Marietta got $27,000 just for
"golf balls and an office Christmas Party."[6]

The issue is rich with irony; the corporations cheerleading privatization are the very ones rushing to gorge themselves on public funds. Policy analysts in Washington have identified at least
127 separate government programs that include "active" forms of
corporate welfare: agribusiness subsidies, military-contractor subsidies, loan guarantees, and other direct giveaways to business.
Above and beyond these are the "passive" forms—the ethanol tax
credit, capital-gains tax loopholes, and other tax breaks—which
Nader argues make up half the federal tax code.

The total sums involved are staggering. The Cato Institute, one
of the few militantly conservative groups to be consistent about its
commitment to shrinking government, writes: "The federal welfare state for low-income families (before welfare reform) now
costs taxpayers between $250 billion and $300 billion a year. But
through an amalgamation of trade policies, selective tax breaks
and spending programs, the federal corporate welfare state is nearing that size. Both of these failed welfare empires should be top-
pled." The Institute probably underestimates corporate welfare
and inflates the cost of public welfare, which—including AFDC,
student aid, housing, food, and nutrition, and all direct public assistance other than Social Security and medical care—came to
about $150 billion in 1996.[7]

The Democratic Progressive Policy Institute has outlined $265
billion that could be saved in five years if reasonable cuts in corporate welfare were made. They note that this amounts "to nearly
half of all the domestic capital dedicated to fixed net business investment of the five years from 1989 through 1993."[8] Unlike the
Cato Institute, the PPI sensibly differentiates between wasteful
corporate giveaways and forms of public investment which add to
the nation's total productive capacity and can be defended as
something other than corporate pork.

The huge size of the pork ultimately makes a mockery of the fiction of corporate privatism. Wall Street financier Theodore Forstmann argues that corporate welfare has created "the statist businessman in America . . . an argument against capitalism even though he is not a capitalist at all."[9] The Cato Institute notes that "the major effect of corporate subsidies is to divert credit and capital to politically well connected firms at the expense of their less politically influential competitors." The Progressive Policy Institute agrees that "many current subsidies and protections have not come from economic logic, but from political influence first exercised long ago."[10] The Cato Institute's conclusion? "Corporate welfare fosters an incestuous relationship between business and government" that turns corporations into dependent protectorates of the state.[11]

The Cato Institute goes so far as to charge that the whole practice is unconstitutional and should be abandoned. "Nowhere in the Constitution is Congress granted the authority to spend funds to subsidize the computer industry, or to enter into joint ventures with automobile companies, or to guarantee business loans to favored business owners."[12] Yet even if all the specific subsidies and tax breaks the Cato Institute identifies were eliminated, it would not create the pure private economy or mythical private corporation that Cato thinkers espouse. There are many other ways in which government and corporation are intertwined—which, if eliminated, would sink the entire economy.

The Iceberg of Dependency

Corporate welfare, for all its size, is just the visible tip of the huge submerged iceberg of corporate dependency. The fact is that corporations are wards of the state whose overwhelming dependency has rendered them undeniably public creatures with unacknowledged public responsibilities and accountability.

The massive reality of the iceberg crushes the illusion of the private corporation. The iceberg is made up of the many billions of dollars spent by governments on schools to educate the workforce, on roads, railways, and ports that allow corporations to transport their goods, on research and development that funds corporate technology, on military and foreign-policy spending that protect and promote exports and foreign markets—to name only some of the building blocks. At first glance, these seem like public expenditures in the service of the public good—which some of them are. But a closer look also shows that these are critical government investments or subsidies essential to the operation of business and indispensable to corporate profitability. While many yield benefits to the public, such subsidies disproportionately reward the corporations themselves. And since they are paid for by government, they should, logically and ethically, render corporations accountable to the taxpaying public.

About twenty-five years ago the American economist James O'Connor, a specialist on fiscal and budgetary affairs, argued that a vast and growing percentage of the entire federal budget was made up of expenses paid by the government to help ensure the profitability of corporations. O'Connor called this the "socialization" of the costs of private production. Prodded by increasingly powerful corporations, government historically picked up more and more of the business costs necessary to operate profitably in a complex high-technology global economy. Such government spending, O'Connor argues, is a kind of social capital: social or public funds going to underwrite "private" business. These expenses include both benefits for specific corporations or industries (some of which qualify as what we now call corporate welfare) and generalized spending that benefits the corporate community as a whole.[13]

In earlier periods, the federal budget remained small because corporate needs were less costly and corporations covered most of the costs of production themselves. In the nineteenth century, he writes, government budgets remained small: "transportation investments were chiefly private, and natural resource, conservation, public health, education and related outlays were insignificant . . . State subsidies to capital as a whole were confined to the state government and local level."[14]

In the twentieth century, however, corporations began to turn to the state to cover risky and rapidly growing production costs. Many changes drove the corporation into the bosom of the state. "The most expensive economic needs of corporate capital as a whole," writes O'Connor, "are the costs of research, development of new products, new productive processes, and so on, and, above all, the costs of training and retraining the labor force, in particular technical, administrative, and nonmanual workers." Also of crucial importance was the massive new cost of infrastructure, from electric or nuclear power stations and world-class airports to a global satellite network.[15]

Government increasingly footed the bill. After World War II, through both military and civilian agencies, the federal government sank billions into the nation's infrastructural foundation—and into the research and technological base of the modern corporation. "It's hard to find a major industry today whose principal investments were not first made by the government—in aerospace, telecommunications, biotechnology and agribusiness. Government research and development money funds the drug and pharmaceutical industry. Government research and development funds are given freely to corporations, but they don't announce it in ads the next day."[16]

O'Connor's analysis suggests a new way of thinking about everything from the interstate highway system to commercially exploitable government research and development projects. These are properly seen as sound public investments, but they also constitute a transfer of resources from the government to the corporation. Such socialization of corporate costs gives the public a largely unacknowledged stake in private production—and a legitimate claim on its return.

Ralph Nader makes clear both the nature of the claim and how it is received. He points out, for instance, that Taxol, a new cancer-fighting drug, "was produced by a grant of $31 million of taxpayer money through the National Institutes of Health, right through the clinical testing process. The formula was then given away to the Bristol-Myers Squibb company. No royalties were paid to the taxpayer. There was no restraint on the price. Charges now run $10,000 to $15,000 per patient for a series of treatments. If the patients can't pay, they go on Medicaid, and the taxpayer pays at the other end of the cycle too."[17]

Socialized production costs represent only one of several kinds of public spending that go largely unacknowledged as forms of corporate subsidy. Spending on the American military and on the development of the United States as a global superpower has decisively cleared the path for corporation expansion and production abroad. Spending on the environment has cleaned up pollution which, if untreated, would have destroyed the ecological conditions for sustainable production. Spending on social programs continues to help dissipate the kind of social unrest that could ultimately lead to populist revolts against corporate power.

The government engages in a wide variety of other corporate services that don't necessarily involve spending money but are no less crucial to the success of American business. These range from trade policies that shape international commerce on American terms to tax policies that massively favor corporate priorities. On taxes alone, corporations have seen their own percentage of the national tax burden fall from 35 percent in 1945 to a projected 11 percent in 2000. Most important, the government and the Federal Reserve System help to manage, coordinate, and stabilize the national and global economy in ways that sustain demand, control inflation, and regulate interest rates in the service of corporate profitability.

None of this suggests that the government should not be engaged in such aid to corporations, or that the acceptance of this assistance makes corporations nothing but wards of the state. Much of the integration of government and corporation contributes both to the corporate and the public interest, and could not be eliminated without unacceptable damage to both business and society. The scandal here is not so much the intertwining of public and private arenas as the widespread denial of such interdependence and its implications. America is long overdue to discard the notion of the purely private corporation and start insisting that the public get its fair return on its corporate investment—as well as a system of public accountability proportional to the contribution it has made.

And perhaps the greatest irony in this scandal has been the extent to which corporate interests have turned the issue on its head. The government assumption of corporate costs has been a major source of the rise in the federal budget, the ballooning of the federal deficit, and the rise in taxes; yet these are all now attacked by the corporations themselves as the evil result of big government, socialist thinking, the irresponsibility of the poor, and the over-entitled middle classes. In fact it is the government-sanctioned entitlement of the American corporation and its own irresponsible willingness to shift costs onto the taxpayer, that accounts for much of the problem.

Private Corporations, Public Powers

During the 1996 elections, public outrage over the role of big money in politics exploded. More than two billion dollars were spent on campaigns—the greatest sum in American history. The resulting demand for campaign-finance reform became a symbol of the new concern about the prostitution of democracy to those who can pay.

As the biggest contributors, corporations bought by far the greatest share of political influence. As in the Gilded Age, such spending has allowed them to help set the agenda for both political parties. Gaining such influence over government itself is another one of the ways in which corporations are gaining political and public power. Like their increasing public dependency, this massive purchase of government influence is another way in which corporations are becoming public institutions that should by all rights be accountable to the people.

There is scarcely any pretense now about the corrupting influences of political money, even from those who shell it out. Don Tyson, chairman of the board of Tyson Foods Inc., said in 1995 that the business of politics "consists of a series of unsentimental transactions between those who need votes and those who have money . . . [it is] a world where every quid has its quo."[18] Robert D. Brown, VP for government affairs at AT&T, one of America's biggest corporate donors in an era of epochal telecommunications legislation, unapologetically summed up AT&T's money-giving approach: "We look to where the power is."[19] Reviewing the influence of corporate contributions on health care, tobacco, and agribusiness legislation, Archibald Cox, former Solicitor General of the United States, wrote in 1996 that the "dependence of our elected representatives in Washington on the flow of special-interest money is corrupting our democratic process . . . lawmakers are not beholden to the voters who elected them, but to the political action committees (PACs) and other special interests which finance their elections."[20]

President Clinton ran for office in 1996 promising to end the "cliques of $100,000 donors" who can buy access to Congress and the White House. Instead he became a virtuoso at the game, the first Democratic president in a generation to rival Republicans in raising huge sums from corporations. On his birthday in 1995 he took in $10 million at one event. In 1991, during Clinton's first race, corporate donations to the Democrats had been only four times that of labor, but by 1995 corporate contributions to the Democratic party had skyrocketed to nine times those of unions. The number of corporations who joined the Democratic Business Council, which requires contributions of at least $15,000 per company, jumped from 200 in 1992 to 1,900 in 1995.[21] The corporate financial embrace of the Democrats paid handsome dividends in the most pro-business Democratic agenda of the twentieth century, with Clinton claiming that the most important objective of his second term would be to prove that the era of big government is over and bring the deficit down to zero.

The cascade of rhetoric about the role of "special interests" in politics is a polite mask for the overwhelming influence of corporate money on campaigns at all levels of government. While much was made about the $35 million spent by unions in the 1996 presidential and congressional campaigns, corporations spent at least seven times as much, dwarfing all other contributors. The biggest single "special interest" contributor in the 1996 elections was Philip Morris, a paragon of unabashed corporate immersion in politics. Darlenne Dennis, director of communications for the huge food and tobacco company, said: "Philip Morris supports those who share our thoughts. We have a responsibility to our employees and shareholders to be in the political process and we are happy to do so."[22] The tobacco companies and the wider corporate community helped to reelect a conservative pro-business Republican Congress in 1996, even as they were covering their bases by donating vast sums to President Clinton at the same time.

The right of corporations to engage in such expansive funding of elections is gradually being written into the Constitution. In the 1976 case *Buckley v. Valeo* the Supreme Court defined money given to parties, candidates, or ballot issues as a form of free speech protected under the First Amendment of the Constitution. The Court ruled that "A restriction on the amount of money a person or group can spend on political communication during a campaign necessarily reduces the quantity of expression by restricting the number of issues discussed, the depth of their exploration, and the size of the audience reached." Explicitly protecting corporate as well as individual contributions for the first time, the Court thus used democratic logic to justify a decision that might obviously impair the democratic process. In the process, it began a major new judicial offensive to constitutionalize a new broad package of corporate political and public powers—the most consequential legal aggrandizement of corporate power since the Gilded Age.[23]

In another important case, 1978's *First National Bank v. Bellotti,* the Court underscored its view of corporate giving as protected free speech. The Court declared that corporate contribution designed to influence a ballot referendum "is the type of speech indispensable to decision-making in a democracy, and this is no less true because the speech comes from a corporation rather than an individual." The Court rejected the notion that vast inequality could distort the democratic process, since "the people in our democracy are entrusted with the responsibility for judging and evaluating the relative merits of conflicting arguments."[24]

It was by no means a unanimous ruling. Justice Byron White, along with Justices William Brennan and Thurgood Marshall, expressed a profound dissenting opinion: "Corporations are artificial entities created by law . . . the special status of corporations has placed them in a position to control vast amounts of economic power which may, if not regulated, dominate not only the economy but also the very heart of our democracy, the electoral process. . . . The State need not permit its own creation to consume it . . . Such expenditure may be viewed as seriously threatening the role of the First Amendment as a guarantor of a free marketplace of ideas."[25]

This was one of several times that dissenting justices or even a Court majority have expressed qualms about the new Constitutional protections they were generously awarding. In a 1986 decision Justice Brennan wrote that "Direct corporate spending on political activity raises the prospect that resources possessed in the economic marketplace may be used to provide an unfair advantage in the political marketplace." In 1990, in *Austin v. Michigan State Chamber of Commerce,* the Supreme Court for the first time upheld state laws limiting the amount of money that corporations could spend for candidates in state elections. Justice Marshall wrote that the state could limit the corporation's right to free speech, since there was a compelling public interest to prevent "the corrosive and distorting effects of immense aggregations of wealth that are accumulated with the help of the corporate form and that have little or no correlation to the public's support for the corporation's political ideas."[26]

The Court did not justify this infringement on the ground that great wealth inequalities made democracy impossible, nor did it seek to equalize the relative financial influence of different political actors. Rather, it argued that the special status of the corporation as a creation of the state provided it with special qualities enabling it to amass vast wealth—and that it thereby owed the public some accountability to prevent it from using this "publicly created advantage to undermine the public's own political expressions."[27]

The Austin case is significant not only because it imposes real limits on corporate political money, but because it does so in ways that recognize the corporation as a state-created artificial entity that should rightfully be publicly accountable. However, it does not fundamentally change the trend established in the *Buckley* and *Bellotti* cases. As Scott Bowman points out, the *Austin* case does not place any limits on corporate contributions in federal or local elections, or on other kinds of political advocacy. No meaningful constraints on corporate lobbies, PACs, or soft money have been enacted in over two decades. Bowman concludes that the corporation's new political rights are not in jeopardy; the privatization and personification of the corporation established in the Gilded Age thus continue to haunt us. When corporate freedom is equated with the freedom of individuals, any restriction on corporations becomes an attack on individual rights. In the name of protecting the constitutional rights of the citizen, the Court has given its backing to full-blown corporate political rights that endanger citizens themselves. Given the enormous wealth controlled by corporations, such political rights ensure them a level of governmental influence, or public power, that is hard to reconcile with the notion of a private entity. Its supposedly private status has become a guarantee of the corporation's inescapable public identity and weight.

The corporation's influence over government does not, however, derive simply from its massive election contributions. Even if Congress were to pass laws tomorrow eliminating all private campaign financing, corporate influence over government would remain overwhelming. The reason is inherent in their prize power resource: mobility.

In 1996, the Fidelity Corporation made it clear to the Commonwealth of Massachusetts that it would relocate many of its facilities to New Hampshire and Rhode Island if some specific, very generous tax breaks weren't forthcoming. Raytheon had successfully made the same case to the beleaguered legislators earlier that year. The prospect of the loss of thousands of Fidelity jobs was enough to ensure quick capitulation from the Massachusetts leaders.

The rise of the corporation, as observed in Chapter 2, was based on its exquisite rootlessness. The musical-chairs game by which corporations have historically pitted one state against another— just as today they pit nations against each other—is a splendid tool for persuading governments of the political correctness of the corporate agenda. Those that don't play the game of carrying out the corporation's legislative wish list will lose jobs and ultimately their tax base—ensuring that the public powers of government are being wielded, surely if indirectly, for and by the "private" corporation.

Privatism Run Rampant

In 1988 President Reagan's Commission on Privatization delivered its final report, announcing itself as the harbinger of a privatization revolution that "may well be seen by future historians as one of the most important developments in American political and economic life of the late twentieth century."[28]

While the Gilded Age and much of the twentieth century has been spent privatizing the corporation itself, a new agenda looms: the spread of the privatism agenda to the whole of public life. With corporate privatization largely achieved in the eyes of the law and the public, the stars in the postcommunist political firmament seem favorably aligned toward the privatization of everything else. The new privatization movement is an explicit effort to turn public resources, services, and functions—for centuries operated by governments—over to corporations. As the movement grows, corporations are already assuming new public powers—not by influencing government but by spinning off its component parts and swallowing them whole.

The new privatization rests on many of the same fictional assumptions that the process of corporate privatization did. Stripping a function away from government—whether it be education, policing, or tax collection—does not necessarily take away its public character. It is more of a shell game that transfers something to a nominally private institution from one that is transparently public. It expands the private sector, but only by engorging it with public authority. Privatization thus deepens the public identity of the corporation and expands its public power without increasing its public accountability.

The president's commission noted three approaches to carrying out the revolution: selling off government assets, contracting out key services, and creating vouchers. One of the three could be fruitfully applied, it suggested, in almost every area of government. Targets included schools, the FAA and air-traffic control, low-income housing and other housing programs, the post office, prisons, military commissaries, Amtrak, Naval Petroleum reserves, federal loan programs, urban mass transit, international-development programs, and medical programs. In the 1990s the old Reagan Commission roster was expanded to include the prospect of privatizing Social Security, Medicare, and other more ambitious targets.

The commission could not have foreseen how rapidly the new

privatization would spread. Since 1988, giant for-profit hospital corporations have established a major niche in medicine, while the Republican congressional majority has proposed to privatize the heart of Medicare. Governments have contracted out a huge chunk of their services—from garbage collection to prisons to welfare. Corporations are buying schools and supplying them with curricula—complete with commercials in the classroom—while governments distribute vouchers to make them viable. Huge parcels of federal land, as well as public airways and satellite bands, are being handed over, free or at bargain prices, to corporate giants.[29]

This turns much of the public good of any society—whether caring for the sick, teaching wisdom to the young, or preserving the environmental commons—into simply another arena for generating corporate profits. In this sense, privatization is anything but fictional, tearing apart the public quilt that binds people together and turning it into the raw material of capital for the already wealthy. The economic result is not only evident in the bottom lines of the media, mining, agribusiness, and hospital corporations that have already plucked their public plums, but in the Wall Street firms now spending millions to promote Social Security privatization in anticipation of plums to come—the stupefying profits to be made from investing billions of privatized 401K and other retirement funds.

The new privatization would redistribute not only wealth but public authority as well. The powers to educate, jail, rehabilitate, heal, care for the poor, and manage nature itself are all being turned over to corporations. And as these functions are sold off, government itself is transformed, if not dismantled, into a creature of private enterprise.

Finally, it would be negligent to ignore the most expansive of public or quasi-public powers that corporations have been accumulating long before the current waves of privatization and corporate political influence. These are the core market powers at the heart of their being, including the power to determine who will work and at what reward, to decide what products will be produced at what quality and price, to determine how land and natural resources will be used, squandered, polluted, or saved, and to determine the form, content, and distribution of ideas and images that shape culture through the mass media. These are the decisions that shape our everyday lives and broadly define our culture and way of life.

Even if one accepts that governments should stay out of such decisions, the power to make them nevertheless remains a public or quasi-public power. Such decisions have more impact on our own lives as citizens than virtually any other. They not only help shape each of us personally, but in large measure mold our collective identity and shared values.

Such publicly influential market powers are neither new nor necessarily illegitimate. But their concentration in an increasingly small number of giant global corporations foreshadows important social changes. As the public impact of such market powers keeps growing, inevitably coming to touch populations all over the world, the circle of corporate decision makers is also shrinking, becoming less accountable every day to any public authority. Since multinational corporations now increasingly take action without any parochial loyalty to a particular nation, decisions that can make or break whole societies are being made by those without either loyalty or accountability to them.

This brings us back to Abe Lincoln. In an age defined by almost universal belief in the fiction of the private corporation, the corporation itself has become ever more public—in its growing role as both public dependent and prime public mover.

Even Lincoln at his most cynical might have hoped that the American public would see through the bill of goods we've been sold under the brand name "private enterprise." Seeing how the corporate mystique is created and sustained, however, is one thing; knowing how to change the illusions it sustains and the power it bolsters is another.

NINE

Five Reasons Americans Don't Think about Corporate Power and Why They Should

It was Pat Buchanan who created the only real excitement of the 1996 elections. In a conservative-populist campaign that mixed virulent rhetoric and jingoistic bigotry with valuable perceptions about American business, he relentlessly skewered corporate executives as "corporate executioners." He rallied laid-off workers in Michigan, characterizing unbridled capitalism as "the law of the jungle." He shouted to Bible Belt churchgoers, self-styled patriots on motorbikes, and other militant conservatives, "When go-go global capitalism is uprooting entire communities and families, I ask conservatives what it is we are trying to conserve."[1]

Buchanan charged quite rightly that corporate values are no longer friendly to family values. He harangued corporations as moral criminals for fleeing abroad in search of cheap labor and selling out America. For a short time, he made it almost fashionable to attack corporations. At the height of his popularity, *Newsweek* ran a scathing story on corporate "hit men," splashing the label "Corporate Killers" in big, bloodred letters on its cover.

Buchanan fancied himself a charismatic populist for the 1990s. "The peasants are coming with pitchforks," he would bellow at campaign stops. In his eyes, it was time to make Wall Street answer to Main Street. As the *Wall Street Journal* put it sarcastically, "Mr. Buchanan has a distinctly nineteenth century view of the economy, in which capitalism is dominated by robber barons who work with their lackeys in government to oppress workers." Alan Brinkley wrote that "Buchanan draws from powerful impulses in the American past. His rhetoric echoes the agrarian populism of the late nineteenth century with its harsh attacks on the railroads, corporations and banks, its suspicion of 'international finance' and its deeper fears that in a new and alien economy individuals were losing control over their own fates."[2]

But while Buchanan created a brief national moment of populist consciousness, there is no movement today anything like the populists of the robber-baron era. The populists of the 1880s and 1890s helped turn the presidential campaigns of 1892 and 1896 into a national seminar on corporate power. The populists lost, but they succeeded in bringing about the consciousness and outrage about corporate greed that led to the Progressive reforms a decade later.

In today's new era of corporate power, on the other hand, a near taboo seems to have descended about the subject. Politicians, with the exception of heretics like Buchanan, never talk about it. The media expose sensational business scandals, such as the savings-and-loan crisis of the early nineties, and periodically focus on issues such as downsizing, yet rarely do they ask why corporations collectively have so much power, or what we can do about it.

Most of the rest of us don't spend much time thinking about the question either. In the classes I teach, most students acknowledge they have never really thought about how much power corporations have or whether it is good for America. When the corporation has become not only our employer but our church, government, and opinion maker, this ignorance is far from bliss. Corporate power is a dominant reality of our lives. To fail to understand or question it is to live in a mental prison, and to foreclose the possibility of living differently.

Usually, people give great attention to the forces or people that control them. Children spend a lifetime trying to understand the parents who have shaped them. Graduate students obsess about the professors who help determine the course of their careers. There is something unnatural about not thinking about the most powerful forces in our lives.

In this era when unfettered corporate power has begun to threaten democracy itself, it is time for Americans to take off their mental blinkers. There are at least five reasons we have not done so thus far. Together they help explain one of the sacred taboos of our culture, and its end result—our deafening silence about corporate power. It is this taboo, one of the signal elements of the corporate mystique, that keeps things going on their present course and blocks the kind of thinking that could change our lives.

The Politics of Diversion

Not thinking about corporate power does not come naturally. It is a trained incapacity.

Buchanan was a Democrat's dream come true—a Republican spoiler who split his party not only on social issues like abortion but on its core doctrines of free-market economics and faith in the corporation. This was like splitting the Catholic Church on the issue of the divinity of Jesus. The legitimacy of the corporation had not been a proper question in the Republican party since Teddy Roosevelt at the turn of the century, and he would eventually leave the party over the issue.

Buchanan's real contribution, however, was to shake up the terms of political conversation that have prevailed in the nation since the presidency of Ronald Reagan. Reagan's legacy was to redefine big government as the evil presence in American life. Buchanan, by lambasting corporate patriotism and greed, changed the fundamental terms of the debate. He seemed for a while to be inadvertently ending the Reagan era's overriding preoccupation with big government and turning the spotlight on big business.

His ultimate lack of success reflected the persistence of a Reaganite strain in American political thinking that long preceded Reagan himself. At the birth of our nation, the Founding Fathers called the power of government the central threat to liberty. This, of course, was a popular sentiment at a time when government meant King George III. The goal of the Revolution was to challenge the tyranny of the British monarchy, and the Constitution devoted much rhetorical flourish to the idea that the freedom of the people depends first and foremost on checking and balancing the powers of government.

The Founding Fathers did not address the threat to freedom that could be posed by the emergence of unchecked private power. Although he opposed a national bank, Madison wrote that private property was in fact the key bulwark of liberty, a notion firmly built into the Constitution. And the Founders' perspective is hardly surprising, since the drafters of the Constitution were all part of the propertied elite. Collectively, they were as much concerned with limiting the power of the people as they were with limiting the power of government. The protection of private power served their own interests, and one of the great dangers that John Adams, Alexander Hamilton, and others sought to head off was a populist challenge to property rights.[3]

The definition of unchecked government as the primary threat to freedom became a central and enduring tenet of American political thought. During the Gilded Age hostility to big government actually grew, even though it was the rise of corporate power that defined the age. The robber barons, political leaders, and great thinkers of the era, the definers of the corporate mystique, sang in one great choir of the overwhelming threat posed by government. Henry Jackson, a leading corporate attorney, summed it up: "The great curse of the world is too much government."[4]

The focus on government became the centerpiece of what

might be called the politics of diversion. Then, as now, it distracted people from thinking about the corporation by riveting their attention on the dangers of government. By discrediting government, such diversion undermines the most important check on corporate power, even as it distracts people from paying attention to the real problem.

The politics of diversion creates a climate in which hostility to government overwhelmingly dominates political discourse and popular consciousness. Government gets blamed not only for the very real problems in which it is implicated, but for virtually every other problem as well. It is true, of course, that government carries out much of the corporate agenda and creates plenty of its own social ills. Big government can, indeed, become a threat to freedom; the focus on government is compelling because it is not entirely illegitimate as a diversion. The problem is that by loading virtually all economic and societal problems on big government, it blinds Americans to the role of big business in creating our current morass.

The politics of diversion has made for an American populace largely disinclined to think clearly about social problems. Elites from the robber barons to the Reaganites and Gingrichites have succeeded in lulling average Americans into believing that the checks and balances necessary to preserve democracy apply only to government, not to the corporation. In the Gilded Age the populists felt no such deterrent, and mobilized a social movement that focused American attention on corporate power. The politics of diversion has proved stunningly effective today, but it need not always be so.

Creature Comforts

When first presented with a critique of corporate power, most of my students react with astonishment. As noted earlier, many say they cannot imagine Disney or Microsoft being too powerful. These corporations are, after all, the source of the lifestyle pleasures and magical technology that make their lives fun and their studies easier.

The thought of criticizing or tampering with the business of corporations seems nothing less than a threat to prosperity and the American Dream. Americans see our corporations as the source of the creature comforts that make us the envy of the whole world. If our corporate system were to be weakened or brought down, so might our whole way of life. Most Americans would likely say they are prepared to tolerate great corporate power if the only alternative were losing their standard of living.

Americans, in other words, feel both grateful to corporations and profoundly dependent on them. This is not just because they are our employers, the forces that keep us sheltered and fed: Our corporations deliver the goods, in ways our Gilded Age forefathers could hardly have dreamed of. The corporation is responsible for all the enchanted goods that seem to make our lives worth living, from color computer monitors and new cars to the comfortable sneakers on our feet. The corporation not only produces these goods but makes them affordable. Americans know that tourists worldwide come here to shop for bargains. No other corporate system provides so many different consumer products, in so many different varieties, at such affordable prices.

Americans are also keenly aware of the convenience in their lives that corporations have helped make possible. Though the media in 1997 reported an upsurge in consumer discontent about rude and unsolicitous service, no other national economic system appears as customer-friendly or so eager to oblige to make a sale. From credit cards to home deliveries to twenty-four-hour service,

American corporations have attuned themselves to the habits and tastes of their customers. In a consumer culture, and probably in most others, this is not a trivial blessing.

This sense that the corporation delivers the goods is undoubtedly a cornerstone of our broadly positive feelings about the corporation, and a key reason that Americans spend so little time thinking about corporate power. To do so might be profoundly personally threatening: A line of thought that challenges the corporation might suggest compromising not only one's job but all the comforts that make America unique.

This is not false consciousness, as many corporate critics might suggest. The American corporate system does deliver convenience, creature comforts, and a level of material well-being that few Americans would like to see endangered. Populists must challenge rampant consumerism, but any critique of the corporation that calls for the elimination of these privileges is a nonstarter in American culture.

The truth is that any politics of the corporation must begin with an appreciation of its successes. It is possible to be critical of overwhelming corporate power without seeking to undermine the many benefits that the corporation has brought the consuming public. Part of the problem is not the production of abundance but its obscene maldistribution. America's consumer paradise is becoming even more heavenly to a small sector of the population, but moving out of reach of the 40 million Americans officially designated in poverty and the even greater number in the downsized middle class. The brand of new positive populism that would benefit America would seek to increase productivity and redistribute its fruits by engaging more Americans as stakeholders in corporate governance.

The new division between the classes is only one of the devastating societal costs of the current corporate system. There is no free lunch for the creature comforts delivered by the corporation. The ravaging of nature, the erosion of economic security, the destabilization of the family, the commercialization of all human relationships, the corruption of democracy, and the dissipation of spiritual meaning in the face of rampant materialism—these are all part of the cost of the corporate system as we know it. And they add up to a very high price to pay for the bounty of the great American shopping mall.

No Exit

The question is whether many of these costs can be alleviated through populist reforms without drastically compromising our prosperity. Most Americans seem not to think so. The carefully preprogrammed view that there are no alternatives to our current corporate regime is a third reason Americans rarely question the system.

It is always difficult to imagine significant change. Like children who do anything to hold on to parents who abuse them, we tend to hang on to what we know even when it is bad for us. The risk of change is attractive only when terrible crises plague us, and a clear alternative exists.

The end of the Cold War seems to have played a major role in eroding our collective ability to conceive of an alternative to our current corporate order. While communist and socialist regimes hardly seemed like attractive options to the great majority of Americans, they were omnipresent reminders that there were dramatically different ways to organize society. For a small sector of activists and intellectuals in America—and for many more people around the world—they provided some continuing faith that it was possible to arrange things so that corporations served the people rather than the reverse.

With the collapse of the gray realities of communism and the ideals of socialism, that hope was dealt a blow. The new mood was summarized by Francis Fukuyama, who wrote that "what we may be witnessing is not just the end of the Cold War, or the passing of a particular period of postwar history, but the end of history as such: that is, the end point of mankind's ideological evolution and the universalization of western liberal democracy as the final form of human government." Western liberal democracies and corporate capitalism, suddenly, were the only game in town.[5]

After the collapse of communism, some social critics such as Lester Thurow pointed to the profound differences in the various capitalisms that rule the globe, suggesting that Americans might learn from other models.[6] The corporate systems in Germany and Japan, for example, are different species from those in the United States, marked in Germany, at least, by much greater countervailing governmental and labor power. But while Japan's Confucian capitalism and Germany's social democratic system became, for a while, a source of hope, the bloom now seems to have left these alternatives as well. The American media have relentlessly portrayed high unemployment rates in Europe, the continuing sluggishness of the Japanese economy, the collapse of other Asian economies, and the new dynamism of America's corporate giants in the mid-nineties as evidence that no sane American would give up our system for theirs.[7]

But while neither Japan nor Germany nor any other European society offers any panaceas, they do demonstrate that there remain many different ways to organize world-class economies. The United States does far better than either Japan or Europe in many economic arenas, particularly recent job creation, but lags in other major economic indicators and is far worse on many societal ones. The United States not only suffers dangerously greater economic inequality than Japan, Germany, and other advanced nations, but also has much higher rates of poverty, violence, urban and public-school decay, malnutrition, and family breakdown. We also tolerate disproportionately large numbers of people lacking medical coverage, day care, adequate public transportation, affordable housing, and any secure form of emotional and community support.

The problem is not so much the lack of alternatives, but a failure of imagination and will. As we shall soon show, there is no dearth of possible reforms to corporate rule. What is needed is a clear analysis of our crisis and the courage and hope to take action.

The Couch-Potato Syndrome

A fourth explanation of why Americans don't focus on corporate power is the immensity of the power itself. Polls suggest that many Americans are aware of the existence of the vast power that corporations exercise, and of the greed and exploitation that goes with it. A 1996 national poll commissioned by the Preamble Center for Public Policy in New York showed that 46 percent of Americans saw corporate greed as the main force behind our national economic problems and the current wave of downsizing. More than 70 percent agreed that current corporate trends toward moving production abroad, outsourcing, higher executive compensation, lower health-care and other employee benefits, and escalating political corruption were serious problems requiring national attention. The pollsters conclude that "the American people have become firm in their belief that corporations are good investments but bad citizens."[8]

Why, then, is there no populist movement like that of a century ago? The power of corporations has become so vast that many Americans feel lilliputian in contrast. Their sense of their own power has faded as the corporation has closed itself off from public accountability and from any real influence by either worker or consumer.

It's a reliable truth that concentration of corporate power is inversely related to a public's feelings of personal power. As corporations like GE have grown larger and more economically powerful than whole countries such as Israel or Denmark, individuals who work in their shadow feel increasingly diminished. The growing sense of disempowerment among Americans reflects current corporate realities, and as it grows it perpetuates itself.

To launch a movement for social change requires a real belief in one's own power—and in that of one's friends and neighbors. Americans still believe they can make a difference in the life of a single poor or hungry person. Fully one-quarter of college students, and a substantial percentage of Americans, do some voluntary service in soup kitchens, battered women's shelters, and the like. But when it comes to changing the corporation or larger system, that sense of hope is far more difficult to find.

Isolated individuals, in truth, have little prospect of transforming big institutions on their own. This kind of change requires social movements or countervailing institutions to mobilize large-scale resistance. In an era of declining countervailing powers and social atomization, the sense of helplessness is understandable. Challenging large-scale power requires both the time and the hope that people can come together to make a difference. Economist Juliet Schor has documented the time crunch that faces growing numbers of low-wage, overworked Americans: Squeezed for time with their families, they are hard-pressed to find a way to make public commitments or even go to evening meetings. In an era of community decline, where Americans are more likely to "bowl alone," as political scientist Robert Putnam has put it, finding the hope for coming together also takes a courageous leap of faith.[9]

These factors have contributed to America's new couch-potato syndrome, a blow to the chances of collective behavior generally and populist movements in particular. Harried, exhausted, and helpless, many Americans retreat after work to the cocoon of their television room. There we are comfortably seduced by corporate messages about the world, pacified by sitcoms and soaps, and removed from the contact with others that might begin to elicit a sense of empowerment and hope.

Disempowerment breeds couch-potato apathy, which breeds

greater powerlessness: It's a cycle that corporations may not be conspiring to create, but it undoubtedly helps their ascendancy. Seduced by the tube, we spend little time dwelling on where the pictures on the screen might have come from. Picking up the remote and changing the channel is, ultimately, an all-too-comfortable substitute for trying to find a way to change the world.

What's Left?

In the spirited days of the sixties, Martin Luther King, Jr., articulated his dream of a "beloved community," embracing blacks and whites, old and young, men and women, coming together to fight for justice. King started as a civil-rights activist, but ended up a populist. He had learned that ending legal segregation would not bring justice to African Americans or white Americans: That would take changing the values and power structure of a corporate world.

King was killed before he could lead that struggle forward. Since his death, no other leader or movement has been able to lead where King hoped to go. In the absence of a strong populist movement, critical thinking about the role of big business has become idle fantasy in the eyes of most Americans.

In the Gilded Age, when a great populist movement swept through the Midwest prairies and fired the imagination of hundreds of thousands of farmers and workers, the power of the corporation became a household topic. If you lived in Lincoln, Nebraska, you could read this in a farmers' journal: "The corporation has absorbed the community. The community must now absorb the corporation. . . . Has there been a better system in the world? Does not the problem of humanity demand that there shall be a better system? There MUST be a better system."[10]

If you didn't live in Lincoln, the issue of corporate power would still have been part of the conversation. In their 1892 founding platform, the new People's party created by the populists asked every American to vote for stripping away railroads, telephone and telegraph services, banks, and land from corporations and returning them to direct government ownership or community control. They did not persuade most citizens, but every American of the time was obliged to think about what limits were appropriate on corporate power.

The populism of the nineteenth century failed. In part it fell victim to the vast power and political resources of the robber barons, who won control over both political parties: Both the Republicans and Democrats worked to undermine a populist third party. The Democrats ultimately succeeded by co-opting them, nominating William Jennings Bryan as their candidate in 1896. Bryan, as we see shortly, was far from an authentic populist, but his nomination and defeat spelled the end of populism. Since then there have been periodic resurfacings of left- and right-wing populist movements, but most have taken demagogic, paranoiac, or xenophobic forms such as Buchanan's, and they have tarnished populism as a viable American political idea. The original populism, despite flaws of its own, became the last mainstream political movement to raise a radical and legitimate challenge to the new sovereign American corporation.

Today we need a new, positive populism. While the seeds and vision of such a movement are already emerging, its prospects for success depend on the chances of making a major change in the political culture of the progressive forces that are its natural leaders.

In the twentieth century, what Richard Flacks calls the "tradition of the Left" has been the main political hope for raising the issue of corporate power. Flacks defines the Left as "that body of thought and action that favors the democratization of history making, that seeks to expand the capacity of the people themselves to make the decisions that affect the conditions and terms of everyday life." Populism was part of that tradition; historically, the Left has targeted the corporation as the arch antidemocratic institution. The Progressives of the early twentieth century were no radicals, and created a system of regulation that helped consolidate corporate capitalism, but they raised deep questions about the purpose and public accountability of the corporation—questions that dominated the thinking of the era. During the Depression, similarly, the New Dealers reformed the corporate order to help save it, but they also pushed the question of corporate power and responsibility onto the national agenda.[11]

The question of corporate power gradually faded in mid-century as business accepted a pact with labor and a modest contract of social responsibility. After business abandoned that contract in the Reagan era and brought back the specter of the robber barons, the issue of corporate power should have returned to the center of American thought, as it did in the Gilded Age. But at that very moment, the Left community was decomposing into the fragmentary movements of multiculturalism. These movements for racial, sexual, and ethnic emancipation—which made up the new "politics of identity"—had profoundly important missions, but they no longer constituted a common cause, and they no longer claimed the problem of corporate power as their own.

There is every potential for a natural marriage between multiculturalism and populism, but there are many barriers to its consummation. It will take radical new thinking to reconstitute these movements and bring them together around a set of shared populist interests that they have yet to articulate completely. Such change would electrically revitalize both the Left and a larger populist movement, yet the prospects at this writing remain to say the least, uncertain.

Moreover, in order to accomplish such a sea change, any new breed of populism would require a far broader base in the population than populist movements have traditionally enjoyed. The Left is too marginalized in American political culture to foment that kind of movement on its own, its historic approach too un-suited to mass appeal. For too many years it has shared some of the negative features of "paranoid populism," including the kind of unqualified denunciation of business that tends to threaten rather than energize most Americans.

We need a new approach to politics, and to the role of the corporation as America's dominant institution. The next two chapters outline the vision and practice of a positive populism with the potential to change the country. While it is nowhere to be found in Washington, the seeds of positive populism are beginning to sprout in grassroots communities, a new labor movement, socially committed religious congregations, and innovative multicultural movements all over the country. Surprisingly, signs of nascent populism are also emerging within the corporation itself, among workers *and* a growing number of managers and shareholders who believe corporations should be serving the public rather than the reverse.

T E N

How to Be Politically Hopeful
for the Next Century

When I speak in public groups about why we should start thinking about corporate power, I often ask people to look at their feet. Who made the shoes they are wearing? Where were they made? What was it like to be a worker stitching them together? For many audience members, it is a sobering and sometimes transformative experience.

Typically a good percentage of the listeners are wearing Nikes or Reeboks, so my question leads us quickly into a discussion of working conditions overseas. We talk about the fact that Indonesian and Chinese peasant factory girls often stitch fourteen hours a day for the grand total of a dollar—not enough even to feed themselves. Inevitably, too, we touch upon the profit margins such companies make off each pair of shoes, which can cost them under $5 and sell for up to $150.

Keeping people's attention focused on their own feet also serves to keep the discussion personal. When people reflect that the poverty-stricken lands of Asian workers have shaped the cloth that is touching their feet, the desperate pay and working conditions of such workers becomes less remote. Reactions vary: Some feel outrage, others guilt. Some are tearful. Others see a different story; this is the beginning of economic development in rural Asia, they say. Some listeners hear this as a tale of jobs going abroad, of foreign laborers doing work that used to be done in Massachusetts or South Carolina factories. But every one of them has taken the time to think about the corporation and how it affects everyone around the planet, binding us together and separating us all at once.

Such conversations are beginning to take place all over the country, and not always idly so. Activists come forth regularly, mobilizing to try to help workers or rein in corporate excesses. Labor unions in the United States have organized to call attention to the plight of workers in places from Indonesia to El Salvador, and to demand strict corporate adherence to International Labor Organization standards. Religious groups such as the Interfaith Religious Council have launched their own campaigns to boycott offending corporations, sometimes exercising not just their moral authority but the economic clout of the billions of dollars in pension funds that churches control. Some consumer groups have urged company boycotts or federal government action to cut off subsidies to offending companies, or halt trade with entire nations, such as China and Burma, with poor human-rights records.

The popular pressure has been heated enough for corporations to begin to take action to ward it off. Reebok has taken the lead in developing its own corporate codes of conduct, promising to stop using child labor and paying wages below the Indonesian or Vietnamese national standard. In 1997 Reebok, Nike, and other shoe and apparel makers announced a global industry-wide initiative to limit sweatshops and child labor. Scores of major corporations, from Levi Strauss to General Motors, are adopting their own similar corporate codes.

While grassroots groups are calling attention to corporate conduct abroad, a much larger number of people are responding to evidence of corporate greed or abuse at home. This kind of activism ranges from the popular outcry against downsizing by giants like AT&T and GM, to local community efforts to shut down sweatshops in Los Angeles and New York, to new national union initiatives to organize the unorganized. National legislation for corporate responsibility has been introduced, and President Clinton has sponsored high-profile White House conferences on the subject. Former labor secretary Robert Reich has argued that a new social contract is good not only for the country but for the corporations themselves. A growing number of corporations appear to agree, partly in deference to public relations, but also partly after a reevaluation of the potential economic payoffs of a socially responsible business strategy.[1]

At their most promising, these initiatives suggest the beginning of a new positive populism in the United States. Positive populism refers to an embryonic social movement that has begun to take form and emerge from within several more traditional social movements, including a revived labor movement, a variety of loosely coordinated grassroots community movements, and various other religious, student, environmental, and other social movements. While the organizational structure and ideology of this movement is still relatively undeveloped, a new vision is now coming into view. But it has many obstacles to overcome. And the well-being of the nation in the next century may depend on whether and how this new populism develops as a national social force. The new populists can learn a great deal from their precursors who rallied the nation briefly in the Gilded Age a century ago, but they have to become a fundamentally different movement to succeed in the next century. It is time to think about the vision and practice of what I shall call positive populism.

Positive Populism

Populism has a bad odor in America. Associated in the public mind with demagogues like Pat Buchanan, it has been largely dismissed as a paranoid style of politics that is more likely to undermine than to save democracy. Paranoid populism has little to do with the reality of the nineteenth-century populists, but they, too, had their flaws.

At least three factors explain populism's bad name, starting with the terms some of America's most famous historians have used to describe the original populists. Richard Hofstadter, the eminent social historian, saw the populists as a reactionary agrarian movement that helped to define what he called the "paranoid strain" in American political thought. Hofstadter noted that some early populist leaders such as Georgia's Tom Watson and the fiery Kansan orator Mary Ellen Lease hinted at vague Jewish or international banking conspiracies lurking beneath the surface of corporate power. Populists wanted to return, in Hofstadter's view, to a preindustrial America, free of foreign influence, immigrants, and the complexities of urban economies. Leaders like William Jennings Bryan, whom the Democrats nominated for president in 1896, were tied to erratic political schemes, such as "silverism," that had little to do with solving the nation's problems.[2]

Hofstadter's indictment is not entirely wrong. Bryan's Cross of Gold agenda was simplistic and narrow. Neither Bryan nor his currency scheme would have saved the nation. The problem with Hofstadter's indictment, as Lawrence Goodwyn, the greatest American chronicler of populism, has shown, is that Bryan and the Silverites did not represent the true stream of populism. They spoke only for its shrunken and deformed spirit, as molded and coopted by the Democrats. Bryan had abandoned the heart and soul of populism to become the Democratic candidate. He never expressed the broad, inspiring vision and democratic spirit of the hardscrabble Southern and Midwestern farmers who had challenged not just the gold standard but the entire fabric of corporate rule.[3]

Populism's bad name also derives from various twentieth-century movements that have spoken in its name. From Father Coughlin to Buchanan they have been mainly demagogic, rightist movements far more xenophobic and paranoiac than the original populists. Drawing their strength from economic insecurity and anger at corporate greed, they have exploited and whipped up popular rage. While using anticorporate rhetoric, seldom have they had any real agenda for curbing corporate power. Such movements deserve to be discredited and should be understood as false, rather than failed, populism.[4]

A third reason for the general mistrust of populism is the very real flaws of the original populists and later Left movements that have challenged corporate power. Gilded Age populism was one of America's great experiments in democracy, but it should not be romanticized. The movement had indisputable nativist and racist currents, and despite its natural sympathies for the downtrodden, never developed a voice that could speak to urban workers. Moreover, like many of the twentieth-century Left movements that challenged corporate America, it based its critique upon a simplified analysis of the economy and tended to demonize business elites at a time when corporations were beginning to bring home the bacon for an emerging middle class.[5]

Why, then, should we look back to the populist tradition at all? Because, for all its flaws, Gilded Age populism was the nation's most genuine and inspiring struggle of ordinary people to free themselves from corporate rule. Populists were the "farmers and workers," writes historian Harvey Wasserman, who "flocked to Omaha to launch a new national party. Many couldn't afford train fare and walked or rode horse and wagons hundreds of miles to get there; they slept in parks and cheap hotels and packed the city's nickel lunch counters to overflowing." When they got to Omaha in 1892, they founded the People's party, which grew rapidly into a national force. In passionate rhetoric, they proclaimed that corporations were being "used to enslave and impoverish the people. The Golden Rule is rejected by the heads of all the great departments of trade . . . Corporate feudality has taken the place of chattel slavery and vaunts its power in every state."[6]

The populists had thrown down their mantle against the new sovereign corporation, thereby defining not only the central struggle of the Gilded Age but that of our own as well. They understood the tension between democracy and the corporate world that was just coming into being. They had no illusions about the struggle to come: "We must expect to be confronted by a vast and splendidly equipped army of extortionists, userers, and oppressors marshalled from every nation under heaven."[7] But they refused to be cowed, inspired by a sense of democratic rights. "We are at the dawn of the golden age of popular power,"[8] they would write in their unwavering hope.

The populists recognized that the corporations of their day were creating an unprecedented concentration of power that could subordinate everything to its own pecuniary logic. They proposed popular control of the economy, and called for stripping corporations of the right to own and operate railways, media, land, and especially banks. They were doers as well as talkers, creating large-scale democratic alternatives—notably producer and purchasing cooperatives—as well as a populist credit and banking system. All of this was theorized and carried out not by experts but uneducated folk of the heartland, many dirt-poor, who took the ideals of American democracy seriously.

The populists stood in the great American tradition of Jeffersonian democracy. Jefferson—along with Benjamin Franklin, Thomas Paine, James Madison, and other revolutionary leaders—had warned that great inequality of wealth would destroy the very possibility of democracy. For this reason, they were deeply suspicious of big business and opposed federal chartering of banks or other corporations. While they were slave-holding men of property, the Jeffersonians condemned bankers and aristocrats alike, with their titles, wigs, and jewelry, valuing widespread civic participation by ordinary people as the highest virtue. They thus wrote populist principles into the American democratic creed, and the populists of the Gilded Age can be viewed as their true heirs, keeping alive the American flame of genuine democratic hope.

Lawrence Goodwyn observes that populism was not a moment of triumph but one of democratic promise. It was, he writes, "a spirit of egalitarian hope, expressed in the actions of two million human beings—not in the prose of a platform, however creative, and not, ultimately, even in the third party, but in a self-generated culture of collective dignity and individual longing. . . . The agrarian revolt demonstrated how intimidated people could create for themselves the psychological space to dare to aspire grandly—and to dare to be autonomous in the presence of powerful new institutions of economic concentration and cultural regimentation."[9]

Neither the Progressives nor the New Dealers of this century would reassert such a profound or democratic challenge to the corporate order. Instead they created a governmental regulatory system administered by experts. Like the populists, they were preoccupied with the question of the corporation. But the regulatory apparatus they put in place, as we have seen, ultimately served to stabilize corporate power. The lawyers, engineers, and other experts who would regulate the corporation shared corporate values of profit and efficiency, and were as removed from poor and uneducated Americans as the corporate elite.

As Goodwyn writes, the Progressives and New Dealers "reflected the shrunken vistas that remained culturally permissible" after the collapse of the populist challenge.[10] Twentieth-century Progressives were, in the main, elite reformers with a social conscience. They accomplished reforms of great importance. But unlike the populists, who built economic alternatives operated by and for the people, Progressives resorted to public administration that would help manage capitalism—in the name of the people, but not by them.[11]

Positive populism needs to distinguish itself from this twentieth-century liberal tradition, and become a movement of ordinary people seeking to reclaim control of their lives. It has to put back on the table a politics of sovereignty, reviving the daring challenge of the populists but in a new way suited for the twenty-first century. The ultimate goal is not to bring about more regulation or more corporate social responsibility—although we need new forms of both—nor to tear down the corporation. It is to awaken Americans to the threat to democracy and civility inherent in the current order, and to generate hope for new populist alternatives. A new populism will have to tear down the fiction of the private corporation, and devise new forms of economic accountability to bring the corporation in line with the public interest.

But the most difficult work of the new populists will be to challenge corporate power without denouncing all business or threatening the American standard of living. The populists and later movements of the Left all invariably lost touch with the American people on this critical point. By attacking the corporation, each has fallen into the trap of seeming to want to dismantle the great American engine of prosperity. Populists and Leftists have unnecessarily made the problem worse by embracing a demonizing rhetoric about capitalism that has made it easy to interpret attacks on corporate power as a generic assault on business and the American Dream.

A positive populism will have to begin with an appreciation of the remarkable successes of the corporation. Corporate America, by delivering the goods as discussed in the last chapter, has earned a measure of the gratitude and appreciation most Americans feel. A new populism must acknowledge this or lose all credibility. Moreover, it will have to identify itself with the kinds of changes in corporate governance and new economic alternatives that promise to increase economic well-being rather than destroy it.[12]

This may seem like a paradox, since the more profound its challenge to the corporation, the more of an economic threat populism would appear to represent. And contradiction is not entirely illusory, as the next chapter will show. Corporate accountability and profitability do not always go hand in hand. Challenging corporate sovereignty, however, is not the same thing as demonizing the corporation or calling for its elimination—strategies that can only fail. Positive populism seeks new economic arrangements that offer greater economic security for all Americans, without undermining the competitiveness or performance of business. While many forms of regulation and public control of corporations can kill the golden goose, certain forms of economic democracy—which we explore shortly—can actually increase productivity and even profitability.

But first we must look at how a positive populism can go about raising the question at its center—the question of sovereignty, of who has the right to control American lives. Positive populists must take a set of issues already on the American political plate—from downsizing to corporate welfare to corporate money in politics—and remind America of what they really are: questions of democracy.

ELEVEN

Why You Shouldn't Be Liberal or Conservative

Choosing a side in contemporary American political debate is like looking for your car keys under the lamppost because that's where the light is. The real answers are somewhere in the dark, like the key, because nobody is shining the light on the right questions.

The populist task is to raise the questions that the debates between liberals and conservatives make invisible. Merger mania, downsizing, and America's new economic insecurity have laid the foundation for a new populism, but issues of corporate power and responsibility have not yet become central to our political discourse. The major political parties fear them like the plague. When forced to address them because of public anxiety or rage, legislators tend to reframe underlying issues of corporate power as merely a matter of fine-tuning the economy.

Positive populists need to redefine the terms of traditional American two-party politics. Liberals and conservatives agree on more important issues than the ones that divide them. While they disagree on how much government regulation we should have, both groups accept the dubious notion of the private corporation. While they disagree about how much economic inequality is appropriate, they accept the underlying corporate assumptions that make extreme levels of inequality inevitable.

America's most pressing issues—including downsizing, inequality, and the erosion of democracy—are not being solved because the real questions they raise are obscured. Neither liberals nor conservatives have the language for them. These are the questions of democracy that remain hidden by the law and by the shared consensus between liberals and conservatives about freedom and private enterprise.

The success of positive populism depends on exploding the fiction of corporate privatism and helping Americans come to their senses about the corporation as a public institution. This will require long-term, widespread education about the meaning of the public and private spheres. We will need a new language to clarify the public nature of private enterprise, and how public institutions have come to be dominated by private interests.

Positive populism can learn from other movements, such as feminism, which started with personal consciousness-raising initiatives and moved toward calling for legislative and institutional change. Though Americans often fail to recognize it until they're troubled personally by some corporate decision, corporate issues have deeply personal ramifications. Positive populism has to begin by revealing how private anxieties about money, work, respect, and security are rooted in the public structure of corporate life. Only as they begin to see the connection between their own private lives and public power—what C. Wright Mills called the task of the sociological imagination—will they come to perceive politics as relevant to them.

Such personal engagement is only the first necessary step in the populist remaking of American politics. The next is to reexamine America's leading political issues from a populist perspective, in order to move beyond the comfortable diversion of the liberal-conservative debate and get to the heart of the matter: corporate sovereignty and the democratic alternative.[1]

The Populist Approach to Economic Insecurity

No issues carry more electric charge in the public mind and more populist significance than downsizing and job insecurity. Downsizing, along with outsourcing and the shift to contract temporary or other forms of contingent labor, are generating—even in an era of great wealth and prosperity—a Depression-like shock to the American public. Millions of Americans are living in fear of permanent insecurity, and of the end of the middle-class lifestyle to which they've grown accustomed.

Liberals and conservatives both tend to treat downsizing and contingent jobs as inevitable responses to merciless global competition. Downsizing is market-driven emergency "surgery," as the most famous corporate downsizer, Albert Dunlop former CEO of Sunbeam, has put it. It saves the corporation and sustains profitability. Conservatives and liberals disagree about how to deal with its victims, but they tend to accept downsizing as inevitable within the context of relentless and deeply threatening global competition, thus transforming the issue from one of corporate power to one of corporate vulnerability.

But as we've seen, both downsizing and contingent labor are by-products of the greater trend of emerging corporate ascendancy. Corporate mobility and the availability of an inexhaustible global labor supply have nearly wrecked the countervailing power of organized labor. Contingent labor institutions will seal labor's fate, undermining the full array of New Deal worker rights. Yet both liberal and conservative discourse has framed the emerging contingent workforce as a symbol of the weakened corporation—a new endangered species struggling to survive in the global habitat.

Yet polls suggest that the public is surprisingly skeptical of such ideas, with 70 percent saying in 1996 that greed rather than competition causes downsizing and outsourcing. It should be the mission of populism to support that feeling with facts, explaining how the shift to contract labor is eroding the Wagner Act, the Fair Labor Standards Act, and the entire legal edifice or worker rights.[2]

Positive populists can offer two new insights on this issue. First, they must make the case that the trend toward contract labor reflects seismic changes in corporate political authority, rather than competitive adjustments in labor-market strategy. The public needs to understand that corporations are changing the nature of jobs to reduce the power of unions and workers, not simply to compete better; in fact, temporary and contract jobs may hurt productivity and competition in the long run. Ultimately, what's at stake here are the basic rights of workers, not whether they can be retrained or assured of benefits. Contingent labor is a political rather than an economic strategy, and requires a political solution: corporate accountability to workers.

Furthermore, populists need to make clear that such accountability can *enhance* competitiveness, rather than hinder it. Data is accumulating that downsizing and outsourcing both tend to hurt corporate performance. Morgan Stanley chief economist Stephen S. Roach, once a champion of downsizing and outsourcing, now says, "If it turns out that all we have done is squeeze out labor, then I have to reverse what I have built a reputation on. And it is increasingly clear to me the improvements in operating performance and profits have been built on a steady stream of downsizings and cost cutting that is just not sustainable."[3] The low road doesn't always promote profitability, especially in the long term. Positive populists must show how empowering workers can be part of a high-road strategy to improve the bottom line.

The public may be ripe for the positive populist message that a corporate shift to contingent labor can only lead to institutionalized economic insecurity. Surveys suggest that Americans view downsizing and other such strategies as moral issues, and as evidence of a disloyalty, bordering on gross immorality, on the part of corporate America. As one Connecticut focus-group member said in 1996, "I still don't understand how you can have all these big executives laying off all these people. They're making millions and they've got these stock options. I just don't understand it. I'm sorry. I have a problem with that." Another, in Illinois, says simply, "It's all about the dollar . . . see how much more we can make and give to the executives."[4]

Such sentiments are leading the American public, as shown by a 1996 national poll, to support a surprising degree of public intervention. Seventy-seven percent would support a law "requiring that all employees receive a basic package of benefits, so that corporations cannot cut costs by replacing current workers with new ones." Seventy-four percent would deny "tax deductions to corporations whose executives receive large pay increases at the same time they lay off large numbers of employees." Seventy percent would force "corporations to pay substantial severance to employees and penalties to the community when they lay off workers." Sixty-two percent favor "eliminating tax breaks for profitable corporations who lay people off."[5]

Such public support is leading to unusual initiatives by legislators. Representative Richard Gephardt, the Democratic leader of the House of Representatives, has introduced federal legislation which would create tax disincentives after a company downsizes. Both Gephardt and Senator Edward Kennedy of Massachusetts have introduced their own corporate-responsibility bills to offer favorable tax treatment for companies that do not downsize when profitable. These are modest government initiatives, but they reflect the new sense that corporations must be held accountable when they violate the public interest.[6]

But the real populism is arising at the grassroots level. In 1997, a Massachusetts coalition of labor and community groups filed an omnibus bill, cosponsored by many legislators, designed to "ensure livable wage jobs and workplace rights to contingent workers." The bill required "parity" in the wages and working conditions of conventional and contingent workers, and mandates equal prorated benefits packages, including health insurance and disability and welfare benefits. Corporations who cheat will not receive contracts as vendors or suppliers to the Commonwealth.

The bill also gives legal standing to temps, contract workers, and others to sue if discriminated against in ways outlawed in the bill. This not only erodes the key financial incentives for hiring disposable workers, but begins to provide a new legal foundation for employee rights in the era of contingency.[7]

Just as important, the Massachusetts coalition views contingent labor as the cutting edge of a new populist politics. The coalition brings together a large number of labor unions and grassroots community groups—arguably, the two most important positive populist movements—in common cause. The coalition is linking contingent workers up with unions, and helping members become employee owners of their own employment service. Such imaginative alternatives are critical to a new positive populism, which should seek to build positive economic cooperative alternatives that provide employee-ownership rights and economic security in tandem with the labor movement. Moreover, partly through public hearings on their bill, the unions and community groups have mounted a long-term educational campaign to raise the broader issues of corporate accountability and economic democracy.

While labor and community forces will be the main populist leaders on these issues, some sectors of the business world may make their own challenge to the practice of contingent labor. Employee empowerment has become a buzzword in business itself, and few managers deny that loyalty has an impact on the bottom line. Many corporations understand the tension between contingent work and worker commitment, creating a near schizophrenia about their own labor-market strategies. As discussed in the next chapter, self-interest is propelling some businesses toward a corporate variant of populism, which promises to help erode corporate contingent practices from within.

The Gap

I recently asked an undergraduate class what they viewed as the most pressing problem in America. Virtually all put the gap between rich and poor at the top of their list. Later in the class, I learned that these same students nevertheless viewed large corporations in a mainly positive light. They did not see them as responsible for our main social problems, and saw no connection between corporate power and the gap. Once again, here was the basic problem with political discourse in America: Liberals and conservatives frequently debate the question of inequality, disagreeing about how much we should have and what to do about it, but the debate has deflected attention from underlying causes—and distracted Americans from real solutions.

The gap those students perceived is actually a set of several different gaps which together represent an ever-wider gulf between rich and poor. Our population is growing more and more polarized on any number of levels—wages, income, and wealth among them. Even within subgroups of the population, such as the technologically skilled or women or African-Americans, the gap in wages and incomes is growing.[8]

A growing number of Americans have become aware that the gap is growing and threatens to divide Americans into separate classes who feel no sense of common destiny. The *New York Times* reported in 1996 the findings of several studies showing that America had become the most unequal industrialized nation in the world. Our fabled land of opportunity is now polarizing rich and poor more severely than the ancient class societies of Europe. Trends show the rich pocketing most of the growth in national wealth, while the poor face increasing obstacles to education and to jobs paying living wages. Wages at the bottom have been falling catastrophically, creating a national scandal: millions of new workers who work full-time remain in poverty. Meanwhile, wages in the middle brackets are stagnating—and those at the top are increasing, sometimes astronomically. Moreover, with one in every four American children growing up in poverty, a rate ten times greater than in any of the European countries or Japan—and more than 50 percent of black children raised in poverty and a million more expected to join them because of welfare reform—the hope for the new generation has been fading.[9]

Both liberals and conservatives tend to acknowledge this as one of America's great problems, but their debates haven't done much to clarify the basic issue. Part of the problem is the tendency to treat the gap as the key issue itself rather than a symptom of more fundamental disturbances. The liberal-conservative debate about how much income inequality there should be never seems to address the deepest causes of inequality and the solutions. That conversation would quickly move from a focus on income distribution to a focus on power and who holds it.

This is not to say that income distribution is not important in its own right. Societies characterized by enduring deep divisions of income and wealth, such as most third-world societies, are wounded societies with little sense of the common good. Societies with mass poverty and shrinking opportunity are usually violent and politically unstable. As America drifts in this direction, ending poverty and redistributing income should be at the top of the national agenda. It is this populist issue that can mobilize Americans more surely than any other.

But populism would refocus the debate on the underlying issue—that of the dangers of corporate ascendancy. The growing gap has many causes, including globalization, rapid technological change, the expansion of the low-wage service sector, and the growth in single-parent families. Inequality cannot be dismissed simplistically as an inevitable outgrowth of corporate power, but it *is* ultimately, the fruit of the quiet political revolution led by corporate and political elites to rewrite the social contract and erode popular sovereignty.

The corporate redistribution of economic and political power drives the redistribution of income, a revelation at the heart of the populist message. It is so little understood by my students and the larger American public that it may be worth a short detour, after which we will return to the new populist solution to the gap. Virtually all analysts agree that up to 30 percent of the increase in the gap is due to the weakening of unions. Careful statistical analysis by Harvard economist Richard Freeman has shown that unions not only increase wages among their own members but help drive up everyone else's. Historically, when unions have been strong, as in the 1950s and 1960s, the income gap has closed. In the 1980s, when President Reagan set the tone by breaking PATCO, the air traffic controllers' union, and corporations launched an unprecedented attack on unions, wages fell dramatically, and the gap shot up. Since unions are the best resource workers have to help them push for their own fair share of the pie, the political assault on unions—intended to bring about a union-free world—is the most effective way to redistribute income to the wealthy.[10]

Contingent labor is another political strategy that expands the gap by consolidating corporate ascendancy. With ever more temps, contractors, and part-timers going without benefits, an economic iron curtain has descended that divides core and contingent workers. Contingent workers typically receive lower wages, fewer benefits, and a far less stable income, creating a devastating gap within the working class at the same time that the gap between executives and workers widens. The rush toward contingent work, as discussed above, is driven by the corporate desire to consolidate power by stripping workers of legal protection—a political aim whose economic fallout is institutionalized inequality.[11]

Corporate influence over the major parties and government itself is the third great force propelling inequality. Corporations are winning this power in surprising ways, discussed in the next section, but the result is a bipartisan agenda that enlists government in designing a new corporate social contract. Its aim is fundamentally political, but its main by-product is a host of specific policies that directly redistribute income from the poor to the rich.[12]

Corporate ascendancy depends on fundamental shifts in legal and regulatory arrangements, which in turn have major effects on economic equality. Franklin Roosevelt set a revolution in motion by exhorting workers to organize and signing into law the Wagner Act. The New Deal social contract shrank the inequality gap for the next thirty years, until President Reagan tried to unmake this revolution by crippling unions without directly repealing the Wagner framework. Government has taken a newly permissive stance toward corporations that fire organizers, invent endless legal and bureaucratic obstacles to certifying unions, renege on existing contracts, and replace strikers wholesale.[13] This quiet unraveling of New Deal labor arrangements is government's most important contribution to both corporate ascendancy and the inequality gap. The objective—disempowering labor—is political, but the main economic consequence is more poverty and inequality.

The shift in regulatory philosophy and law has the same impact. Regulation has become the paramount symbol of "big government," leading the Republican party to crusade against it as an assault on freedom and property rights, and leading even the Democratic party to view it, increasingly, as an unacceptable drag on corporate competitiveness. The new age of deregulation reflects the consensus in both parties that the New Deal regulatory framework creates an "overburdened" corporation, whose supposed sluggishness might threaten American prosperity. This kind of thinking, needless to say, is directly contrary to the populist ideal of public sovereignty over the corporation; it puts political authority into the hands of the private government of the corporation. Indirectly, meanwhile, it increases the income and wealth gap by freeing the corporation from costly environmental or other regulations and shifting the burden onto the taxpayers.

In 1945, corporations paid about three times the share of national taxes they pay today. Since 1979, despite moderately progressive tax changes by President Clinton, America's wealthiest families in 1995 paid lower taxes than they did before President

Reagan. Tax policy signals the way a government under the sway of business directly redistributes income. President Reagan's massive reduction in tax rates for the rich is only one of many tax shifts that have redistributed income to the wealthy. Reductions in corporate tax rates and more favorable business depreciation rates, as well as increased reliance on state and local taxes (which are more regressive than those of the federal government) all redistribute income from the poor to the rich. So too does the assault on social spending that came with the deficit-reduction efforts of recent years. Once President Clinton embraced the corporate priority of a balanced budget, he effectively signed on to a massive redistribution of income from poor to rich. Clinton is presiding over the abolition of the Democrat-designed welfare state—the economic equivalent of Republican Richard Nixon going to Communist China.[14]

The populist message is that the growing inequality between rich and poor in America is a symptom of political revolution, not merely the result of technological, market, demographic, or cultural shifts. Since the problem is political, so too must be the solution, suggesting strategies entirely different from those advocated by either conservatives or liberals. Conservatives want to reduce poverty and inequality by ending welfare and eliminating the culture of dependency. Liberals want to make the tax code more progressive and increase government social spending. Both views have merit, but neither will solve the underlying problem.

The redistribution of income is a by-product of the redistribution of power. To close the gap, then, we have to revisit our understanding of the fundamentals of democracy. It will take a rebuilding of the labor movement, a challenge to corporate power, a political empowerment of the poor, and revitalized democratic movements all over the nation to shrink the gap.

A Populist Approach to Campaign Finance Reform

Money in politics has become a hot political topic. Speaker Gingrich and President Clinton shook hands on it in 1994 and then proceeded to do nothing about it beyond finding new creative solutions to finance their own war chests. According to Republican party documents, Gingrich raised over $100 million for GOP candidates in the 1996 elections. Clinton's creative financing schemes have made the politicians of the Gilded Age look like amateurs.

Influential national public-interest groups such as Common Cause have proclaimed that now is the time for real campaign-finance reform. In 1997 both the president and Republican leaders gave their rhetorical blessing, and bipartisan legislation has been introduced to limit "soft money," Political Action Committees (PACs), foreign contributions, and other campaign largesse. Despite all the sound and fury, however, the real issue is being obscured—and the proposed solutions, even if passed by Congress and signed into law by the president, will not solve the underlying problem.

One diversion is the mantra of "special interests" endlessly repeated by the players on all sides.[15] The term *special interests* brings to mind all kinds of competing groups—from unions to industries to nonprofits to public-interest groups such as the Sierra Club. True, all these groups seek to influence the political process—something that is supposed to happen in a democracy. But lumping corporations in with a huge body of other political actors obscures their overwhelming dominance in the $2 billion electoral sweepstakes. It also obscures the more fundamental question of what kinds of groups are entitled to political rights in the first place.

Of the top fifty big-money contributors—including PACs, "soft money" sources, and individuals—between January 1, 1995, and June 30, 1996, thirty-one were corporations or their PACs and trade associations. The roster is practically a list of America's

Fortune 500 corporations, with Philip Morris and AT&T topping the tally and RJR Nabisco, Atlantic Richfield, Lockheed Martin, Goldman, Sachs and Co., Joseph E. Seagram and Sons, and the American Bankers Association not far behind. Each of these contributors gave more than a million dollars in federal elections alone during that eighteen-month period. There are fourteen unions on the list, but the ratio of overall corporate to union contributions is greater than seven to one. Analysts generally agree that it was the shift of corporate money toward Republicans in the last few weeks of the 1996 campaigns that made the difference in saving the Republican Congress.[16]

Even a clear focus on corporations and elections obscures the real issue. The flooding of big corporate money into campaigns—more than $2 billion in the 1996 elections—is a serious problem, and genuine reform is needed. The huge political corruption scandals that enveloped Speaker Gingrich and President Clinton—from Gingrich's GOPAC and outright influence peddling to Clinton's opening up the White House to the highest bidder—are the bitter fruit of the current campaign-financing arrangements. Passage of legislation restricting "soft money," shrinking PACs, or giving candidates incentives for voluntary caps would be a good start toward reform, and movement toward complete public financing of campaigns would be even more important.

Campaign-finance reform will be fruitful only when linked to a broader discussion of corporate ascendancy. As discussed in chapter 8, courts have been constitutionalizing the right of corporations to finance elections, by equating corporate giving with free speech as protected by the First Amendment. Populists need to move this discussion to the center of the campaign-finance debate: The presumption of corporate First Amendment rights goes to the heart of the corporate takeover of America.[17]

While corporations have always been able to circumvent the details of new campaign-reform legislation, their most important accomplishment has been preventing the issue of campaign reform from leading to a national debate about the political rights of the corporation and the broader question of corporate sovereignty. The idea that corporate election financing is merely free speech needs to be aired on the mass media and discussed in the schools. The cumulative vesting of inalienable rights in corporations—rights that were originally conceived to protect citizens—is central to Americans' loss of control over our lives. It will fall to the populists to open a long-needed discussion of how the Bill of Rights has been co-opted to justify the emergence of corporate "rights" that threaten individual citizens and democracy itself.

Richard Grossman, an outspoken populist who heads the Massachusetts-based Program on Corporations, Law, and Democracy, has proven this is not too abstract a conversation for the ordinary American. He goes to churches, unions, and even law schools around the country asking why corporations are treated as private persons with the constitutional rights of citizens. He asks why the Bill of Rights, intended to protect individuals, is being extended to protect institutions with the power to disenfranchise individuals. Since corporations are neither persons nor citizens, he asks why we pretend that they are when it comes to political participation.

This is the kind of populist conversation that needs to go on in schools, union halls, and town halls around the country. The answers to Grossman's questions are not obvious, and Americans will not agree on them, but they are the central questions that are carefully avoided in American political discourse. Such discussions inevitably put the spotlight on the key unexamined myths of our culture, and ultimately call into question the rights of corporations to exercise their spiraling forms of political influence.

Such discussion could catalyze the most important political education that Americans have had in decades, and might even lead to more meaningful campaign-finance laws; yet corporate influence on government won't be seriously eroded by even robust campaign reform. As discussed in Chapter 8, corporations derive their influence from many different sources, notably now their understood threat to move elsewhere if legislators don't oblige their interests. States now routinely compete to see which can accommodate more quickly to corporate legislative wish lists and deliver the most enticing tax breaks, subsidies, and regulatory arrangements. In the global economy, this exquisitely orchestrated game of musical chairs, pitting government against government, has become the most important instrument of corporate political power—and would be largely unaffected by restrictions on corporate campaign contributions.

Corporations influence politics in many other ways. Politically influential business groups like the Business Council, a body of Fortune 500 chief executives, help shape business policy on issues ranging from taxes to regulation to trade. Along with other national business groups, trade associations, corporate foundations, and powerful individual corporations, they saturate Washington with business views on all the major issues of the day. They underwrite leading institutes in Washington, such as the American Enterprise and the American Heritage Institutes, to draft position papers that help mold elite opinion. They spend vast sums on electronic and print advertising to get the word out to the public—evidenced in gestures such as the Mobil message that appears regularly on the *New York Times* op-ed page. They bankroll referenda campaigns across the country. More than 500 corporations maintain political offices in Washington and, along with trade associations, employ thousands of lobbyists who often end up writing the bills affecting their own industries.[18]

Populists have to move the conversation from the typical issues in campaign finance reform to questions about—and struggles against—this multiheaded political octupus. Limiting corporate political influence—a core populist goal—will take discrediting the corporate mystique and building the countervailing powers that are up to the job, the subject of our next few chapters.

Sex and Race

Sexual and racial inequality are burning populist issues. While women and minorities have made important gains, they are still America's second-class citizens, disproportionately poor, under-employed, underpaid, underfed, and undereducated. Corporations are hardly responsible for all the historical ills associated with patriarchy and racism, and many corporations, under the mandate of affirmative action, sponsor diversity and promote women and minorities. But corporations today not only inherit sexism and racism—as seen most famously in the taped comments of Texaco executives about their African-American workers as black jelly beans stuck to the bottom—but are creating new superexploitive labor markets for women and minorities both at home and abroad.

Liberals argue that affirmative action is a solution, while conservatives contend that it only fuels the problem. Both are partly right and partly wrong. Conservatives are right that affirmative action can create reverse racism and sexism, as well as undermine the self-esteem of those it helps, but they are wrong that affirmative action is not needed to overcome persistent opportunity differences. Liberals are right that carefully tailored affirmative action is necessary, but they are wrong that it will fundamentally improve the prospects of the great majority of women and minorities.

The unspoken agreement of liberals and conservatives—that affirmative action is the central issue—is the mistake uniting both groups. This is not to say that affirmative action is unimportant, but that the endless seduction of the issue draws attention from the underlying problems and solutions. Sexual and racial inequalities are endemic to the corporate order as we know it—in surprising ways. Blindness to sex and color—part of a broader code of impersonal individual rights—is one of the underlying ideals of the market system that distinguishes it from feudalism, slavery, and other economic systems. Capitalism helped end slavery and the most brutal forms of patriarchy, reflecting the reality that liberal market principles of meritocracy and universalism clash with both racism and sexism. But the corporate order—a deeply contradictory system—has long fed on sex/race inequalities that it helped create.

Sexism and racism have historically been highly profitable in the United States. Business has seen dollar signs in a second-class citizenry that at the time of the American Revolution was legally excluded from both property and the vote. After the Civil War, the rising robber-baron corporations turned freed blacks, emancipated women, and penniless immigrants into a source of endless cheap labor. In the twentieth century, corporations slowly developed special institutions to segregate women and minorities from other workers, enshrining sexism and racism in the bowels of the corporate order.[19]

Economists now speak of "secondary labor markets," where women and minorities compete for second-tier jobs. Unlike "primary" labor markets that are mainly open to white men, these involve mainly low-wage, disposable jobs unprotected by labor laws and union contracts. The secondary market created a "reserve army" of females and minorities who are fired first and hired last, buffering corporations and white male workers from the risk of business cycles. Corporations described these jobs as natural for mothers who belonged in the home, or fit for irresponsible minority workers who had no serious work ethic. Corporations also helped create sex-segregated occupations, such as secretaries and clerks, in which exploitation of women and minorities without labor rights and union protection yielded exorbitant profits, while also making white male workers feel better about their own paychecks.

In creating secondary labor markets, corporations are exploiting traditional patriarchal assumptions about male and female social roles. Until men assume more equal roles at home, women will be unable to get equal opportunity in the corporation. Corporations did not invent this division of family roles between the sexes, but over two centuries in Europe and the U.S. they have helped to create a sphere of paid male work outside the home and a world of unpaid home labor defined as female. While unpaid female labor produced the "human capital"—that is, the male workers—necessary for the corporations to function, women were treated as unproductive workers whose role in the corporate sphere was to serve as a cheap reserve labor force. The secondary labor markets today, which are rooted in historical notions about the proper place of women at home, allow corporations to draw women more fully into the paid labor force without having to pay the wages or benefits that men get.

The corporate political dividend is perhaps greater than the economic one. By creating gendered and racialized labor markets, corporations dropped an iron curtain between the white male workforce and the second tier. Unions—especially craft brotherhoods—collaborated in this great divide, seeing immediate gains for their members while ignoring the long-terms costs of splitting the labor force. Stanley Aronowitz, one of the nation's most prominent labor theorists, argues that the carefully organized division of labor by ethnicity, race, and sex is the main factor explaining "American exceptionalism"—that is, the inability of American workers to create the kind of powerful labor movement or socialist or social-democratic alternatives enshrined in most European nations.

While sexism and racism are thus old tools of corporate America, the rise of global corporate ascendancy is creating new problems for women and minorities, partly disguised by the impressive but selective economic gains they have won. The rise of a black middle class, and the emergence of a female professional elite breaking through the glass ceiling, is dramatic progress, reflecting the power of both affirmative action and the mainly middle-class feminist and civil-rights movements. Unfortunately, the majority of women and minorities, both here and abroad, are in a different world from these professional and managerial elites; they are increasingly vulnerable to poverty, family instability, and loss of control over their own lives.

Corporate ascendancy is being built on the backs of a super-exploited global contract-labor force composed almost entirely of young women. These mostly nonwhite girls and young women who may stitch sneakers or assemble stereos are the backbone of the labor force in special industrial zones all over the world. They are paid between one and two dollars a day, are forced to work for twelve to sixteen hours without sleep, are exposed to toxic chemicals that make them sick and old at an early age, and are frequently sexually harassed. Corporations say that the girls are the most dextrous and hardworking, but the truth is that they are being hired because they are compliant and accustomed to brutal authority.

This is a new global twist on the old practice of sex- and race-segregated labor markets. Ironically, such exploitation perversely helps to break precapitalist forms of patriarchy, bringing young nonwhite peasant girls in Asia or Central America a measure of economic independence. Nonetheless, this feminized third-world proletariat is the "secondary labor market" of the world capitalist system, delivering bonanza profits to Wall Street and American corporate shareholders. It drags down the wages and working conditions of American women and minorities in U.S. secondary labor markets, and is a threat to many white male workers in the United States and elsewhere, whom corporations can now credibly threaten to abandon.

Since the sixties, corporations have been employing their "new girls" in export processing zones, such as the Maquiladora region on the border of Mexico and the United States. Corporations operating in these special zones typically do not pay customs or tariff fees, enjoy tax holidays, and are often exempted from the labor or environmental laws of the host countries. Unions and state authority virtually vanish. These zones are the closest thing in the world to true corporate sovereignty, since corporations literally make the law, and young, mostly nonwhite women are their disenfranchised citizens.[20]

In the United States, corporate ascendancy is built around the corporation's domestic fiefdom of contingent work, which is hardly new to women and minorities. While corporations recruit high-level women and minorities into the dwindling primary labor market, most poor and working-class female and minority workers are losing ground in dead-end secondary jobs that are being legally restructured as temp, leased, home-based, or contract labor. Corporations are forcing hordes of white male workers, along with millions of additional white-collar women and minorities, into these disenfranchised contingent jobs. Such strategies can fan the flames of sexism and racism among newly insecure white male workers, but can also create potential populist bonds across race and gender. The crumbling of the male primary labor markets makes men, women, and minorities vulnerable together to a world stripped of enforceable labor laws and union contracts.

Contingent labor markets threaten all workers' legal rights, but women and minorities are especially endangered, partly because it is so difficult to enforce antidiscrimination and harassment laws among temps, part-timers, and contract workers. In interviews, I have heard repeatedly from women and African-American temps that they feel helpless in the face of blatant sexual harassment or racial discrimination, noting that their temp status seemed to free bosses not only from following the law but maintaining customary civility. Managers who want blond, blue-eyed receptionists simply put in a request to the temp agency, and minority temps are sent packing—or are forced to endure overt racial or sexual slurs reminiscent of days before Title 7, the antidiscrimination law that makes most bosses more cautious with their long-term employees.

Disinvestment from inner cities and capital flight abroad, as well as the corporate assault on welfare, have made one of every three African-Americans and Hispanics poor. One of every two African-American children is poor, and more young black males between eighteen and thirty-four are in jail or on probation than in a job. The typical black family in 1996 earned half the white family median income of $47,000. The growth of a black middle and managerial class with the means to move up the corporate ladder and out of the ghetto may ironically have contributed to the agony of the black poor and working class, who are now both race- and class-segregated and lack civil-rights leaders fully committed to class issues.

The same irony pervades feminism, as the class division among women grows. Educated women have unprecedented opportunities under corporate ascendancy, even as the majority of poor and working women struggle to survive. The new corporate assault on wages, welfare, and family support puts intolerable stresses on uneducated, low-wage women, particularly single parents who are losing fragile safety nets for themselves and their children. As educated women, aided by affirmative action, gain unexpected corporate rewards, their own commitment to class issues declines, supplanted by a feminism more attuned to postmodern issues of culture and identity.

The new populism would put class back into the feminist and civil-rights agendas. Populism has historically been flawed by its neglect of women and minorities, but corporate ascendancy, globally and in America, has now inextricably joined the questions of class, race, and gender. Reconstructed feminist and minority movements, as we shall see, must lead the new populism to make a difference in the lives of women and minorities all over the world.

Corporate Governance

Corporate governance is not exactly a sexy topic for the public, but how corporations are governed is at the heart of populist politics.

The leading players, however, are anything but populists. Takeover artists such as T. Boone Pickens, who tendered a hostile offer for Gulf Oil with the financial help of Drexel Burnham Lambert, a Wall Street firm, symbolize the elite standing of the main actors. Pickens, Drexel, and other rich investors began in the 1980s to challenge all-powerful executives in the name of the shareholders. Pickens proclaimed, "I am fighting as an investor to create value for Gulf shareholders, and I am shocked at the hostile reaction from Gulf. I can't figure out what they're afraid of."[21] So began the war between shareholders and executives that propelled issues of corporate governance into the headlines—but left most of the population on the sidelines.

Pickens helped start a movement of huge new institutional shareholders—the Fidelitys, Vanguards, Merrill Lynches, and huge pension funds such as TIAA-CREF—who had their own interests in challenging corpocracy and enshrining shareholder value as the holy grail. The shareholder revolution these financial giants have launched is among the most important developments since the New Deal, raising the question of who really owns the corporation and what the corporation is for. Today there simmers a struggle among shareholders, executives, and corporate boards about who will govern the corporation. Shareholders are the first shock troops in what could be a larger populist campaign for corporate accountability. But they no more represent the public interest than do the chief executives they publicly skewer.[22]

Populists must move the issue of corporate governance from a conversation among shareholders, corporate executives, and corporate board members to a discussion with the general public. The first step will be to make apparent how the debate is relevant to ordinary Americans—to show that neither institutional shareholders nor executives speak for them. Second, populists must make the case for a populist alternative to both shareholder and CEO governance—an alternative that can not only safeguard democracy but increase both corporate performance *and* accountability at once.

Shareholder activists do have a persuasive argument that corporations should be accountable to their owners. Their frustration in getting even a foot in the door has helped demonstrate just how closed the corporation has become. Corpocracy has transformed shareholders into a countervailing force challenging the authority of their own institution. Such a contradictory development confirms Adolf Berle's analysis of fifty years ago, when he argued that the corporation had "exploded the atom of private property" and undermined the owner.

Shareholders exercise enormous clout as trillion-dollar institutional investors. They have begun to increase the independence of corporate boards from chief executives—a much-discussed business trend that has landed on the cover of *Business Week* and constitutes a small step toward ending corpocracy. While institutional shareholders remain influential outsiders with no direct control over day-to-day corporate decisions, they have forced corporations to acknowledge that shareholder return is one of their prime obligations, and imposed substantial short-term financial discipline on even the largest companies.[23]

The shareholder movement, however, has ignored the more important side of Berle's analysis, which is that the forces that separated ownership from control have also undermined the legitimacy of traditional ownership claims. Berle showed that the death of traditional corporate ownership rendered corporations logically accountable not just to shareholders but to the wider community. As absentee owners, he argued, shareholders are just one corporate constituent, whose interests do not take precedence over the community's.[24]

Corporate executives, ironically, have used a variant of Berle's analysis to defend their own authority. They ward off shareholder demands by claiming that they represent and balance multiple stakeholders. They have enthusiastically embraced "stakeholder statutes" in thirty-one states, which give executives discretion to consider the interests of workers, local communities, and other stakeholders in making their decisions. Such statutes have potential social importance, as we'll see in the next chapter, but they are mainly used today by executives as a new legal club to thwart shareholders and protect their own authority—all in the name of the public interest.

This surprising executive defense has some credibility, since the 1990s have proved that what's good for the shareholder may be bad for both the public and the corporation itself. Downsizing, contingent work, and other current corporate assaults on the community are, arguably, the bitter fruit of the shareholder movement's success. CEOs have carried out these strategies with relish, but they devised them under the relentless pressure of Wall Street and the big institutional investors. In repeated surveys, CEOs say that the heavy breathing of investors for quarterly profits— what they call the "day-trader mentality" of the institutional investors—is their greatest headache, and a major force behind short-term moves like downsizing that can damage long-term profitability.[25]

Many executives go so far as to claim that institutional investors are not really owners, since they are such fickle short-term holders: "I don't think many of them *are* shareholders," says the treasurer of Lamont Company. "Not the way I'm defining a shareholder." A shareholder, in his eyes, is "someone who is an investor *in the company,* rather than an investor *in the shares* of the company." Another former chief of several large companies agrees that, "Money managers are not owners. When the computer kicks in, they sell their shares." Ultimately this logic has been used as a convenient rationale for corpocracy, but it tells us something real about the financial markets and the conflict between the shareholders' interests and those of the public.[26]

As almost 40 percent of American households become stockholders, largely through their 401K and other retirement plans, we hear more and more that shareholders themselves represent the public interest. Yet this is misleading: The majority of Americans are *not* shareholders, and the shareholder movements don't adequately represent the long-term interests of even those Americans who own stock. Most are small investors, and their core economic interests are in their own jobs and communities—which the shareholder movement is helping torpedo in the name of maximizing quarterly profits.

But if shareholders do not speak for most Americans, even less do executives. CEOs may cleverly claim to represent all who have a stake in their corporation, but at bottom what they are defending is their own sovereignty. The shareholder movement has challenged the absolute rights of unchecked corporate management, and in so doing has ironically performed a public service even while undermining some basic public values. A new shareholder activism speaking for the common good—which is beginning to emerge among some unions, churches, and other nonprofit pension-fund activists—could become an important part of a broader social movement for corporate accountability. Indeed, the most socially conscious players, including a few of the big union pension funds, are emerging as populist underwriters by funding large-scale urban development, job creation, and employee-ownership experiments. CEOs, on the other hand, will defend corpocracy— their own monarchical system—to the very end.

The debate about corporate governance, then, smolders on today mainly among parties who have little to offer the general public—CEOs and institutional shareholders fighting for rights that aren't theirs, Democrats and Republicans whose interests are so tied up with corporate dollars that they're unable to question corporate power. No wonder most Americans remain indifferent and uninvolved. They have not been invited to the table; they have nobody speaking for their interests. It is time for a populist movement to help remedy the situation.

TWELVE

What's Right and Wrong with Corporate Responsibility

Arnold Hiatt, former CEO of Stride Rite, helped make the children's shoe company a hopeful symbol of America's new movement for corporate responsibility. During Hiatt's tenure, which lasted from 1967 to 1992, Stride Rite created the nation's first in-house day-care center for employees and community residents, while also having one of America's most generous family-leave policies. It paid workers to tutor inner-city kids on company time. It gave 5 percent of its annual pretax profits to its corporate foundation that sponsors community projects, and gave away more than 10,000 sneakers to children in war-torn Mozambique. None of these exemplary programs for workers and the community hurt the company's bottom line, since the company grew during Hiatt's administration from a 36-million-dollar firm to a 1.5-billion-dollar giant.[1]

In an age of downsizing, Stride Rite's philosophy seems a breath of fresh air. Hiatt says that a successful company should "take a broader view of what the role of business is and not separate stockholders and the bottom line from employees and the community." When the company demonstrates sensitivity to the needs of employees and the community, Hiatt argues, its payback will include increased worker loyalty, greater customer and community support, and the satisfaction of stockholders and corporate executives who know they are doing something worthwhile for the world.[2]

In 1992, however, Hiatt stepped down within the context of a growing controversy about the company's mission and strategy— and, more specifically, about a decision to close a distribution center in Roxbury, an inner-city Boston neighborhood. The company relocated the center to Louisville, throwing workers out of work and abandoning a community in which they had invested significantly. The company explained that Kentucky was closer to its nationwide customer base, offered a 24-million-dollar tax break, had lower wages, and had streamlined bureaucratic hurdles. As one of the company's financial officers said, "After the numbers were added up, it wasn't even a close decision."[3]

Hiatt argued against the move, saying it was a test of the company's commitment to a social vision. "If you're pro-business, you also have to be concerned about things like jobs in the inner city and the 39 million people living below the poverty line."[4] But Hiatt had to admit that he himself had moved jobs out of Roxbury, and had presided over the relocation of thousands of Stride Rite jobs out of the country.

By the late 1960s, Stride Rite had already begun moving jobs overseas to get the benefits of cheap labor; by the early 1980s, only half of Stride Rite's shoes were being made in the United States. In 1984 the company closed three plants, including a production facility in Roxbury, laying off more than 2,500 workers. Now, almost all of Stride Rite's shoes are manufactured abroad, mostly by contractors in Indonesia and other Asian nations. The effects on communities like Roxbury have been devastating. Speaking of the effects of the Stride Rite shutdown and two other plant closings in the community by Digital Equipment and Ames Department Store, Roderick Dowdell, a community resident, said, "It is like back-to-back grand slams by the opposing team."[5]

The Stride Rite story is a morality tale about one of America's great dilemmas. The rise of the corporate responsibility movement, symbolized by Hiatt and Stride Rite, represents the potential for a new way of thinking in corporate America that could help heal the ravages of what some call the new "ruthless economy." But Stride Rite's failures suggest the pitfalls of the social-responsibility movement, and the existence of deep contradictions in the strategic thinking of American business. Moreover, it shows that there are fatal flaws in the corporate-responsibility idea which can only be remedied by a fundamental rethinking of the idea itself.

Corporate Social Responsibility

As we move toward the millennium, corporate social responsibility seems an idea whose time has come. Arnold Hiatt has gone on to be one of the founders of Business for Social Responsibility (BSR), a national organization that Fortune 500 companies are joining in growing numbers. Major companies such as Levi Strauss, Johnson & Johnson, Procter & Gamble, Motorola, and Saturn are making money while making a reputation for themselves as leaders in corporate responsibility. Smaller companies such as Ben & Jerry's, the Body Shop, Tom's of Maine, and Stony-field Farms attract attention for more visionary social commitments. Even companies not known for their commitment to responsibility speak the new gospel. Gerald Levin, CEO of Time Warner, has said that "Our position as the world's leading media and entertainment company could not have been reached—and could not have been sustained—solely from business success. It rests equally on our tradition of social responsibility and community involvement. At the core of this enterprise is the determination to make a difference as well as a profit."[6] William Norris, founder of Control Data Corporation, puts his case for responsibility more succinctly: "You can't do business in a society that's burning."[7]

Beyond the chorus of business leaders themselves, the idea has caught fire among business writers, politicians, and the general public. The business section of any Barnes & Noble or Borders bookstore is bulging with books by management gurus on employee empowerment, community involvement, and the like. When a Massachusetts mill owner, Aaron Feurstein, kept paying his employees after a disastrous fire burned his plant to the ground, he got more media attention as a local hero than the New England Patriots in their SuperBowl appearance.

The social-responsibility movement comprises both a set of socially oriented business practices and a fashionable new managerial ideology that has grown up around them. Although there is a good deal of distance between the rhetoric of responsibility and the practice, both speak to the counterintuitive idea that business can be more profitable when it does not prioritize profit above everything else and respects the needs of workers, communities, and the larger society. The spread of this high-road approach signals an emerging contradiction in corporate America's strategic vision. Many of the corporations, such as Reebok or General Motors, that preach and practice modest variants of the new gospel are the same ones who downsize indiscriminately and pay third-world workers less than two dollars a day. High- and low-road strategies coexist in individual companies, as well as in the economy as a whole.

Social responsibility, as practiced by America's leading corporations, involves intriguing small steps toward a new kind of relation with employees, local communities, and the environment. Companies such as Motorola, Shell Sarnia, Corning, and GM's Saturn have taken the lead in introducing employee-participation programs that seek to nurture workers' skills and offer more job autonomy. In the most ambitious programs, such as the well-known experiment at GM's Saturn, managers become partners rather than bosses, and the plant operates more like a Quaker meeting than like a military command system. The trend toward distributing stock to workers, through employee stock ownership programs and 401K retirement plans, raises the stakes and seeks to institutionalize responsibility by turning the worker into an owner.[8]

Big companies such as Levi Strauss, Honeywell, and Reebok have applied the same philosophy to their local communities. All of these companies give workers incentives to help the homeless, serve in soup kitchens, tutor in local schools, or help renovate low-income housing. Honeywell pours money into local Minneapolis schools, and has built a much-acclaimed new high school for teenage mothers and pregnant girls right in its own corporate headquarters. Some of the new "responsible" community practice falls within the tradition of corporate philanthropy, with corporations giving about $6 billion, or 1.6 percent of their pretax income, to charities and the arts in 1992.

What makes today's social-responsibility movement interesting, however, is that it is not mainly conceived as philanthropy. The emphasis is on the bottom line—with responsibility seen as a powerful new way to increase profits. As such, it seems to challenge pure market-oriented capitalism on its own terms, arguing the far-from-obvious proposition that the best way to make money is to treat people well and to invest in communities and the environment.[9]

Bob Dunn, formerly VP of Levi Strauss and now national director of BSR, has said that "Ultimately, the success of business is linked to the prosperity and stability of the society that hosts it." BSR notes that giving to the local community gains a corporation goodwill among customers and employees—as well as among politicians who have some power to regulate your business. When Dunn was at Levi Strauss, he noted that as the company shifted to team work "a lot of the skills that people need are skills that some people have cultivated as a result of the work they've been doing in community volunteering." Community service, he adds, "has really developed them and made them more valuable employees in ways that far exceed anything we could cook up in a training program."[10]

FedEx makes a particularly striking case for employee empowerment in its mission statement: "The U.S. Constitution, Bill of Rights, Civil Rights Act, and other important legislation—particularly in the United States since the Depression—mark steady progress in the elevation of human dignity. . . . Slowly these values have appeared as the centerpiece of progressive company policies, always with remarkable results." By results, FedEx means growth in the bottom line: "Federal Express' philosophy is that if you take care of the people, they provide the service which gives you good returns and your profits."[11] In the words of a former Citibank CEO in recommending training programs and decision-making roles for employees, "The organization that can harness the collective genius of its people will blow away the competition."

While the responsibility movement is often seen as corporate liberal "do-goodism," this is a distortion of the new thinking. The movement's main incentive is the same that has always motivated business—the traditional goal of making money. Robert Haas, chairman of Levi Strauss, is explicit about social responsibility as a strategy to survive under new market conditions. He says; "If companies are going to react quickly to changes in the marketplace, they have to put more and more accountability, authority, and information into the hands of the people who are closest to the products and the customers." Most corporations have not accepted Haas's view that corporate success now requires "an enormous diffusion of power," which Haas claims was the secret to Levi Strauss's turnaround in the eighties. But the emergence of such unconventional rhetoric in high corporate circles signals the possibility of dramatic shifts in corporate behavior even among major corporations largely wedded to traditional bottom-line priorities.[12]

There is an emerging body of research that supports the notion—central to both the corporate responsibility movement and positive populism itself—that a high-road corporate strategy in which companies work fairly with unions and treat the community and the environment respectfully—can be profitable, and often more profitable than low-road strategies. The Council on Economic Priorities (CEP), a prestigious resource council that rates companies annually on their social performance, has found that the highest companies on the list are also more profitable than less responsible companies on many bottom-line economic levels, including income growth, sales-to-assets ratios, return on equity, and rate of asset growth. A Dickinson College study in 1992, based on the CEP data, confirmed a strong relation between social and financial performance. A 1993 Rutgers study found that the top 25 percent of firms rated on a "best practice" index of democratic and responsible workplace practices had an 11 percent higher gross rate of return on capital than other firms. A 1994 study at the University of Florida found a statistically significant relation between social performance and return on assets and growth in sales revenue.[13]

Sociologist Severyn Bruyn has compiled the results of many other research studies showing that "self-managing" corporations—that is, those with high levels of employee participation and decision-making authority—have lower turnover, absenteeism, and tardiness rates, and higher productivity and profitability. Business scholar Sandra Waddock has conducted empirical studies showing a significant statistical correlation between social performance, as measured by various corporate research and consulting groups, and profitability indices such as return on equity. A great deal of academic research over the last twenty-five years on the relation between social and economic performance points to the economic benefits of "doing the right thing," leading some scholars to talk of a "dual bottom line" that promotes both profit and human value. While this research does not in the least prove that high-road practices are always more profitable than low-road ones, and is in no way evidence that market behavior *typically* promotes social responsibility, it does strongly suggest the high road can be profitable in many circumstances, and that companies do not always have to trade off doing well economically for doing good—a conclusion that a growing number of companies are coming to through their own experience.[14]

The movement is most interesting among the most visionary companies, where the new way of thinking raises broader questions about the nature and purposes of business. James Rouse, founder of the Rouse Company, argues that "Profit is not the legitimate purpose of business. The purpose is to provide a service needed by society. If you do that well and efficiently, you earn a profit, perhaps an enormous profit."[15] This paradoxical view that profits may increase by rejecting profit as the bottom line reflects a basic tension at the intellectual core of the movement about whether it represents a challenge to underlying capitalist values.

Joel Makower, who has written a manifesto for the corporate-responsibility movement, explicitly rejects Milton Friedman's thesis that the only social responsibility of the corporation is to make a profit. His analysis returns to the basic fact that corporations originated as chartered entities created by the state to serve its purposes. Robert Dunn of Levi Strauss and BSR argues that today "there has to be a charter of some sort" to affirm the corporation as an institution with new fundamental responsibilities to society at large. By discussing charters and new forms of social accounting, Dunn begins to raise significant questions about the constitution of the corporation, and the legal framework necessary to create a different type of institution.[16]

While few companies have yet to live up to the lofty language of the movement, the language itself has potential significance. A growing number of business leaders and management consultants argue that what is really going on is a shift in the understanding of values in a capitalist system. Management gurus Tom Peters and Robert Waterman—speaking for a growing community of corporate leaders—argue that a company's culture, "the shared values that give its people a sense of purpose"—is by far its most important resource. Corporate leaders and management thinkers are beginning to perceive values as the bedrock of economic life.

Even the philosopher Adam Smith, the "Father of Capitalism" acknowledged that all markets are based on trust and values that transcend pure self-interest. Corporate theorists today are rediscovering the social foundation of the economy, looking at social relationships and morality as keys to successful production. "Social-capital" theorists, who have provided some of the academic foundation for the corporate-responsibility movement, view the quality of community both inside and outside the corporation as its most important economic resource.[17]

In the new corporate ideology, profits will flow from a cultural revolution inside the corporation. The reformed corporation places employees, customers, and the larger community as partners in a larger community of values. The communitarian corporation can then expect long-term paybacks in motivation, productivity, and quality, and expects to prosper by increasing social well-being among all its stakeholders.

A basic shift toward value commitment is the most radical edge of the responsibility movement. Robert Waterman goes so far as to argue that companies facing trade-offs between values and profits "should always favor values," which he argues is the case in highly competitive companies such as Levi Strauss. Makower says: "We believe that responsibility is less programmatic than philosophic. It stems from a deeply held vision by company leaders that business can and should play a role beyond making money."[18] The Caux Round Table of Principles, signed in the 1980s by a group of international executives, says the purposes of business, beyond "creating productive employment," are to "contribute to human rights, education, welfare, and revitalization of the comunities in which they operate."[19] In response to Milton Friedman, Kenneth Mason, president of Quaker Oats, wrote that "Making a profit is no more the purpose of a corporation than getting enough to eat is the purpose of life. Getting enough to eat is a requirement of life; life's purpose, one would hope, is somewhat broader and more challenging. Likewise with business and profit."[20]

Making the Best of Corporate Responsibility: Populist Possibilities

In an age of market fundamentalism, the rise of a corporate-responsibility movement is both surprising and refreshing. It offers a new way of thinking about the corporation that has great public appeal. It suggests that there are ways to make corporations more responsive to the public interest which are also in the corporation's own financial self-interest. The fact that so many corporate leaders have begun to embrace the rhetoric of responsibility is a sign not only of opportunistic public relations in the face of growing economic insecurity and public unrest, but of some embryonic new thinking within the corporation itself about its own mission.

The idea of corporate responsibility as currently conceived has fatal flaws that have diverted public attention from the fundamental changes we need. It nonetheless offers something very important to positive populists. It represents an acknowledgment by hard-nosed corporate leaders that traditional low-road strategies are not necessarily best even within the capitalist logic of profit maximization. This is a major crack in the prevailing capitalist consensus. It lays the groundwork for populists who insist that there are ways of making the corporation more publicly accountable that won't destroy prosperity and may increase profitability itself.

Populism in America has previously foundered on the public's assumption that any attack on corporate power implies an attack on its own standard of living. The responsibility movement—largely a movement within corporate America itself—has begun to follow the positive populist's argument that an economic system reprogrammed to meet the needs of workers, communities, and the environment can be more efficient as well as more just. While a great deal of the corporate-responsibility movement does come down to public relations—and, in some regrettable cases, an effort to undermine the labor movement and other sources of popular opposition to corporate power—it should not be dismissed by even the most skeptical.

Corporate leaders have more credibility than any other group in American society to raise questions about the corporation, largely because no American doubts their commitment to the institution and its financial objectives. The corporate chieftains speaking the language of responsibility have launched the first corporate attack on the dominant corporate logic of our times. The motivation among some may be to deflect popular criticism and manipulate employees into an illusory world of corporate community, but they have opened the door to a new public discourse about the future of the corporation.

Their rhetoric, moreover, holds a deep emotional appeal to many in the workforce and the public. The possibility of creating human development in business, and giving business itself a social, even spiritual purpose, has an irresistibly idealistic character, addressing profound hungers that now go unrecognized in our society. It begins to create among workers and the public the view that it is legitimate to expect corporations to respect their emotional needs and human rights as well as deliver a paycheck. Simply put, it mirrors the basic concern of both organized labor and the populist movement: putting people first.

The responsibility movement has sponsored thousands of small workplace reforms and strategic innovations, and in those details can be found the key to another important imperative of the new populism: how to engage local communities and involved workers in the work of improving both the community and the corporate bottom line. Some managed-health-care companies offer free day care, mental health, and educational benefits to employees and community residents, thereby reducing staff turnover, increasing enrollment in the neighborhood, and reducing health costs for the company. A number of America's biggest banks are going well beyond the requirements of the Community Reinvestment Act, partnering with community activist groups in urban ghettos to

provide millions of dollars for new locally controlled businesses—
which also provide a new commercial clientele for the banks. Jack
Stack, president of Springfield Manufacturing Corporation, has
demonstrated how opening financial books to employees can lead
to better financial returns. Such corporate-driven innovations are
proof from the most credible source that one way to improve financial performance is to infuse corporations with a modicum of
democracy and a respect for humane values.[21]

Moreover, because the new vision is not merely a matter of philanthropy but a new corporate strategy, many such small changes
can add up to a profoundly different type of corporation. The old
philanthropic approach created community-relations departments that dispensed corporate charity without affecting the way
a corporation conducted its business. Robert Dunn, leader of BSR,
argues on the other hand that only complete systemic change can
make the new vision possible. Beyond a new corporate charter, he
argues for a new management culture that "gives people permission to venture out beyond where others are . . . There have to be
reward systems so that people are not measured on the basis of
gross profit margin."[22] The new corporate-responsibility model,
unlike philanthropy, is not an add-on program divorced from the
essential business of the company. It requires cultural and organizational shifts toward that oft-heard mantra, putting people first.

Unfortunately, as currently conceived, it will never do so.

Why Corporate Social Responsibility Has Not Produced a Socially Responsible Economy

Stride Rite abandons the communities it invests in. Levi Strauss
pays less than two dollars a day to its overseas workers. Ben &
Jerry's increases the salary gap between their new CEO and their
ice-cream workers. Clearly, not all is right in the new corporate

world of social responsibility. Anyone who reads Dilbert cartoons would have to conclude that corporations are getting meaner even as the social-responsibility movement supposedly grows stronger.

Just as it is a mistake to dismiss the responsibility movement altogether, it is equally foolish to view it as the answer to our problems. Because it is a movement within the corporate class itself, it is hardly surprising that it does not reflect the concerns or interests of the population as a whole—and serves, in considerable measure, to divert the public from the issues that should be on the table. The problem lies not simply in the huge gap between rhetoric and practice, but in the vision itself. Corporate populism is not the populism we need.

There is both a conservative and a liberal critique of corporate responsibility, and each has merit. Conservatives mock the movement as the folly of executives gone soft in the head. Making a profit, they argue, is the most socially responsible thing a corporation can do. Milton Friedman writes that if social responsibility is not "pure rhetoric, it must mean that he [the executive] is to act in some way that is not in the interest of his employers. For example, that he is to refrain from increasing the price of the product in order to contribute to the social objective of preventing inflation . . . Or that, at the expense of corporate profits, he is to hire 'hardcore' unemployed instead of better-qualified available workmen to contribute to the social objective of reducing poverty. In each of these cases, the corporate executive would be spending someone else's money for a general social interest."[23] Friedman is arguing that responsibility will inevitably clash with the goal of maximizing profits. And he is certainly correct.

Liberals make a similar critique. Robert Kuttner argues that "No matter how hard the enthusiasts of the new corporation try to infer social values from the logic of competition itself, markets remain fundamentally amoral; values need to be found elsewhere—and then imposed on corporations lest they overrun everything else we hold dear. . . . A recent spate of books pointing to cleaner air and water . . . conveniently ignored the fact that environmental progress was entirely the result of citizen consciousness translated into public regulation, and not at all the result of newly enlightened oil company executives realizing that, as one ad put it, 'we have to live here too.'"[24]

The notion that profits and people go together is an illusion, adds liberal philosopher Bernard Avishai. Even if they genuinely wanted to, he writes, "the companies of the new economy cannot maintain anything like loyalty to employees. . . . Nor can they train the less well-educated people of our society in a way that will make them fundamentally employable. Only the government can do that. . . ." Avishai correctly notes that, ironically, the responsibility movement can make things worse by supporting business initiatives that "dilute support for government action while unloading unsustainable expectations onto the private sector."[25]

Kuttner and Avishai, like Friedman, are reminding us of some of the fundamental realities of the market system. Even if we assume that people and profits can often go hand in hand, as the responsibility enthusiasts correctly insist, the market and human values are also constantly in tension. In certain contexts, exploitation pays off. Corporations in the Gilded Age made huge profits off sweatshops and child labor which no responsible corporation of the era could have matched. Today, when corporations go to China or El Salvador to find the cheapest labor available on the planet, not even a responsible executive like Arnold Hiatt can stem the tide. Sometimes no amount of social responsibility can make up for market laws, which—without public intervention, a new macroeconomic policy, and a rewriting of the rules of the market system itself—drive the corporation to the low-road strategy we see everywhere today.

The responsibility movement has hoped to wish away the inevitable conflict between profit and people, but in the end it's a conflict that must be faced, and bravely. It is vital that corporations act responsibly when it is consistent with profits—but it is equally important that they do so when it is not. The responsibility movement has tried to duck the critical question of whether people or profits take precedence when a choice between the two arises. It has also diverted attention from the fact that true corporate responsibility will require not only well-intentioned executive action but more responsible macroeconomic policy and a new legal and governmental framework that changes the rules and incentives under which corporations and government itself operate. Most important, the responsibility movement fails to address who gets to define the meaning of responsibility and who has the power to decide the values a responsible corporation will put into practice.

The popularity of Dilbert makes clear that few Americans feel corporate America is on their side. Responsibility-movement enthusiasts say that this simply reflects the youth of the movement, and that as more companies join in the economy as a whole will become more responsible. But even the companies most fully dedicated to responsibility today—whether Levi Strauss, Reebok, or the Body Shop—continue, quietly, to pursue low-road strategies such as going abroad to contract with the world's cheapest and most disposable labor force.

The contradictions that ensnared and finally defeated Arnold Hiatt at Stride Rite will eventually entangle the entire movement. As at Stride Rite, the effects on the movement itself could be devastating. Promoting idealistic rhetoric that raises people's hopes is dangerous if companies fail to follow through. In the former Soviet Union, the terrible disparity between communist ideals and their brutal practice turned much of the population into permanently hardened cynics. Because the idealism of the responsibility movement cannot be realized within our current market framework, it could have the same debilitating effect on an already cynical American public.

The contradictions in the Stride Rite story reflect the limits of a responsibility movement created of, by, and for the corporation itself. This is not the first time corporate America has invented its own responsibility movement, and the historical record is not reassuring: In the Gilded Age, the robber barons embraced a patriarchal religion of responsibility, arguing that there was no need for workers to organize because God had entrusted their care to industrial leaders. Rockefeller, Carnegie, and others lavished billions in philanthropy to prove their commitment to the common good, though in their own businesses they hardly practiced what they preached.

In the 1920s, business embraced "welfare capitalism," another variant of corporate social responsibility. Corporations created medical and insurance plans for their workers, built housing for them, and designed employee stock ownership and "participation plans." Under the name of the "American plan," these programs were actually designed to destroy unions and buy worker loyalty at the expense of true worker empowerment.[26]

Even if we assume good faith on the part of today's corporate-responsibility leaders, their vision is deeply flawed. The movement assumes a common good among corporations, workers, communities, and the larger society that can be defined and put into practice by enlightened executives. This has long been a hope that has captivated even New Deal liberals, such as Adolf Berle, who believed that corporate executives would ultimately embrace and carry out a consensual vision of corporate responsibility for the whole society. But this engaging communitarian vision of the common good obscures the painful reality that our market system is founded on conflicts of interest among the corporation, its various stakeholders, and the larger public interest.

These conflicting interests are built into our legal system and market arrangements. Downsizing yields benefits for executives and shareholders while costing the workers their jobs. Contingent labor yields corporate savings while depriving workers of their rights. Corporate executives and their various stakeholders have some interests in common, but just as many that clash. What is good for the shareholder is not always good for the worker or the community; what is good for the executive is not necessarily good for either the shareholder or the worker. Moreover, what is good for the corporation as a whole in a global economy may not be good for society. Corporations have always been able to make profits at the expense of social needs, but as the world becomes their terrain, the link between corporate interests and those of their host societies weakens dramatically.[27]

This does not make it impossible for corporations and society to pursue a common agenda, but requires an honest acknowledgment of their deeply conflicting interests. The corporate "community" is deeply stratified by the play of power, rights, and rewards. Within our current legal framework, corporations are bound to pursue the interests of some stakeholders at the cost of others—and to pursue profit even when it undermines the social fabric. Most members of the community are legally disempowered, while executives and, secondarily, shareholders have been made virtually sovereign.

This allotment of power has profound implications which the responsibility movement obscures. Empowerment has been one of the buzzwords of the corporate-responsibility movement, but the movement has not addressed the underlying constitutional rights and powers of the corporation, its different stakeholders, and the larger public. That would require a rethinking of the rights of ownership and property—a set of concerns far removed from the radar screen of responsibility leaders.

Despite the empowerment mantra, the responsibility movement subtly discourages real democratization. The kinds of employee or community empowerment it nurtures can be beneficial to individuals and their circumstantial comforts, but such changes fall short of challenging the existing legal structures of ownership and control. Giving teams more control over their work schedules or job design is not the same as giving them the real clout needed to assert their own interests when they clash with those of shareholders or executives—as in the case of a corporate decision to downsize or contract out jobs. In other countries, such protection has come not through corporate-responsibility movements as understood in the United States, but through constitutional shifts brought about by powerful labor or public movements—as in

Germany's codetermination and works council system, which vests employees with ownership authority. In the United States, when the responsibility movement promotes employee ownership, it typically strips it of real power by setting up employee stock ownership plan (ESOP) arrangements that deny worker-owners the right to vote.[28]

The responsibility movement's spirit, despite its rhetoric of empowerment, has been to deny the significance of formal power arrangements—and, ultimately, of power itself. To presume that corporations and workers share a common good is to suggest that power is irrelevant: If all interests converge, after all, it hardly matters who makes the ultimate decisions. Moreover, the emphasis on values and corporate culture taints virtually any mobilization of power from below—including the building of strong, democratic unions—as sectarian disloyalty, a betrayal of the very vision of the common good.[29]

The language of responsibility—rather than accountability or democracy—reflects the depoliticizing of a movement that claims to speak for empowerment. Corporate accountability and economic democracy are part of a political vocabulary that requires attention to who governs.[30] The language of responsibility, on the other hand, puts things in cultural rather than political terms, emphasizing changes of the heart over changes in power. If the will to work together and treat one another with respect is present, the argument goes—from the CEO all the way down the ladder—the needs of workers, communities, and the public itself will be realized.

Such language of the heart is emotionally gripping, and makes sense in democratic communities where everyone has a voice. But in systems of corporate hierarchy it is deeply misleading. Even the most enlightened corporate leaders cannot discover and give voice to the needs and values of disempowered workers and consumers. Such needs and interests can only be expressed through full participation in the process of governing, and then only by the people themselves.[31] The language of the heart can help guide the whole community when everyone has a voice, but the first step is to create genuine voice itself—which will require a fundamental shift in corporate governance.[32]

The failures of corporate responsibility—whether at Stride Rite or Reebok or Ben & Jerry's—partly reflect this depoliticization. Responsibility is defined at the top by those making the rules. When Stride Rite left Boston's inner cities, no worker or community member was brought into a democratic discourse on the board of directors about what the company should do. Stride Rite workers might have come up with alternative strategies that could have anticipated and prevented the loss in both profit and morale that followed the shift to Kentucky. Until a top-down system is fundamentally democratized, the values and culture it embodies will always reflect the narrow interests and perspectives of those in command. The limited "responsibility" of the current movement serves only one sector of the community, and wastes the wisdom of others that the responsibility movement says that it wants to empower.

And, as our previous treatment of corporate power suggests, the responsibility movement never addresses any of the other issues of corporate ascendancy—among them the question of corporate power in the larger society. Corporate-responsibility leaders do not challenge the political influence of corporations on the state, the shift of constitutional rights from citizens to corporations, the need to limit corporations from taking over areas of public life where they don't belong, or the fundamental rights associated with ownership and property. This reflects not only the obvious interests of corporate leaders in feathering their own nests, but their circumscribed focus on the corporation itself rather than the larger corporate and political system.

True corporate responsibility will ultimately require changes in the structure of the larger economy and political system, as Arnold Hiatt must now recognize. Under current circumstances, even responsible corporations tend to be compelled to make socially irresponsible choices. Robert Reich says we should not blame the corporation for downsizing or outsourcing abroad, since it is only pursuing profit as the larger market and legal system require. His premise is misleading in implying that the larger system reflects our collective choice; it is clearly the construction mainly of the corporate elites themselves. But he is correct that a real solution cannot be limited to changes within the corporation itself.

Trapped into its narrow focus on the individual corporation, the responsibility movement should look instead at the systemic forces that are encouraging corporate irresponsibility. We need not only responsible corporations but, for starters, a socially responsible macroeconomic policy. One of the most responsible things corporations could do, for example, would be to oppose the long-standing policies of the Federal Reserve, which defer to the financial community's inflationary fears and keep the growth rate unnecessarily low. A higher growth rate would facilitate a thousand responsible initiatives that even the most socially conscious corporations would find difficult in a low-growth environment, from reaching out to low-income workers in a tight labor market to instituting more generous wage and benefit settlements and more ambitious community-outreach programs. The high growth rates of the postwar era were a major factor in the corporate acceptance of unions in that era, and would be crucial to the embrace of a responsible social contract.[33]

While a new macroeconomic policy might lead to a cornucopia of responsible initiatives by business, the responsibility movement must also accept that there are many problems that only the public sector can solve. Individual corporations—or even corporations acting in concert with their industry—cannot solve on their own the entrenched problems of education, training, poverty, unemployment, and urban decay that beset the nation. The responsibility movement does the larger society and business itself a serious disservice by implying that responsible corporations can step in and provide its own answers to these crises. While corporations can and should help in many ways, all these problems call for new assertive approaches—and often new spending programs—by local or national government. Rather than setting itself up as an illusory alternative to the public sector, the socially responsible corporate community should lend its weight to supporting essential government and community intervention.[34]

To make the corporation responsible and accountable will require deeper changes in the market system. These changes must come from the larger society, and should include overall democratic reconstructions of American institutions, including government, the law, and financial markets, as well as the corporation itself. Corporate responsibility in its current incarnation focuses on the vital but limited potential of corporate leaders to bring about a more enlightened corporation. Authentic populism, on the other hand, is a societywide movement that seeks both to create a new, enlightened corporation, and to keep it from invading or controlling the many sectors of society where it can only do damage. It requires prime movers both within and without the corporation who can work together to craft a more thoroughly democratic system. Responsible corporations will have to find their own way to support these populist movements, recognizing that while it may challenge the current ascendancy of business, the new populism seeks to create an environment in which most corporations will join their cause. Only a larger social movement, in concert with current corporate advocates, can move a meaningful corporate-responsibility agenda from the fringes of the business world to its cutting edge. The corporate-responsibility movement should not be abandoned. But it should be redefined and absorbed within a new, authentic populism. How to do that is our next subject.

THIRTEEN

How to Be Against Corporate Power and For Business

As the saying goes, "democracy doesn't work all that well, but it's a hell of a lot better than the alternatives." Americans have historically accepted that view, but many now appear to be cynically giving up on democracy as incompatible with prosperity. John and Jeanne Q. Public don't like the way that big corporations corrupt politics with huge infusions of cash, control the media, or manipulate consumers, but they seem content to view it all as the inevitable by-product of a system that delivers the goods.

The populist task is to challenge that fatalism, and show that more democracy may offer the best hope for the economy itself. Economic democracy is emerging as one of the genuinely new ideas for the next century. Corporate leaders have not fully grasped the concept, but many, such as the Citibank executive quoted in the previous chapter, are beginning to realize that power to the people may be a surprising corporate strategy to "blow away the competition."

The irony is that as corporate power becomes ever more threatening to democracy, democratization is becoming ever more necessary for the success of the corporation. This helps explain the myopia of both social-responsibility theorists within the corporation and corporate critics outside business. The social-responsibility theorists have begun making the case for democracy within the corporation, while having nothing to say about the corporate threat to political democracy. Corporate critics, on the other hand, attack the corporation as a threat to democracy, but have little to say about how democratization might end up benefiting business.

The populist challenge is to show that democratization in both business and society can advance both social well-being and business itself. The attack on corporate ascendancy will be resisted by business, since no institution willingly gives up power. The creation of economic democracy will require more profound shifts in business organization than the most ardent champions of corporate responsibility entertain. Populism will only be able to overcome this resistance by mobilizing forces outside of business to push it where it will not go on its own.

At the same time, the populist movement cannot expect to succeed without persuasive evidence that such basic changes will increase prosperity and aid business. Corporate responsibility leaders have begun laying the foundation for this way of thinking by developing their own critique of low-road capitalism and offering their own high-road alternative. Their corporate high road will not end corporate ascendancy. But they have hinted at a new way of thinking about democracy and prosperity, which might help win ordinary Americans and a critical sector of the business community over to a new populism.

The populist democratic agenda goes beyond corporate responsibility in five key ways. In the public eye, it seeks to create a national seminar on the role and morality of markets. In the boardroom, it aims to empower all stakeholders rather than just literal shareholders. In the law, it seeks to recharter the corporation as the public entity that it is. Then, too, it advocates wholly new forms of ownership and networks of cooperative community-based businesses. And it seeks to recommend ways in which we can rewrite the rules of our current economic and political environment to increase democracy, even in an age of vast global corporations. Some of these changes can now be entertained because they are increasingly in the interest of business. Others are becoming the priorities of new popular movements that will help shape the next century.[1]

Saving the Market from Itself

We have to go back to the Gilded Age to find a time when the religion of the market had such a grip on intellectuals and much of the public. Billionaire financier George Soros writes that "Let the free market decide!" is the spiritual mantra of both eras. Soros, the archetypal capitalist, now seems almost radical in arguing that today's market fever "undermines the very values on which open and democratic societies depend."[2]

Populism starts with a challenge to the values of the unfettered market—a challenge voiced in the name of democracy. But it is not opposed to markets per se, and seeks to show that democratic reforms can help preserve a more sustainable market order. Populists seek to keep markets in their place, but also to help them function better in areas where they belong. By remodeling markets on social principles, the new populism seeks to revive democracy and strike a more appropriate balance between markets, government, and civil society.[3]

It takes a supercapitalist such as George Soros to speak frankly about how today's imperial market undermines democratic and human values. "As the market mechanism has extended its sway," he writes, "the fiction that people act on the basis of a given set of nonmarket values has become progressively more difficult to maintain. Advertising, marketing, even packaging, aim at shaping people's preferences rather than, as laissez-faire theory holds, merely responding to them. Unsure of what they stand for, people increasingly rely on money as the criterion of value."[4]

Soros tells us that after a lifetime of opposing communism, he has come to believe that "the capitalist threat" is now the biggest threat to democracy. "Laissez-faire capitalism holds that the common good is best served by the uninhibited pursuit of self-interest. Unless it is tempered by the recognition of a common interest," writes Soros, our democratic open society "is liable to break down." Rather than protecting liberty, he argues, unfettered markets in the long run produce the kind of social disorder that can breed authoritarian or even totalitarian regimes.[5]

Soros suggests that Americans have been hoodwinked less by corporate leaders than by an economics profession increasingly wedded to free-market absolutism. Nobel Prize winners such as the University of Chicago's Gary Becker and Milton Friedman carry enormous prestige when they argue that unfettered markets are the bulwark of liberty and solution to all our social problems. For them, even the family and community are markets—for love, sex, and babies. Becker says we should deregulate them. At the extreme, this would mean such absurd policy as permitting buying and selling of infants. Soros views such free-market extremism as the flip side of communist dogma.[6]

Soros, America's least likely populist, has opened the national dialogue we need on the meaning and place of markets. The new market fundamentalism that he challenges has taken over intellectual and political life, deeply misleading Americans about the causes and solutions of our democratic crisis. Both Democrats and Republicans now attribute poverty, family breakdown, and the decay of democracy to big government, and equate liberty with market values.

Adam Smith, the great originator of market theory, would not have appreciated this American consensus. Like Soros, he instinctively understood the dangers of unfettered and imperial markets. Smith recognized that the values of trust and sympathy on which the market depended originated in premarket institutions such as the family and community. The greatest threat to markets was their potential to undermine themselves by destroying family values and any sense of the common good.[7]

The new populism needs to create a national public dialogue that builds on Smith's and Soros's critiques. Part of the aim is to show how the morality of the unfettered market contributes to the breakdown of community and civic participation. This new conversation about market values—which will finally take the national discourse about morality out of the grip of morality czars such as Bill Bennett and Pat Robertson—is at the heart of the populist project. But it needs to be connected with a view of how promiscuous privatization can undermine the market system itself, and how democratizing the market—increasing the voice of workers and communities—can strengthen business as well as reduce the need for government.

A first step is keeping markets in their place. By 1995, Columbia/Healthcare Corporation, the largest for-profit hospital chain, had become America's fifty-third largest company, with roughly the same market value as Boeing, Chrysler, Time Warner, or NationsBank. Columbia/HCA, which in 1997 was charged with multiple counts of fraud and forced to rein in its most predatory practices, had led the charge to corporatize medicine, but education, welfare, and other human services are all being reengineered for profit. Chains of for-profit schools complete with TV curricula (such as Channel One, acquired recently by a huge Wall Street leveraged buyout firm) are part of the emerging corporate educational package. Children are required to watch daily commercials for potato chips or sneakers, which are programmed seamlessly into the history and biology curricula. Meanwhile, as General Mills, AT&T, Microsoft, and other giant corporations flood schools with the greatest advertising campaign ever seen, states like Massachusetts are contracting with Raytheon, the giant defense contractor, to take over welfare services.

Introducing modest forms of privatization to increase choice and reduce bureaucracy can serve public needs. There is some evidence of this in public enthusiasm for certain kinds of charter schools, which on a modest scale can provide useful spurs to public-school improvement. But radically privatizing medicine, education, and other social services will not in the long run serve the market system or even the big corporations any better than it serves the sick and poor. Markets work efficiently only where there is free and informed choice by consumers, free entry for providers or sellers, and no major social externalities to complicate the issue. Spheres such as medicine "violate several conditions of a free market," writes Robert Kuttner, among them the lack of free entry for anyone who wants to be a doctor or operate a hospital, the inability of consumers to know enough about their doctor and choose freely among insurance plans, and the overwhelming presence of "'positive externalities'—diffused benefits not calculated in the instant transaction. The value to society of mass vaccinations far exceeds the profits that can be captured by the doctor or drug company. If vaccinations and other public-health measures were left to private supply-and-demand, society would seriously underinvest." A free market in medical care would not only fail to provide such necessary social goods as vaccinations and care for the poor, but, as Kuttner notes, would create incentives that would reduce efficiency. "In ordinary markets, sellers maximize profits by minimizing costs. But in health care, the profit maximizer's objective is to maximize insurance reimbursement. . . . All this inflates the costs of the whole system."[8]

Efforts to make imperfect markets more marketlike, observes Kuttner, often create greater inefficiencies and lower quality. The failure of corporate medicine to universalize care, deliver to the sickest, or provide efficiently even for the well will ultimately drive up the costs of the whole system, with long-term damage even to the big corporate providers.

Columbia/HCA will no doubt eventually pay the piper by being required to assume some responsibility for the extravagant costs of treating very sick poor people who are triaged by the privatized system—much as the cigarette companies are now incurring major financial liability for illnesses created by irresponsible marketing of cigarettes. By 1997, in fact, Columbia/HCA was already a besieged company, its grossly predatory practices leading to multiple legal suits leveled by aggrieved patients and communities. At this writing, in 1998, Columbia is seeking a new name and divesting itself of many of its community hospitals—its story a corporate morality tale of the dangers of imposing radical market solutions where what is called for is actually radical restriction.

In many other imperfect markets, such as banking or telecommunications, the effort to create more perfect markets has perverse effects that ultimately backfire on both society and corporations themselves. Deregulation has become a free-for-all in which the big players cash in short-term at the expense not only of the public but of long-run systemic efficiency. This gave rise to the S&L crisis, hardly a model of deregulatory efficiency, which will ultimately cost both the public and the banks hundreds of billions of dollars. Deregulation is also creating new problems in telecommunications and airlines, involving collusion among global giants and price increases. Heated political struggles over new regulation ensure not more efficiency but short-term bonanzas for the best-connected companies, at the cost of their competitors and the public. In the long run, however, even the corporations may suffer, since the social costs and systemwide inefficiencies that result will be absorbed partly by the corporations themselves.

The long-term social and economic costs of radical privatization in areas like medicine are unsustainable for all the players. In other areas privatization can make sense, but only if new democratic market arrangements can be created that give greater voice to workers and communities. Populists support social markets that can spread economic power evenly among multiple stakeholders who can speak to the social results of corporate decisions. These innovative arrangements are the most intriguing part of the new populism, since in the main they don't depend on government regulation, and they can have real economic payoffs for business.[9]

The best social markets—based on employee ownership and corporations chartered in the public interest—will not eliminate all the conflicts between profit and people. But they can be attractive to business as well as its critics, since they increase profits as well as democracy, and reduce the need for government intervention. Nonetheless, even social markets require a modicum of government regulation in the interests of society as a whole.

The fundamentalist impulse to purge government entirely is an impractical fantasy: Not only is it impossible to achieve, since all markets are organized by governments and constituted by property, finance, and contract laws, but government intervention is necessary to protect human needs. While the new populism seeks the common ground between business, social needs, and democracy, it recognizes that there will always remain deep contradictions among them. Left to itself, business might choose child or prison labor as a rational profit-maximizing strategy. Even an employee-owned business might decide to spew pollution in faraway communities as a way to cut costs. We need government to make clear that many profitable strategies are unacceptable on moral or social grounds.

Furthermore, government intervention is often essential to increase the efficiency and profitability of business enterprises. This is obviously the case in monopolistic markets, like the U.S. mail or utility monopolies, where it would be irrational to introduce competition and irrational not to regulate. In highly imperfect markets like medicine, even the most socially responsible private insurer makes less economic sense than a governmental system of public insurance. And in more naturally competitive markets, regulation can still often increase efficiency and profitability in thousands of ways, as Robert Kuttner and others have demonstrated in painstaking detail. More broadly, business depends on the kind of careful monetary and fiscal policy that all governments must seek to provide. A government that withdrew from the obligation of crafting a macroeconomic policy would instantly sink the private-enterprise system.

Beyond all these economic considerations, a reaffirmation of government—which is quite different than espousing a government solution to every problem—is desperately needed to restore faith in democracy and make it possible. Quite simply, there can be no popular sovereignty without a real belief in the value of government. If government does not assume and carry out public responsibilities, less accountable institutions such as the corporation will do the job in their own self-interest.

Stakeholder Capitalism and the Public Corporation

In the American model of shareholder capitalism, even Jesus Christ might have a hard time practicing economic democracy and social responsibility if He were running a large corporation. The laws of the land require that he give top consideration to his shareholders. As long as corporate directors owe their fiduciary responsibility to shareholders alone, there is little chance that any corporation can serve the public interest, no matter how saintly the chief executive. Profit will rule above the needs of workers, communities, or the environment, if only because our laws require that it be so.

In Japan, Germany, and some other capitalist societies, corporations operate on a stakeholder rather than shareholder principle. Corporations are legally directed to recognize the interests of workers and other social stakeholders—and sometimes to put them in the corporate boardroom. A stakeholder is anyone whose contribution is essential to the success of the corporation and has a stake in it. This includes not only the owners—those who put in money—but workers who put in labor, governments that provide support, and consumers who buy products. A stakeholder system moves closer to the model of a public corporation, since it recognizes the claims of many different social groups, and makes the corporation legally accountable to all of them.

Many economists now recognize that workers and other stakeholders invest their own kind of capital in the firm—and, like shareholders, have something important at risk. The skills of the labor force are just as important to the bottom line as the money invested, and they are often firm-specific—that is, not easily transferred from one company to another. Today's shareholders have diversified portfolios and often do not know where their money is invested, a very attenuated kind of ownership compared to the owner who founded and ran his own business. Meanwhile, the worker who has invested much of his life in a firm may have far more at risk in that firm, since he or she may not be able to transfer firm-specific skills to another company. This argument has led even conservative economists to recognize the ownership claims of stakeholders other than shareholders.

A new stakeholder system has serious potential flaws, but could serve both the public and the corporation itself, making it a key part of the positive populist conversation. Workers, consumers, and other stakeholders in the corporate boardroom would ensure that the needs and values of the larger community would get greater attention. Society would literally get a new voice, if not necessarily a vote, in corporate America. But such a system should also pay positive dividends for the corporation, since its financial bottom line depends so heavily on the skills, loyalty, and motivation of workers, consumers, and other stakeholders. A growing body of managerial theory argues that building social capital— that is, cooperation, trust, and a sense of community among all the stakeholders—is the most effective strategy to increase profit, an argument for embracing the stakeholder vision on economic grounds as well as moral ones.

The stakeholder vision has gained increasing political attention in the United States. Many states, as noted earlier, have amended their incorporation laws by adding so-called "stakeholder statutes," designed to change the corporation from a shareholder to a stakeholder model and give directors legal permission to take into account the interests of workers, customers, communities, and other stakeholders. In the new charter, corporations are no longer violating their fiduciary responsibility to shareholders if they act to protect other stakeholders, even at the expense of profit maximization.[10]

As noted in the last chapter, some such statutes amount to no more than tools to help executives ward off shareholder activism. Yet in some states, such as Connecticut, the new statutes are not simply permissive, but mandate that directors *must* take into account the interests of stakeholders. A proposed shift in the Massachusetts statute uses strong language: "A director *shall* consider the interests of the corporation's employees, suppliers, creditors and customers, the economy of the state, region, and nation, community and societal considerations, including the ability of the corporation to provide, as a going concern, goods, services, employment opportunities and employment benefits and otherwise contribute to the communities in which it does business. . . . Consideration of any or all of the community or societal considerations is not a violation of the business judgment rule of any duty of the director to the shareholders . . . even if the director reasonably determines that a community or societal consideration or considerations outweigh the financial or other benefits."[11]

The new stakeholder statutes are weak; while they mandate attention to stakeholder needs, they give workers and other stakeholders no new legal decision-making authority. This is one of several deep problems in the current stakeholder movement. It could be partially overcome by creating real stakeholder power rather than rhetorical deference to their needs. America differs from virtually all European countries in its legal disenfranchisement of workers and other stakeholders: In Germany, for example, a codetermination charter requires that 50 percent of the board of directors of all large corporations be representatives chosen by the workers. Other German laws require "works councils," which are legally mandated representative bodies corporations must negotiate with before they introduce new technology, lay off workers, or change schedules. Such representation complements strong national German unions that have far greater political power and legal bargaining authority than American unions. Some variant of these German stakeholder arrangements exists in every European country, but in the United States workers have no legal stakeholder authority at all.[12]

To remedy this situation, we need new laws requiring accountability to stakeholders. This could begin with simple disclosure rules requiring that corporations issue reports and information of interest to different stakeholder communities. It might also take the form of stakeholder advisory groups—representing shareholders, workers, communities, customers, or environmental groups—who would confer regularly with executives or board members about how better to serve their constituency needs. This would help build trust, and serve not only the stakeholders but the corporate bottom line.[13]

Further steps would bring the system closer to real stakeholder empowerment. One approach would be the European model mandating representation of workers or other stakeholders on the board of directors. Stakeholder representatives would speak and vote for both the interests of their own stakeholder group—whether shareholder, worker, consumer, supplier, or community—and the interest of the company as a whole.[14]

Despite its great attractions, the dangers of this more enlightened approach include the potential alienation of stakeholder representatives from their grassroots constituents, the balkanization of competing stakeholder groups, and a tendency to favor the demands of individual groups over the needs of the corporation or the larger society as a whole. Bundling together groups of stakeholders each looking out for their own interests may be a formula for undermining both the corporation and the larger public interest. The stakeholder model fails to indicate how stakeholders can be induced to guard the interests of the wider society. It also fails to address the broader issues of corporate power, including the political influence of corporations over government and the problems of growing poverty and inequality.

The current stakeholder vision may ironically end up undermining the very power of stakeholders themselves. Giving stake-holders voice in a firm does not ensure a new way of doing business, since under current market and political arrangements many corporate decisions are likely to be decided on low-road criteria no matter who sits on the board. In Germany, worker representatives have often found themselves voting much like shareholder or management directors, shackled by the established constraints of financial markets, laws governing fiduciary responsibility to shareholders, and other similar forces. Stakeholder power will have to be exercised politically at the level of the state—not just in the corporate boardroom—to change these constraints.

The most serious flaw in the prevailing stakeholder vision is its inevitable focus on microsolutions within the firm. While stakeholder voice within the corporation *is* assuredly important, it is not a substitute for necessary macro-level political and legal change. By working to assure "insider" representation, it can undermine the necessary countervailing forces seeking to change the corporate order from outside. Social stakeholders such as workers and communities must ultimately assert themselves as populist political movements on the outside, as well as reformist voices from within. While these two approaches can coexist, the insider stakeholder movements may create a sense of identification with the firm (among workers or other stakeholders) that can undermine the "outsider" movements necessary to change the larger market order. This has happened to a substantial degree in the stakeholder corporate system of Japan, which has weak unions and a high level of unchallenged corporate paternalism, but to a lesser degree in Germany and Sweden, where strong unions and a national labor party give workers and communities a voice in the state as well as the boardroom. To address these problems, new approaches that go beyond the current stakeholder vision are called for, both at the micro- and macro-levels.

Chartering the Public Corporation

We can now speak of King Boeing. Newly merged with McDonnell Douglas, it is the only commercial airplane producer in America, and one of only two in the world. It is also one of America's two dominant aerospace and defense corporations. Boeing is a world power, bigger and more dominant in global civilian and military matters than most countries.

Boeing is chartered as a private corporation, but it is codependent with the state, and exercises transparent public powers. Boeing and the American government are intertwined in so many ways that it is sometimes hard to distinguish them. The Pentagon has produced much of Boeing's technology and funds the lion's share of the research and development that makes the company's products possible. The federal government is the exclusive purchaser of many important Boeing products and makes possible many of its sales to governments around the world. Boeing's monopolistic power over products that help make and break the economy and military might of whole nations gives it a quasi-governmental standing all its own.

Boeing is only one of several hundred giant corporations whose transparent public powers and dependency on government demand that we rethink their charters. The fiction of the private corporation is, as we have seen, the dominant myth of our era. But it now collides so profoundly with reality that it is time to attack it head-on by rewriting the corporation's constitution: the incorporation laws that define what a corporation is for and who governs.

In Chapter 6, we saw that Americans once relied on charters as instruments of popular sovereignty. Early charters made clear that corporations had to serve the public interest and were accountable to the people. When corporations violated these terms, legislatures would revoke their charters and the corporation was dissolved.

Populists need now to call for a new system of corporate chartering to protect and serve the public interest. Specifically, populists should propose the creation of a new "public corporation" with its own distinctive charter. The new charter must express a clear vision of the corporation's public purposes, reserve for citizens all powers not expressly delegated to corporations, and establish not just corporate responsibility but real accountability. It would apply to all corporations over a certain size—those worth at least $1 billion—and should, as discussed shortly, involve dual chartering at both state and federal levels.[15]

While this will require long-term public education and must proceed politically in stages, the issue of corporate responsibility is already in the limelight, and the potential for a new system of corporate charters is already politically in play. Senators Kennedy, Bingaman, and Daschle, as well as House Minority Leader Richard Gephardt, have all proposed the creation of "R corporations," a new species of "responsible" corporation that would be required to invest in training, avoid layoffs when profits are being made, provide fair medical and pension plans, and generally abide by responsible codes of conduct. In exchange, they would be given tax relief and other incentives.

These legislative initiatives are useful tools for starting a public debate about what we expect from corporations. They are modest in scope and nonpunitive toward corporations. They are a carrot to restore a few of the New Deal social protections that corporations used to provide to employees. While constructive, they still do not constitute a full effort to recharter the corporation as a public entity, and do not pretend to be a step toward greater democracy either within or outside the corporation.[16]

Chartering the public corporation means going beyond ideas like R corporations and stakeholder representation to create corporate governance in the public interest. What is needed is a chartering system that redefines the purpose of corporations to serve clear public needs, such as respecting the environment, creating dignified and secure employment, and nurturing the local community. Such aspirations are already built into the mission statements of many companies, but need the strength of constitutional sanction to be effective. Only then will they begin to be taken as seriously as the bottom line.

A public charter will not transform the profit-seeking dimension of the corporation, nor eliminate conflict between corporations and workers or communities. The corporation will always be a creature of the market, and it is neither realistic nor desirable to expect it to become the main guardian of the public interest. That is—and should be—the role of government, unions, grassroots social movements, and other civic institutions. A corporate chartering system would instead codify and help the people to enforce the notion that corporations should ultimately answer to citizens.

A central aspect of the chartering system would be the creation of a new system of federal charters. The huge companies that would be subject to public chartering are all national or global in scope. A dual system of federal and state charters—the details of which have been proposed in several books by Ralph Nader and others—would help to keep the playing field level, enforce uniform national social requirements, and prevent corporations from playing one state against another—which ultimately destroyed the nation's original chartering system.[17]

Creating real accountability would be the goal of a new chartering system. In early America, this was achieved by imposition of strict conditions on the scope and duration of corporate activities, reservation by the state of all powers not expressly delegated to the corporation, and regular legislative consideration of whether to renew the corporate charter. Many such charter restrictions on corporate internal policy could undermine corporate performance and would not be realistic today. But constitutionally reserving to the people all powers not expressly delegated to the corporation remains vital and should be paired with a reexamination of all the rights previously vested in corporations as legal persons under the Bill of Rights.[18]

A public-charter system would dispense with the idea of the corporation as a private individual. Corporations would still be invested with important, specific rights—such as the right to conduct business, issue shares, enjoy limited liability, etc. But since the new system would explicitly reject the premise of the corporation as a private person, the current set of corporate "constitutional rights" would be subject to review.[19] This would be a major step toward a dismantling of corporate sovereignty, leading to a new publicly debated and democratically ratified vision of what rights and obligations corporations should have.

The notion of periodic public reviews of corporate adherence to its charter is worth exploring. If America's largest corporations were required to give public accounting of their contribution to the public interest, it might lead to both a new level of corporate responsibility and an upsurge of populist democratic participation. Moreover, such a reviewing system would help clarify both popular and legal standards of corporate behavior in the public interest, a matter that will necessarily evolve over years of national public discussion and evolution in the law.[20]

Accountability would also require introducing forms of public representation into corporate governance. For many years, the European Union has debated proposals to require public or "general interest" representatives on the board of any large corporation chartered to operate throughout Europe. One idea has been to divide the board into three groups: one-third shareholders, one-third employees, and one-third "general" or public-interest advocates. The members might be jointly chosen by employee and shareholder representatives, or, more democratically, chosen in elections much like local or national candidates for other public offices. These public board members would speak for the society as a whole rather than for any particular stakeholder constituency, and would help all Americans to judge what falls within the realm of corporate public interests. The "public interest" cannot be perfectly defined by any universal blueprints, but in broadcasting and other areas the concept has developed a clear legal and political meaning cable television providers, for example, must offer public access programming and fair rates, a first step toward defining their public obligations.

Public representatives, empowered by the language and teeth of the new charter, would inevitably help raise public consciousness and expectations of the corporation—and help bring about new standards of practice that could serve both business and democracy.[21]

Attorney Christopher Stone has proposed a detailed scheme for public-interest representation on American corporate boards. Stone notes that more than a century ago Congress mandated public representatives for Union Pacific Railroad (reflecting a huge gift of free public lands to the railroad); in the 1970s, similarly, President Nixon nominated three public representatives to the Comsat satellite corporation. Stone proposes that public directors be appointed by a new Federal Corporations Commission—representatives whose role will be to ensure that the public interest is protected in major corporate decisions.[22]

Employee Ownership and Cooperativism

Web Converting is a midsize manufacturing company operating in five states. It calls its management style Theory O, meaning that the company will succeed only when workers feel like—and act as—owners. Web is now an ESOP (employee stock ownership company), and is moving toward 100 percent employee ownership.[23]

Web has become symbolic of the national movement toward employee ownership. One of its executives, Charles Edmunson, is a leader in the employee-ownership community nationwide. A Web worker, Rob Zacharias, has talked about the merits of employee ownership with President Clinton and has gotten presidential assurances of support.

Web sees itself as a community that can do well in the market by caring for its workers and doing everything possible to promote their spiritual as well as economic development. One of its workers, a former convict, says he would have dropped off the face of the earth if the company had not picked him up, hired him, and put faith in him. He is now a leader in the company, speaking frequently and movingly to people about the redemptive aspects of an employee-ownership system that trusts workers with real authority.

Web is moving toward a new corporate model that marries democratization and business success. Web views employee empowerment as a moral imperative but also as a competitive strategy. It is going beyond traditional corporate responsibility by investing workers with the real powers of ownership. This means not only a formal voice in corporate governance, but an effort to bring workers into real decision-making authority on every corporate issue. Web sees ownership as the only way to deliver fully on the high promises of the social-responsibility movement. Without ownership, workers are not really empowered. Moreover, it is only with the power, respect, and financial incentives of ownership that workers will deliver back to the company the financial payoffs that it is seeking.

The corporate responsibility movement has made much of the idea that increasing the worker's control over his or her own job—often through cooperative teamwork—can increase both worker satisfaction and corporate profitability. But individual or team participation in conventionally owned companies can actually disempower employees and erode profitability, since it typically limits participation to low level or superficial decisions and disenchants workers whose hopes for more autonomy and fulfillment are raised and then cruelly dashed. The insight that democratic participation is good for both worker and corporation is a key to positive populism—which is at heart a movement for increased participation at every level of the corporation and society—but it is only the expansive form of participation associated with ownership—as Web magnificently exemplifies—that truly can empower workers. When strong unions are present, they can help make participation a strong plus for both worker and company even without employee ownership. But since most corporations are non-union, participation without ownership tends to degenerate into meaningless rituals which help neither the worker nor the bottom line.

Unlike the corporate responsibility model, Theory O sets in motion fundamental changes in the practice of capitalism. Wage labor, from the Theory O perspective, will eventually be thought as morally reprehensible as slavery. This is hardly a new perspective; Marx talked about wage slavery a century ago. What is new is that today it is being asserted by corporate leaders, on business grounds.

Theory O challenges the division between owners and workers, and the view that capitalists rather than workers should be in legal control. As such, it is a dramatic corporate challenge to property rights. In the system that Web is building, all workers would be vested with the moral and legal powers of ownership simply because they are members of the workplace community. By awarding ownership democratically, based on the moral claims of labor, this system fulfills the classic populist goal of employee sovereignty. At most companies where employee ownership has begun to sprout, worker ownership is being driven mainly by the capitalist need to increase productivity and profits. At Web moral passions play a larger role, but there, too, everyone understands that employee ownership can succeed only if it delivers the goods.[24]

Employee ownership is catching fire on a surprisingly large scale; today there are more than 10,000 employee-owned companies in America, and at least 11 million workers owning stock in their own companies. Employees were the largest shareholders in almost one-fifth of all corporations by 1990, with 12 percent employee ownership in Ford, 10 percent in Exxon, 25 percent in Procter & Gamble, 19 percent in Lockheed, and 15 percent or higher in scores of other well-known companies. The largest employee-owned company in 1997, with over 50 percent worker ownership, is United Parcel Service, which has 315,000 employees. Kroger is the second largest, with over 30 percent of its

200,000 employees also owners. Employee ownership is at 5 percent or greater—a potentially controlling share in companies with millions of owners—in the majority of Fortune 500 companies. The 1996 conversion of United Airlines to full employee ownership with strong union support marks the mainstreaming of the movement.[25]

Employee ownership has grown more than fiftyfold since 1974, and the rise of 401K plans, where workers receive pension benefits in the form of company stock, will mean further expansion. Nonetheless, while employee ownership has a major role to play in positive populism, it is not a panacea and faces serious challenges. In most ESOPs, as Joseph Blasi has shown, employee ownership is not associated with any meaningful change in workplace involvement, nor does it typically give workers any real control over the corporation. Executives do often turn to ESOPs to increase employee loyalty and improve productivity. But ESOP laws are replete with arrangements, carefully structured by banks and lawyers, that deny workers voting rights and leave power vested in executives who typically have the lion's share of the employee stock. Outside shareholders or the banks themselves retain far more power on the board than the workers. Most large corporations have adopted ESOPs mainly for the tax benefits, to ward off hostile takeovers, or to achieve other managerial goals which have nothing to do with workplace democracy. The ESOP movement will thus have to be challenged either by workers, unions, or other forces to deliver on its democratic rhetoric.[26]

Even at Web, where the commitment to democracy is more authentic, the democratic vision does not extend beyond the corporation itself to the larger economic and political system. Web's model does not address the corrupting power of corporations over government, nor does it offer any answers for the millions of unemployed, poor, or others not working in the corporations. No model can do everything, but there are serious problems with a narrowing of the vision of economic democracy to the walls of the individual workplace. If workers at a company like Web concentrate only on besting the competition and making profits, they will do nothing to improve the role of the corporation in our political culture—and could even develop an adversarial relationship with the labor movement that speaks in their name.

Web is on the side of the angels and deserves close study as a national model. But Theory O needs to identify itself with a vision of change for the larger economy and society—a broader application of the values and democratization that Web's managers and workers are trying to make real in their own company. This can begin with a coalition of employee-owned companies banding together to solve the common problems of employee education, participation, capitalization, and legitimacy facing all employee-owned companies. Going it alone—a common problem among employee-owned companies—is an invitation to failure. We do not know yet whether employee ownership is a viable strategy for all sectors of the economy, but it is virtually certain that without an organized employee-ownership sector bridging many firms and building a new supportive infrastructure, employee ownership will have a hard time in many firms. Moreover, without building strong links to the labor movement—which is becoming increasingly interested in employee ownership to save jobs and expand worker rights—employee ownership will likely lose its populist potential.

The most famous model of employee ownership in the world—the complex of nearly one hundred worker cooperatives in Mondragon, Spain—offers hope that an entire national economy can be based on cooperative rather than corporate principles. Mondragon should not be romanticized, because it still has authoritarian managers, limits opportunities for women, and has helped undermine a Basque labor movement, confirming the real tension between employee ownership and unions. But the Mondragon cooperatives—including factories, banks, hospitals, insurance companies, retail stores and even schools—have prospered for more than fifty years as world-class producers with strong community roots and worker-ownership based on one person, one vote. The Mondragon co-ops define ownership as a right connected with work rather than investment of money, and workers who invest more money do not get more votes in a co-op. The major Mondragon bank, owned by the worker-owned companies it supports, functions as a form of community planning enterprise that makes investment decisions based mainly on the social needs of their worker-owners and the larger community. Mondragon's economic success—in terms of innovation, productivity, exports, job creation, and job security—is among the best in Europe, and demonstrates the positive populist principle that democratic ownership and participation are a recipe for both healthy business and healthy communities.

Cooperativism has a growing number of advocates in the United States who speak for not just worker-ownership but a community-based economic and social alternative to corporate America. They envision a proliferation of community-based (and sometimes worker-owned or community-owned) small manufacturers, credit unions, banks, retail stores, farms, and other small-scale businesses—which could mushroom as a cooperative haven for the millions of citizens who do not want to be part of corporate America. Unlike the other populist strategies described thus far, this populism seeks an end run around the corporation. Rather than change the corporation from within, the cooperativists would build workable alternatives centered around closely linked communities and co-ops that might lead by the power of positive example toward a new economy and way of life.

Cooperativists imagine their new sector supported by a cooperative culture and emerging forms of cooperation among communities and regions, as well as a macroeconomic national policy of subsidies and taxation favoring such community and worker-owned enterprises. Such a broadening of the cooperativist vision to the national level has great appeal, since it offers not only a concrete alternative to the corporation but a vision of a better way to live. By highlighting the values of local participation, it speaks to the deep desire of many Americans to see values of community, self-development, and democracy prioritized over a life based on consumerism and competition. But to succeed, the community-based alternatives have to be linked with a broader positive populist movement that offers a vision of how to transform the biggest corporations, the national and global market, and the government itself, in the service of all communities.[27]

Toward the Broader Agenda

Corporate public chartering and employee ownership are major parts of the positive populist agenda, but they focus on the individual corporation. A populism oriented narrowly to the managing of individual corporations will produce narrow results. Unemployment, inequality, economic insecurity, moral decline, and corporate power itself can only be meaningfully addressed by linking changes in corporate governance with changes in the larger economic and social order. We need a new, broader approach that can elicit public-sector involvement without reverting to the traditional liberal notion of bigger government and more regulation. It must involve the kind of challenge to market values described in the first section, but also go beyond such critiques to find new ways to construct socially responsible markets that reduce the need for government in many areas while increasing governmental activism in new arenas.[28]

The corporate-responsibility movement has perpetuated the illusion, as noted in the last chapter, that individual corporate responsibility can be a substitute for government programs or systemic changes in the market. Precisely the opposite is true. It will take a new governmental framework and changed market arrangements to make true corporate responsibility possible. It will also take new forms of cooperation among corporations themselves, as well as a new labor movement and a broader populist coalition for change.

This is not to say that corporations are helpless to make change on their own, or that populism is merely a new big-government scheme or a disguised socialist approach. Individual companies can embrace many high-road strategies even if their competitors stay on the low road and if government offers no new rewards for corporate responsibility as the success of participatory companies such as Levi Strauss, Motorola, and Johnson & Johnson amply demonstrates. Employee empowerment and stakeholder participation, as many managers themselves now recognize, can make a company more competitive even within the current legal and economic framework.

Nonetheless there are many real obstacles facing any company trying to change on its own—obstacles that can be addressed, in the first instance, by new forms of cooperation among firms within a given industry or region. The new network capitalism has already created strong links and new capacities for cooperation and planning among firms. Such links work now primarily to increase corporate profits, but the same networks could be put to work for the common good.

Corporate codes of conduct offer one potential arena for change. If companies would agree collectively to outlaw child labor, union busting, unsafe working conditions, or exploitative wage scales, it would reduce the need for regulation and government intervention while helping enable all corporations in the industry to act responsibly. Collective embrace of high-road approaches, orchestrated by the networks of major companies that are already closely intertwined through alliances and joint ventures, is the most efficient way to introduce responsible practice in an entire industry, sector, or region. Nike, Reebok, and L.L. Bean are beginning to work together on shared standards for Asian or Central American contractors, for example—a step in the right direction that could improve and eventually eliminate sweatshop conditions without putting any rival at competitive disadvantage. Their new White House Apparel Industry Partnership, signed in 1997, pledges to end child labor and sub-subsistence wages, a first step in a long but potentially promising path of industry-wide corporate codes.

Such business cooperation can obviously degenerate into another form of corporate collusion or manipulation. Shareholders, consumers, government officials, and workers will need to be involved in the standard-setting process. The more democratized the firm, the greater the prospect that interfirm cooperation will serve both the corporations and the larger public interest. In the making of the 1997 Apparel Industry Partnership codes labor and human rights representatives played an important role, taking the lead in insisting that factories be monitored by public-interest groups. Codes of conduct must be monitored by public-interest advocates with full access to information if the public is to invest its faith in them.[29]

Business cooperation is a potential strategy for reining in low-road corporate behavior. Sociologist Severyn Bruyn has described hundreds of cooperative initiatives that businesses or their trade associations could take—in the areas of environmental and health and safety standards, worker rights and internal judicial tribunals, minimum-wage standards, and labor codes—that would reduce the need for government intervention, increase profitability, and serve workers and the public interest. The new corporate web—along with the existing infrastructure of trade associations and joint labor-management councils at an industry level—creates a latent infrastructure for corporations to act in concert for themselves and the larger public interest. Such corporate cooperation is likely to serve both the public and business, however, only when it can be linked to public corporate chartering, employee ownership, and an engaged labor movement, thereby bringing multiple social stakeholders into the private-sector planning process.[30]

Such new business initiatives must take place within the context of a larger public conversation about how to achieve a more democratic and responsible society. As we have seen, our nation has periodically focused attention on the legitimacy of the corporation and of highly concentrated forms of market power, as in the Gilded

Age and the Progressive Era. The antitrust debate early in this century created a national seminar on the corporation and its place in American life. The Great Depression created another such conversation; even in the seventies the movement toward huge corporate conglomerates once again created a national discussion about corporations, leading national legislators like Texan congressman Wright Patman to launch important investigations into concentration in banking and other vital industries.[31]

Since 1980, however, as corporations have grown to eclipse nations in their power, this kind of discussion has been preempted by diversionary politics and an unabated focus on big government. As discussed in Chapter 4, antitrust arguments are rarely presented in ways today that catalyze a serious public discussion of corporate power. The new consensus among government regulators, executives, and politicians is that the unprecedented size and dominant market share of companies like GE and Boeing only helps these quintessential American companies survive global competition and reap economies of scale. Questions about the political and social—as opposed to economic—consequences of concentrating such power in single corporations and their international webs are no longer viewed as relevant to antitrust decisions, driving the larger questions of corporate power, democracy, and social justice underground. The 1998 antitrust action against Microsoft is limited to questioning whether Microsoft's monopoly hinders efficiency or sabotages competition—not whether Microsoft is gaining too much social power.

The broader populist agenda must first and foremost put these issues back on the table, raising the ultimate question of whether corporate empires with the size and market share of Microsoft, Boeing, General Electric, or Time Warner are legitimate institutions in a democratic society. The 200 leading corporations of the world are so large and dominant that it is hard to know whether even public chartering or employee ownership will prove able to make them democratic and responsive to the public interest. As Justice Brandeis argued almost a century ago, there is a point at which the size and power of a corporate institution becomes so vast that the only solution is to dismantle it.[33]

While some critics have argued on democratic grounds that the principle of the corporation itself is illegitimate, public chartering, employee ownership, and a new populist political culture could potentially make all but the largest companies compatible with a democratic system. But we need a public debate about whether the top 200 have exceeded the threshold of size and unaccountable power that can keep them within the democratic framework. Should Americans decide that this is the case, government with the force of public opinion behind it would have to move to break up the largest corporations—much as AT&T was broken up by government edict in the eighties. In this spirit Ralph Nader has proposed breaking up Microsoft, and others target Time Warner and Intel.

A new populist antitrust movement could help put such questions on the national agenda, but the antitrust bureaucracy will certainly not launch this discussion on its own accord, and the debate must move out of the closed circles of economists and lawyers and become a broad public debate. Beyond a general concern with encroaching monopoly in any industry, the public has a particular vital interest in being part of a political and social conversation about the growing concentration of corporate giants in the media, health care, and other sensitive sectors. When five or six companies such as Time Warner and Disney own most of the television, news, and entertainment industry, it is transparently clear that antitrust regulators, with their concern limited to purely economic issues, will never address greater social concerns. The question, for example, of whether media giants threaten democracy is one that antitrust regulators ignore completely, and can only be answered through a sustained new public conversation.

This conversation should obviously include the voices of the corporations themselves—and shouldn't be considered antagonistic by nature to their long-term interests. Many business leaders, in fact, argue that the current trend toward concentration may be unhealthy for corporations and capitalism itself. Many critics inside business argue that the largest corporations may be ungovernable and will eventually collapse under their own anachronistic weight. Others argue that decentralizing forces within business are already transforming the largest corporations into networks of federated autonomous business units, and that a confederated structure—a new kind of web—may prove to be a more efficient and competitive form.[34] The prospects for positive populism, antitrust activity, and economic democracy are heightened today precisely because there is so much sentiment within the corporate world itself that the old vertically integrated corporate command structure is no longer efficient. Smaller, more decentralized forms may be necessary for the bottom line as well as the common good.[35]

The populist agenda should also call for a new initiative to make markets more accountable to social and human concerns. No change in the corporation will make it socially responsible without changing the rules of the game that define the market itself. As long as social and human costs remain invisible on the corporate balance sheet, such costs will continue to go unconsidered in the making of thousands of everyday business decisions. Corporate public chartering and employee ownership are two ways of trying to "internalize" the externalities within the corporate decision-making apparatus. The greater question is, What kinds of larger systemic changes—in the market itself as well as in government—can we implement to address all the social conditions, such as poverty, income inequality, urban decay, and community fragmentation generated by the market system as a whole?

As was noted in the first part of this chapter, keeping the market in its place—keeping it from encroaching into education, health care, and other public spheres—is an appropriate first policy. Populists need to drive home the principle that has been so miserably ignored so far: Such public functions are clearly the province of civil society and the state and are only degraded and dehumanized when they are put up for sale.

A second priority will be to deal with the social crises at home—especially rising poverty and inequality as well as declining democratic participation—that are the inevitable outcome of current market rules. The traditional left-liberal approach is to look to government regulation and redistribution of resources to help redress the unfairness of the market. As corporations grow larger and financial markets both vaster and more speculative, it is clear, as discussed in the first section, that government must continue to provide that critical countervailing force. No other institution has the power or mandate to regulate, tax, and act in the name of the human values that the market can never fully protect.

Populism will thus have to confront the antigovernment mood of the era, but not from a big government or antibusiness posture. Positive populism looks to government as an advocate as well as countervailing power to business and defends public regulation as an underpinning of prosperity and business health itself. Moreover, the new populism champions employee ownership and public chartering as ways of reducing the need for big government by increasing social accountability within the market sector itself. The role of government will be central in the birth of a new, socially responsible market—a market that will reduce many of the traditional functions of government, while increasing the level of governmental activism that has always been indispensable to the preservation of human values.

FOURTEEN

The Global Populist

Globalization is the great issue of the twenty-first century—both for America's leaders, who see their mission as constructing the new global order, and for ordinary Americans, whose jobs and way of life are at stake. Globalism is a volcanic force fueling corporate power, and it is the ultimate populist issue. Corporate ascendancy in the United States and worldwide are twin sides of the same coin. There will be no lasting populist solutions in America without a global populist agenda—since corporations can respond to any curbs on their power at home by moving out of the country.

In 1996, Pat Buchanan made globalization the centerpiece of his presidential campaign, and demonized both foreign workers and transnational corporations—an old tactic of "paranoid populism." Buchanan charged that U.S. corporations were sacrificing workers on the altar of global profits, and denounced the United Nations and the World Trade Organization (WTO) as agents of a new international financial conspiracy. Unlike Clinton and Dole, Buchanan was willing to talk about the frightening economic insecurity that globalization creates, but he offered only xenophobic rhetoric and misguided protectionism instead of real solutions.

Globalism does in fact threaten the economic security of millions of Americans, and could ultimately undermine both national sovereignty and democracy here and abroad. Positive populists will have to offer their own alternative to corporate-dominated globalization, but they must avoid scapegoating global corporations and recognize the potential virtues of globalization itself. Global corporations bring not only jobs and capital to poor countries, but also notions of law, individual rights and freedom that can help undermine feudal or authoritarian regimes around the world.

The debate in the twenty-first century will not be about whether to have a global economy, but about who will make the rules. Globalization is inevitable, but the kind of globalism we ultimately will live under is still up for grabs. Positive populists need to show that global markets are the creative handiwork of corporations and governments, and that the new rules of the global market can still be rewritten in the public interest. An energized global populist movement could create a new and more just global order, serving both businesses and individuals throughout the world.

The World's Shadow Government

The largest global corporations are swallowing up an ever larger share of the world economy, while also building a new global architecture of governing institutions such as the WTO and the International Monetary Fund (IMF). The same web of vast global corporations that are helping shape America's destiny are working simultaneously to shape the new global order and govern it in their own interests.

There are now some 44,000 transnational corporations; their share of the world gross product has risen from 17 percent in the mid-1960s to about 33 percent in 1995. These companies are spinning money and investments around the world at a dizzying rate, with foreign investment growing 10 percent a year in the mid-1990s. In 1996, global companies invested $1.5 trillion in foreign nations.[1]

Among the thousands of transnational companies, the top 200 account for most of the action. These corporations enjoy greater combined annual revenue than the total income of 4.5 billion people in the world, more than four-fifths of the world's population. The combined income of the top 200 is $7.1 trillion, which is greater than the combined economy of 182 countries. The top 200 are also rapidly expanding their market share of global production, with a few giants, such as Mitsubishi, Sony, Microsoft, and Boeing virtually monopolizing not only U.S. but global production in their respective industries. Oligopoly is increasingly the global norm, where a handful of giant companies compete to control the world's market in each sector.[2]

Global alliances link almost all of these giant oligopolistic competitors, and these vast networks not only help companies manage intense global competition, but bring businesses together to create coordinated economic policy and political global agendas. While most Americans are not familiar with them, global business associations such as the United States Council for International Business, the European Roundtable of Industrialists, the International Chamber of Commerce, and other groups are working intensively together to help shape the new regime of global corporate ascendancy.

At the heart of the new global order is the alphabet soup of new global institutions, from the WTO and the IMF to the World Bank, that help manage the world's economy. While barely known to the public, they are quietly assuming sovereign powers that deeply affect all our lives. They represent a kind of shadow economic government, whose sovereignty extends to the entire planet.

The existence of these organizations is far from the sinister plot described by Pat Buchanan, since any form of globalization requires new governing bodies that write global rules and adjudicate disputes. Global commerce—like all commerce—requires a vast number of rules and protections for all players, including not only corporations but workers, nations, and communities. Populists should be concerned not so much with the existence of such global bodies and rules, but with the players at the table, the kinds of rules they write, and the question of public accountability. The ultimate problem with the new global architecture is not that it weakens national sovereignty—a necessity if globalization is to move forward—but that it so dramatically threatens to weaken any form of *public* sovereignty and global democracy.

The WTO and the IMF are governed by boards of representatives from member states, typically in proportion to the amount of funding they contribute. Both agencies help set the basic rules of the international regime, by setting the terms of international credit and helping write and enforce the global trade rules that are partially replacing the laws of nations. While they seem to represent a legitimate extension of national authority to supranational bodies, the reality is that this new shadow government is profoundly undemocratic and far removed from any process of public accountability. As in America, the real players are political elites and professional bureaucrats, working hand in glove with the global industries they are charged with regulating. While a semblance of popular participation still enters into the national regulatory process, the new global institutions are sealed off from the influence of ordinary citizens.

The real problem in the liberal-and-conservative debates about globalization is less the disagreement over economic strategy than a failure to shed light on the true nature of the shadow government. The economics themselves, of course, are of great importance, since globalism is catalyzing uneven but vigorous development in some countries, while inflicting economic harm on millions of ordinary people in both rich and poor nations. But while populists must enter the economic debate about who wins and loses, the most important populist mission should be to move the conversation to the underlying issues of sovereignty. These largely invisible problems are embedded in the inner structure of the new shadow government and the emerging trade treaties and doctrines at the heart of the new global regime.

Consider the new, proposed Multilateral Agreement on Investments (MAI), a far-reaching treaty on global financial markets and investment rights that some have called a new economic constitution for the entire world. At this writing in early 1998, a full draft of the MAI, sponsored by the Clinton administration, the leaders of other major developed countries, and the WTO, is nearing completion but has not yet been submitted to Congress. Growing popular opposition to the MAI in 1998 may prevent its approval, but key provisions of the MAI are already being submitted for adoption by the IMF and WTO. Whatever its eventual fate, it is a remarkable case study in the making of global corporate ascendancy. The draft was developed with the official consultation of more than 300 transnational American-based corporations, and coordinated by the United States Council for International Business in conjunction with foreign companies. Members of Congress were neither invited nor involved, a sign of the disturbing and familiar flaws at the heart of the new global order.

MAI is a massive document with a simple stated purpose: to ensure that capital can flow freely around the world with the same protections and rights in every country. MAI requires that every country open every part of its economy—its banks, television stations, and all its vital industries—to unrestricted foreign investment or acquisition. "National treatment" is mandated for all foreign companies, meaning they must be awarded the same or better treatment than local firms. National or community regulations requiring the hiring of local workers or community investment would be outlawed, and the ability of countries to regulate the flow of foreign currency would be effectively decimated. Corporations that felt that any country's environmental or labor laws limited their rightful profits could sue governments for expropriation—which the MAI defines in a very expansive way—and receive monetary compensation. A special MAI international tribunal would hear such cases, rather than the nation's own courts. This remarkable "bill of rights" for investors stipulates no corresponding responsibilities for corporations nor any parallel set of rights for labor.[3]

In a preview of things to come under MAI, the U.S.-based Ethyl corporation has sued Canada for $251 million in damages as a result of an environmental law passed by the Canadian government which bans the import and transport within Canada of any product made with MMT, a toxic gasoline additive. Ethyl, which manufactures MMT, argues that the new law is tantamount to expropriation of its future profits. The Ethyl suit falls under an "investor rights" provision of the North American Free Trade Agreement (NAFTA), which allows the corporations of any NAFTA nations to sue any NAFTA government for legislation which, as Ethyl argues in this case, reduces its potential earnings. The "investor rights" and expropriation language of NAFTA is a pale shadow of that in the current MAI draft, suggesting the possibility that corporations around the world could not only sue nations for passing any new protective environmental and labor laws, but could potentially challenge and dismantle the entire existing structure of labor and environmental protections around the world.[4]

The language in use here is especially troubling, for MAI co-opts the language of property and individual rights to legitimize a new set of global investment rights not subject to democratic adjudication. Clinton officials argue that the bill does nothing more than establish fair and nondiscriminatory treatment for global investors. But lurking beneath the remedy for presumed discrimination is a breathtaking assault on popular sovereignty. MAI creates a parallel government with no accountability to the public in any country—and with the power to invalidate national laws.

A group of congressional representatives, angered that MAI was negotiated without their participation or knowledge, has observed that MAI "would require significant limitations on U.S. laws and policy concerning federal, state and local regulation of investment." They also note that "the MAI provides expansive takings language that would allow a foreign corporation or investor to directly sue the U.S. government for damages if we take any action that would restrain 'enjoyment' of an investment. This language is broad and vague, and goes beyond the limited concept of takings provided in U.S. domestic law. Why," these representatives asked, "would the U.S. willingly cede sovereign immunity . . . ?"[5]

Here lie the beginnings of a true national debate about globalization. MAI would put in place a legal infrastructure that would shift sovereignty from nations and democratically elected officials to corporate and legal specialists unaccountable to any democratic process. MAI has the potential to undermine any nation's ability to govern itself, and gives ordinary citizens no way to affect the global rules of the game.

As MAI analyst Scott Nova has said, "The multinational corporations are really happy with the developments in the world of the past 20 years. They want MAI to lock these developments into place."[6] These "happy" developments are the result of years of concerted effort to weave global corporations themselves into the inner fabric of the shadow government they have helped create. The United States Council on International Business participated in every MAI negotiating session as official consultants, and corporate representatives also had input before and after every official drafting session, as well as major additional influence through their lobbyists in Washington and other capitals. As of the end of 1997, there were no major differences between the MAI draft and the proposal initially developed by the most powerful global business groups.

This pervasive corporate representation and influence also marks the WTO, the central pillar of the new shadow government. The WTO, housed bureaucratically in Geneva, Switzerland, was established in 1995 as a successor to the General Agreement on Tarriffs and Trade (GATT), the huge code of international agreements regulating global industries from banking to manufacturing to agriculture. The WTO is the shadow government's judiciary and enforcement agency, with independent tribunals that enjoy astonishing power to review and challenge domestic laws that might create unfair trade.

Like the proposed MAI tribunals, WTO panels are sovereign adjudicating agencies with no public accountability. Howard Wachtel writes that the WTO "has no written bylaws . . . holds no public hearings and in fact has never opened its processes to the public. Its meeting rooms do not even have a section for the public to observe its activities." Yet its professional staff, advised by corporate lawyers and lobbyists, make crucial decisions that are enforceable in national courts. In response to American beef industry and government suits, the WTO overturned the European Union's ban on imports of hormone-treated beef. In 1998, WTO ruled that an American law penalizing countries whose shrimp-catching methods threatened the world's sea turtle population constituted a violation of free trade. Environmentalists had no voice in these proceedings. The WTO and MAI forums are manifestly antidemocractic: The new enforcement bodies have no citizen representation, and no public accountability.

IMF agreements, a cornerstone of the global architecture built by corporations and their political allies, threaten popular sovereignty in other ways. The IMF, created in 1944 at the Bretton Woods Conference that reorganized the world's economy after World War II, is roughly equivalent to the shadow government's executive branch. While its formal responsibility is to help nations deal with debt and balance-of-trade deficits, it has evolved into the world's foremost policymaker, setting terms for receiving credit that essentially dictate the economic and social policies of scores of nations.

Nations afflicted with the economic "Asian Flu" in the late 1990s have learned firsthand about the sovereign powers of the IMF. Massive inflows of capital investment into nations such as Thailand and South Korea helped develop these countries, until the same speculative investors withdrew their funds, creating undertows that swamped whole economies.[8] When the IMF came in to offer credit to these drowning nations, it effectively forced them—as has been its historic practice in scores of countries—to give up control of their own macroeconomic and social policy, typically imposing austerity, privatization, and currency devaluation strategies that make bread and housing unaffordable for much of the population.

Leading mainstream economists such as Joseph Stiglitz and Jeffrey Sachs have begun to raise serious questions about the economic wisdom of such policies; Sachs has also begun to raise populist issues about sovereignty, noting that the IMF is a "surrogate government" with an "all-too-constant presence." Sachs even hints that a new corporate-style colonialism may be at work: "Not unlike the days when the British Empire placed senior officials directly into the Egyptian and Ottoman finance ministries, the IMF is insinuated into the inner sanctums of nearly seventy-five developing-country governments with a combined population of some 1.4 billion. These governments rarely move without consulting the IMF staff, and when they do, they risk their lifelines to capital markets, foreign aid, and international respectability." Sachs, an unlikely source of populist thinking, concludes with a populist manifesto: "It is time to end the IMF's artificial monopoly on policymaking in the developing world."[9]

One task of the new populism will be to shine the light on the new shadow government and focus the debate on the question of global corporate sovereignty. Positive populism is pro-globalist, since a fair system of globalism can benefit both the corporations and the citizenry of the world. But it seeks to derail the corporate-dominated form of globalization that currently threatens democracy, and to replace the shadow government with a publicly accountable global regime.[10]

Populism can achieve this only through a popular education campaign designed to reveal the essentially political—not economic—nature of both the shadow government and the global capital markets it helped create and regulate. These markets are seen by most Americans as "natural" economic formations that flourish, like other markets, mainly by being insulated from politics. If the development of the MIA, NAFTA, and the IMF has a silver lining, it is that they have served to confirm that global capital markets are far from "natural," but instead are meticulously constructed political institutions managed by agencies of the shadow government. While these treaties have been crafted using the rhetoric of free trade and "natural rights," any informed citizen can see that they are purely the creation of global corporations and other groups acting to write global rules to serve their own interests.

Positive populists have no interest in wrecking global governing institutions such as the WTO, or global capital markets, in which a growing number of citizens as well as corporations feel they have major economic interests. Rather, we must show that global capital markets, like all markets, depend on a set of political rules that somebody has to write and enforce. Americans need a crash course in understanding markets and how they develop— as the historical creation of corporations and political elites whose needs they service. Once ordinary Americans understand that capital markets are not "givens" rooted in nature, but changeable products of a political and social process, the real debate about globalism can begin—the debate about who will write the rules and how they can serve the public interest.[11]

Global Solutions

In the Gilded Age, corporations faced with populist movements in Pennsylvania or New York escaped to more accommodating states such as New Jersey and Delaware. Today, corporations have a bigger escape hatch. They can move their headquarters from Delaware to third-world nations, or to offshore havens such as the Cayman Islands.

In the new global economy, populism must also be global. The willingness of corporations to leave the country undermines the strength of isolated populist movements in the United States or other nations. But globalism catalyzes new international relations among workers and environmentalists from different countries, making a global movement possible. The slogan "Think globally, act locally" suggests that even locally oriented groups can act to change the global regime. But positive populism must both think and act globally—with populist groups cooperating and mounting coordinated campaigns around the world. A purely nationalist populism is doomed to failure, and is likely to degrade into a demagogic and politically dangerous movement.

There are many useful things populists can do in their respective countries—especially in the United States, since building widespread employee ownership, legalizing stakeholder claims, or greatly strengthening the labor movement here would have massive effects all over the planet. But there will be no meaningful limits on the corporation in the United States without the rise of global countervailing powers and the democratization of the global economic system. While this may seem to be a tall order, global populist strategies are far from utopian and have already emerged in many parts of the world. They will make the American-oriented populist strategies discussed in the last chapter far easier to achieve, just as American movements for populist change here will immensely help global activists win their battles.

Corporate ascendancy in both the United States and the world is rooted in the ability of corporations to shift capital freely across borders. Corporations move on a whim across whole continents to cut labor costs, break unions, or escape taxes and regulations. As whole countries reel from the destabilizing impact of these dizzying moves, the time may now be ripe for populist ideas about regulating and democratizing the new global corporate order.

The idea of regulating global capital movements recently surfaced in the most improbable of places: a 1998 meeting of leaders of the International Monetary Fund, the World Bank, and executives of the world's largest corporations. With the meeting coming in the wake of the "Asian Flu," Stanley Fischer, an IMF deputy director, acknowledged for the first time that "the IMF recognizes the problem of surges of short-term capital across borders and the need to find ways to deal with that." This was an astonishing assertion, since the IMF has always been the high priest of free trade and unregulated global capital markets. Joseph Stiglitz, chief economist of the World Bank, also unexpectedly supported new regulations that would give bigger tax deductions for global investments longer than a year, and much smaller or no tax deductions for shorter transactions.[12]

These are small steps, but they point to the kind of expansive global regulation that will be vital to the populist agenda. Economist James Tobin has proposed transaction taxes designed to limit how quickly corporations and banks move capital around the world. As William Greider writes, these would "take the fun and profit out of currency trading and other speculative activities . . . but would not inhibit the long-term flows of capital for foreign investment and trade." While also a small step, such financial regulation would help make clear that global capital markets, as well as cross-national corporate mobility, need to be subject to democratic political control if countries and ordinary people are to preside over their own destinies.[13]

Greider has suggested more robust populist forms of global financial regulation. These include tightening credit terms that encourage global financial speculation, expanding transaction taxes to limit corporate or speculative whipsawing of national economies, outlawing unregulated offshore bank havens, and monitoring the social impact of capital flows and corporate flight. The intent is not to shut down global capital markets, but to restructure them so that governments and their publics rather than just speculators or global corporations have a powerful voice in how they run.[14]

Global corporations in tandem with the IMF and the WTO now set the rules governing capital mobility. The global populist agenda must be to broaden the spectrum of political actors and to modify the rules in the public interest. Populist groups in the United States and elsewhere are now not only exposing the assaults on sovereignty embodied in treaties such as the MAI, but drafting alternative treaties for public debate—alternatives that would subject capital flight to public scrutiny, force corporations to report on and pay some of the social costs of corporate mobility, and ensure that labor and environmental stakeholders enjoy the same legal standing in trade disputes as corporations.[15]

The global populist agenda requires rethinking the entire architecture of the current global system, including the structure and policies of both the IMF and the WTO. The goal of global positive populism is not to prevent any erosion of national sovereignty, but to ensure that the new global institutions are themselves democratic and subject to popular rather than corporate control. The same forms of participation and accountability to stakeholders and the general public that we have proposed for the corporation need now to be applied to global institutions such as the WTO. Otherwise, the professional bureaucrats and their corporate advisors will only foster low-road globalism, subverting the public interest all the way.

Globalization also demands a new look at international codes, and a global corporate charter. International codes of corporate conduct, as noted in the last chapter, are already emerging in many forms. Corporations are voluntarily embracing international standards such as the ISO 14000—an ambitious set of global technical and environmental standards created by the International Organization for Standardization, a global association of businesses representing 95 percent of the world's industrial production—to help create uniformity, avoid litigation, and discourage products that would damage the environment and the industry's reputation. Levi Strauss and other giant global contractors have embraced Global Sourcing Guidelines that prohibit child labor, prison labor, and sweatshop working conditions. Corporations such as General Motors have signed on to the CERES principles, an ambitious form of environmental self-audit that will cost companies millions each year.

Such self-imposed social charters are only the first step toward what Tim Costello and Jeremy Brecher call a "global social charter," which would set "a floor under environmental, labor, and social conditions. It would provide both universal rights and rising minimum standards appropriate to countries at different levels of development." This seems a visionary ideal and is not likely to be accomplished in the near future, but the European Union has already embraced a modest version of the idea, spelling out certain minimum labor, health, safety, and women's rights standards for corporations in its 1988 Social Charter and the Social Chapter of the Maastricht Treaty of 1991. One hundred sixty-nine nations are signatories to the International Labor Organization; together they have established 174 conventions that set minimum global standards for wages, free association of labor, social security, health and safety, and rights for women workers and children. A variety of other regional treaties, in the Caribbean Basin and elsewhere, are introducing labor and environmental standards that would apply to all the signatory nations.[16]

Global corporate charters are a key goal for the global populist movement, as they would prevent corporations from fleeing abroad—and gaining the fruits of child or prison labor—if charter restrictions in any one country seem too burdensome. The European Social Charter, which creates a public charter binding corporations to minimal public standards in all the participating European nations, is a partial solution. Any system of federal American charters for a "public" corporation could be a model for international charters sanctioned by the United Nations. A successful chartering movement in the United States would obviously mark a major step in the long-term development of a global social charter, perhaps administered and adjudicated through the United Nations and the World Court, to regulate the behavior of corporations around the planet.[17]

The political prospects for such global change could be dramatically affected by a global downturn or regional crisis. The 1998 crisis in Asia sparked unprecedented discussion even in mainstream circles about the need for regulation of global markets. The rhetoric about free markets seems magically to disappear when bailouts or other forms of radical state intervention are necessary to guarantee global economic stability. At this writing any number of events, from Chinese currency devaluation to an escalating bank crisis in Japan to a dramatic drop in the American stock market could trigger a new international climate in which the populist vision of today becomes the common sense of tomorrow.

The globalist agenda of positive populists overlaps that of global corporations, a fact that only increases the possibility of success. Both positive populists and corporations themselves favor globalization, and both recognize the need for new transnational institutions and a global regulatory regime. Richard McCormick, the CEO of US WEST and the chairman of the United States Council for International Business—the official corporate umbrella group to the MAI—wrote to President Clinton in 1997 that global corporations "rely on having consistent rules of the game" and support a full panoply of international standards for business and all its stakeholders.[18] Global business is starting to recognize that regulation is necessary to manage competition and prevent systemic breakdown. In the wake of the Asian flu, global business has advocated massive government intervention both in Asia and elsewhere to prevent destabilization spreading to Europe and the United States. Just as American national businesses, since the Progressive Era, have asked government to step in and manage economic downturns, so global corporations today must depend on a regulatory regime that will prevent global or regional collapse and maintain the delicate macroeconomic conditions that support global prosperity.

Global business not only supports the worldwide investment rights guaranteed by the WTO and proposed MAI, but is prepared to support certain forms of global labor and environmental rights. Chairman McCormick wrote President Clinton that global business has "a responsibility to our shareholders, our employees and customers and to our communities to be good citizens and to apply high standards of conduct in all our operations. We adhere to voluntary multilateral codes of conduct promulgated by the OECED and the ILO." But beyond this voluntary commitment, which is the corporations' preferred route, many corporate leaders also endorse regulation. McCormick asked the president to be "more vigorous in using the ILO to bring international pressure to bear on governments that commit egregious violations of basic workers' rights" and to "work through the WTO, UN, and World Bank to combat extortion and bribery in international business transactions." He also wrote that business "has a responsibility to protect the environment and it is in our interest to do so. We expect a regulatory regime" to prevent corporate environmental rogues.[19]

Now, this hardly suggests a conversion to populism among corporations: They have also asked the president to "Avoid the use of trade measures, investment restrictions, or government mandated codes of conduct on business operations to address social and environmental concerns."[20] Moreover, they militantly oppose public or stakeholder participation in the inner sanctums of the WTO or IMF. Corporations embrace global regulation, but not yet economic democracy.

Nonetheless, the existing transnational bodies that corporations have welcomed and helped create, such as the WTO, could become part of the solution. The WTO has enforcement powers to review and sanction national laws that violate "fair trade," and this could include unfair labor laws. In 1995, the International Labor Organization initiated work with the WTO to introduce labor standards into WTO' s criteria of fair trade practices. If successful, this would allow the WTO to declare child labor, sweatshops, and bans on unions or other attacks on labor rights as "unfair trade," and to punish the offending nations. While this provoked a storm of internal controversy, and remained secret to the outside world, Howard Wachtel writes that "labor's best hope" for dealing with the problem of a global "race to the bottom" now lies with the WTO—and some unions have already mounted global public campaigns to have the WTO and other international bodies treat labor abuses as trade violations and forms of "social dumping." A populist campaign, led by organized labor in the United States, could succeed in turning the WTO into an unexpected tool for protecting wages and working conditions in both the first and third world, requiring countries around the world to respect and protect labor rights.

Beyond democratization of the shadow government, the ultimate populist aim is to turn globalization into a race to the top. This means preventing corporations from abusing workers or the environment as their ticket to global success. By taking pollution and supercheap labor off the playing field—through regulation and international standards or charters—corporations will be forced to compete by seeing who can motivate and educate their workforce most effectively.

Global corporations will continue to resist most changes of this kind—and further attempts to democratize the new global regime. Nonetheless, stakeholder involvement and public accountability in organizations such as the WTO could serve corporations' long-term interests, much as it could in the corporation itself. To succeed, positive populists, even as they challenge the corporation, need to show how their solutions will ultimately serve many business interests—from preserving political stability and continued demand for global production, to enhancing productivity as well as social responsibility through a global stakeholder regime.

FIFTEEN

The Four Movements to Join

In 1996, John Sweeney was elected America's national leader of labor on a fiery populist platform. He called for a shift in the AFL-CIO from a "Washington-based institution concerned primarily with refining policy positions" to a "worker-based movement against greed, multinational corporations, race-baiting and labor-baiting politicians." He claimed that the labor movement had become "irrelevant to the vast majority of unorganized workers in our country" and feared even that "we are becoming irrelevant to our own members." He is the first such national leader in a generation to call for labor to become a real social movement again, to challenge the corporate culture of greed and hypermaterialism, organize the unorganized, link up with minorities and women—for it to join with community, church, and grassroots groups all over the country to help revitalize American democracy.[1]

The rhetoric comes easy, but words like this coming from the head of the AFL-CIO hint at something new and important. As we move into a new Gilded Age, it is inevitable that the populist and labor struggles of the 1890s against the robber barons will resurface in new movements for justice today. While the social landscape seems far more quiescent than in the 1890s, activists such as Noam Chomsky have argued that there is more grassroots activism in America today than in the 1960s.

This may be true, but the movements today are deeply fragmented and lack any unified vision for a national struggle. The populist struggle for democracy depends on their coming together. As both political parties embrace the priorities of business, no populist leadership is likely to emerge from Washington, potentially for many years. Fortunately, there are at least four resurgent popular forces that are already beginning to assert themselves; but each will have to adjust its focus and goals radically in order to become part of a truly populist movement. They will have to learn a new language to help them connect with the American people; find the strength to discipline their own goals in the spirit of coalition politics; build new viable cultures and economic alternatives rather than just criticize the old; and learn to work in support of business as they challenge corporate power. But the larger goal for which they would all be working is necessary to achieve their founding goals: the return of basic rights from corporations to the citizens to whom they rightly belong.

Putting the Movement Back into the Labor Movement

The first and most important of the four populist forces is the new labor movement, which under Sweeney has claimed that "the Federation must be the fulcrum of a vibrant social movement." Sweeney seems to have recognized that labor is dead if it continues to act as a narrowly oriented lobby for its declining membership. He has traveled the country announcing that labor will now speak for social justice, especially for the poor. Sweeney has begun to articulate a concern for values and human dignity—for people as more important than profits—and he is calling for labor to reach out to all the groups at home and abroad who are suffering from "the over-reaching of profit-hungry corporations."[2]

Sweeney has called for a new national and global organizing

campaign to reach sweatshop workers, temps, white collars, pink collars, and even managers. Putting his money where his mouth is, he has committed one-third of the AFL-CIO budget to the biggest organizing drive since the Great Depression. He has also called for new "capital strategies" which would involve use of the billions of dollars in union pension funds and strike funds to create worker-owned companies and to create new jobs in depressed urban and rural areas. Labor might now be in a position to offer some real economic alternatives, as did the early populist cooperatives, providing real-world models of business enterprise in the public interest that would give Americans some hope for change. Sweeney seems serious about building a strong movement—and is actively seeking coalitions with other social groups long at odds with labor, including women's groups, environmentalists, minorities, and religious groups.[3]

The real constituency of the new labor movement Sweeney envisions is the American public as a whole, as well as workers throughout the world. As the old social contract unravels, the great majority of those in jeopardy are not American union members but unrepresented American workers, as well as workers in the third world. Beyond organizing new members, labor must transform itself into a voice speaking mainly for these expansive constituencies who are not already American union members. Ironically, this will be the most effective way to service its own dues-paying members. In France, for example, less than 10 percent of the workforce is in unions, but the French people as a whole support union work stoppages to protect wages or benefits. In 1997, a majority of the French population virtually closed down the country in support of transportation workers' efforts to protect retirement and vacation benefits. This reflected public appreciation of French labor's long political role in fighting for a social contract to protect the entire French public.

Sweeney has sought not only to advance a new national political agenda around such issues as the minimum wage, fair trade, public education, and social equality, but to join forces with third-world unions. Cooperation among Canadian, U.S., and Mexican unions is mushrooming, reflecting the new post-NAFTA reality of the American continent as a single corporate market. It is impossible to defend the corporate high road in any one nation without protecting wages and benefits in all countries simultaneously. As Peter Smith, a Latin American labor specialist, argues, "United States labor has a stake in helping Mexican unions because it leads to protection of their own self interests." A Mexican independent labor organizer, Benedicto Martinez Orzoco, says that "We're finding that there's a new vision among trade unionists in the United States. They're showing more interest in understanding what we're up against in Mexico: the control, the manipulation, the gangster tactics." When Mexican workers organized by Martinez voted to decertify the corrupt government-controlled official union in a Tijuana Hyundai Maquiladora plant, they got financial and political help from Sweeney's AFL-CIO. Sweeney's political success in 1997 in defeating the president's fast-track trade agreement—which explicitly protected financial but not worker and environmental rights—reflects the promise of a new labor strategy oriented toward the public interest.[4]

As labor activists and writers Tim Costello and Jeremy Brecher have argued, labor will have to make a heroic effort to shed its old skin if it is to live up to its new rhetoric. It will have to clean house completely and internally democratize—a staggering task given the hierarchical bureaucratic structure of existing unions and the corrupt entrenched leadership that dominates many of them. The 1997 corruption-related ousting of Teamsters president Ron Carey, who himself had cleaned up the Hoffa-dominated union, shows how deeply the shadow of corruption continues to haunt labor. The new labor movement will also have to become truly inclusive and create real power for women, minorities, and others who remain deeply underrepresented at all levels of union leadership. It will have to reach out to the poor and unemployed as it has not done since the Great Depression. It will have to sacrifice the cozy political arrangements with the Democratic party that the

AFL-CIO has long enjoyed. And it will have to get serious about being a new social movement broadly committed to human rights, as the Sweeney leadership claims to be, rather than just business unionism servicing the special interests of its members. This will require new thinking in every corner of the house of labor, and can probably only be achieved if its members reach out and connect to other movements that have much to teach it.[5]

Labor is ideally placed to educate the public about the social and human costs of low-road capitalism. In a post-communist world no longer preoccupied with red-baiting, it can offer a more serious systemic critique of the corporate order. Labor is the only major institution in the United States that can sponsor, fund, and disseminate a critical consciousness about low-road capitalism. It is high time to start.

Unions will only be able to recruit American workers if they show that they are willing to contest corporate power and offer credible economic alternatives that will foster real economic security and empowerment. This means working politically for an industrial democracy that gives workers a voice in every business and contributes to the creation of the new publicly chartered corporation. Since unions only represent about 15 percent of the labor force, they will have to seek to represent workers who are not part of unions through various forms of associational membership and services.[6] They will also have to support forms of representation, including an American variant of the German works council, that can empower nonunionized workers in new ways that fall outside direct union control.[7] Most important, they will have to lead the national struggle for full employment, and against the trends toward disposable work and declining wages that can threaten economic security for so many Americans.

While labor will have to contest corporate power in a more serious way, it will also have to learn to cooperate with business. The labor movement has been deeply conflicted about cooperative partnerships with business and the corporate responsibility movement. As discussed earlier, there are serious dangers lurking in cooperative strategies. But unions will gain public credibility and power only if they are seen as acting not just to help workers but also in the interest of the nation's greater economic growth. Labor will have to be seen as an ally of business in the struggle to ensure our viable place in the world market—even as it continues to contest corporate power, with redoubled militancy.[8]

Labor is the only force that can help corporate responsibility become a real movement for democratization. In Germany, strong national unions have played a role on both boards of directors and worker councils that commit workers to cooperation without compromising the independence of the union. The unions act in the works councils and the board to help the enterprise become more cooperative and productive. But they also negotiate in a tough adversarial way to protect the interests of their workers.[9]

American labor has to find the same delicate balance, moving simultaneously toward greater confrontation and greater cooperation. Only more concerted confrontation will lead to successful organizing and systemic change. At the same time, labor can work closely with corporations to move their social responsibility and empowerment rhetoric toward a meaningful form of economic democracy. It is only where unions have taken an active role in shaping employee participation and "cooperation" programs, as at Saturn, that any real prospect of creating a genuinely democratic and responsible company has emerged.

Cooperation is a bad word in many union circles, but it is going to be a rising tide in most American corporations whether or not unions get on board. Shopfloor participation properly implemented is vitally important for the human development of workers as well as for corporate efficiency. The great limit of the European labor model is that it has failed to devise forms of participation that combat the stifling bureaucratic character of much factory and office work. American unions should seize the initiative and fight for partnership on terms that do not compromise their own independence and ensure that cooperation serves workers' interests.[10]

The Third Sector

As labor is being reborn, a new "Third Sector" of grassroots community groups has emerged as a second force that could change America. Called the Third Sector because they are part of neither the public nor the market sectors, these groups are emerging to fight for jobs and living wages, but also for good schools, safe streets, affordable housing, and, most of all, a new sense of civility and community. The marriage of labor with the Third Sector could become the foundation of the new populism.

The leading theorist of the Third Sector has been Jeremy Rifkin, who argues that communities themselves are the prime force that can move America in a new direction. He contends that the Third Sector, which embraces families, churches, schools, foundations, volunteer agencies and other community-based organizations, is the carrier of social morality. Unlike government, it does not represent coercion; unlike business, it does not stand for profit. It breeds the communitarian values of service, responsibility, and love on which the health of civil society, democracy, and the market itself depend.[11]

Rifkin observes that the Third Sector is vast, with 10 percent of the workforce employed by nonprofits and 90 million Americans volunteering. "If it were an economy, it would be the seventh-largest economy in the world; it's made up of 1.4 million organizations dealing with community needs." What all these organizations—which range from the Lions Club to the Girl Scouts to the Catholic Church—have in common is that "they each believe in serving the community. . . ."[12]

As government and business abandon the old social compact, Rifkin believes only the Third Sector can step into the breach. Of particular importance, he argues, is the technological revolution that is displacing millions of workers. As corporations downsize, the Third Sector could employ laid-off people to rebuild the schools, educate the young, care for the elderly, and rebuild affordable housing and our decaying neighborhoods. Third Sector enterprise is the route to a full employment that rebuilds both neighborhoods and social responsibility.

Rifkin details the proliferation of grassroots community organizations that are rising to take over as government and business abandon communities. Like the original populists, these are ordinary people who are taking matters into their own hands. "But this sector," Rifkin acknowledges, "has been marginalized; it has a neocolonial status, relying on government largesse and the goodwill of corporate philanthropy. How does this sector become an equal player with market and government?"[13]

Rifkin argues that the Third Sector can be mobilized as a political force devoted to preserving community. He is right, but to do so it will need a new political consciousness and new allies. Most communitarian writers and the majority of community groups have failed to acknowledge that market values are subverting community values and that the new corporate economy is the biggest wrecker of community itself. As jobs go overseas, wages decline, and people have to work longer hours, the economic infrastructure of community breaks down and everyone becomes an entrepreneur motivated primarily by personal survival. Competition for scarce resources undermines solidarity within Third Sector communities, even as corporate pressure for balanced budgets, welfare abolition, and the like drain the federal government of resources for personal and community relief.

The Third Sector thus has a natural affinity with the labor movement and a larger populist politics, something Rifkin's own analysis implicitly suggests. Rifkin details the devastating effects of the new corporate contract and technological unemployment on communities. But the prevailing way of thinking in the Third Sector subverts its own political development. The current orientation toward service, localism, and volunteerism, unlike nineteenth-century populism, removes the Third Sector from any real political orientation. Rather than contesting for national power, the Third Sector seeks to help individuals and then communities one by one. The Third Sector eschews political polarization in favor of working together. Its motto seems closer to President Bush's "Thousand Points of Light," a prescription for charity and volunteerism, than to any recipe for political transformation. Young people in City Year, a national service organization that is one of President Clinton's favorites, repaint dilapidated slum housing, tutor kids in rotting schools, and feed hungry people in ghettos. When I asked a group of them in Boston whether their work treating symptoms might be complemented with an attempt to cure the deeper disease, they said they had never thought about it. The idea that we might need change in economic and political institutions had not crossed their mind.[14]

The thinking of the City Year kids is mirrored, more or less, in that of leading communitarian writers. They see change as personal, rooted in the neighborhood, coming from the heart—and almost entirely unrelated to national politics. Their lack of interest in building a national political movement is rooted in today's communitarian theory, which sees communitarianism as requiring moral rather than economic transformation. America's leading communitarian sociologist, Amitai Etzioni, focuses on changes in the micro-institutions of family, neighborhood, and church without ever talking about confronting the concentrations of economic power that can have such profound influence over those institutions.[15]

Capitalism is a word that almost never appears in the communitarian lexicon. This reflects the class bias of the leading communitarian theorists, who like Etzioni are rooted in elite universities and close to circles of power in Washington. These influential new theorists of civil society reflect what I have called a Professional Managerial Class (PMC) communitarianism, which is uneasy with challenges to corporate power and the market. While Third Sector activists in community-based organizations are far more diverse in class background, PMC communitarian theorists have had an impact on the way they conceive their agenda.[16]

Populism needs a moral dimension at its core and should be a politics of the heart, as we discuss in the next chapter. It must be a movement grounded in the human spirit. But if the Third Sector avoids challenges to corporate power and the market, it will never revive community.

The Third Sector and the labor movement could help remedy their mutual deficiencies by coming together. The labor movement could provide community groups with a meaningful economic analysis and political consciousness. Labor's concern with civilizing the global market is essential to meeting the economic needs of communities. Unions, in turn, would benefit from the help of the Third Sector in trying to create public support for full employment—while the new neighborhood jobs that could employ millions of Americans and rebuild our communities would benefit both forces. Labor could also bargain for community benefits in its negotiations with companies and lobby in Congress for public-employment and social programs that would rebuild our neighborhoods.

There are many potentially fruitful links between labor and the Third Sector. One is the prospect of hundreds of community-development organizations (CDCs), which create jobs and housing in decaying neighborhoods. Labor is already beginning to invest union pension funds with community-development groups and work with them to demand more financial support from banks. A vibrant coalition between unions and CDCs is critical to both groups.

There is also the larger dialogue between the labor movement and religion. The original populists, as well as America's first national labor movement, the Knights of Labor, were deeply religious.[17] Churches and synagogues are an important part of the Third Sector, and the Catholic Bishops' letters on the economy in the last decade are an example of how the Church can add spiritual meaning to the populist struggle.[18] The Catholic Church has called for a "third way" social economy that speaks for the poor and draws on the best of capitalism and socialism. A dialogue between labor and the Church on these questions could introduce the ideas of the social market and economic democracy into parishes and union halls all over America. The labor movement must remain religiously pluralistic, but infusing the labor movement with a spiritual sensibility would be religion's most important contribution to populism. When labor embraces a crude materialism, it loses its soul. Americans understandably associate the labor movement not only with corruption but with the kind of materialistic and bureaucratic assault on the human spirit that marked Soviet communism. For the labor movement to lead a new populism, it needs most of all to find its spiritual center and lead a challenge to the new religion of consumerism and hypermaterialism. This will happen only in a new dialogue between religious communities and the labor movement.[19]

The Third Sector as a whole could infuse the labor movement with the broader cultural vision, base of support, and grassroots spirit that it so desperately needs. As it moves from business unionism toward becoming a more truly social movement, labor needs to rediscover communitarian values. Just as the Third Sector needs to engage with national politics, labor must remind itself of the real meaning of democratic participation and community. The Third Sector embodies these ideals today far more than most unions, which have become bureaucratized and removed from their own members. The Third Sector could bring the labor movement closer to the people and help them understand their needs for community and respect outside the workplace as well as within it.

Populist Multiculturalism

When President Clinton spoke of the connection between the Gilded Age and today, immigration was on his mind. Both periods, he noted, have been marked by huge waves of immigration that suit the appetites of global corporations. In the process, corporate America has been a breeding ground for the multiculturalism that increasingly defines our social landscape.

Multicultural politics has grown to become almost synonymous with politics. The most vibrant social movements today are the full spectrum of identity groups that speak for the interests of not only immigrant and ethnic communities, but for a new politics of race, gender, and sexual preference. Their only common cause is the celebration of difference and the search for rights and respect denied them by the dominant culture.

We have long had a multicultural politics, but its new postmodern form—especially the rise of identity politics—is a unique development.[20] It has helped connect personal identity and politics in a way that makes politics more meaningful for millions of Americans. By conceiving all forms of life, including marriage and the family, as political arenas, the rise of identity politics has created new forms of political consciousness rooted in everyday life experience. By virtually reinventing politics, the women's movement has become arguably the most influential political movement of the twentieth century. Identity politics more broadly has created hope for millions of women, African-Americans, gays and lesbians, and others who had never seen their private suffering as political. Building on Jesse Jackson's mantra to poor teenagers, "I am somebody," it has offered a new political language for building self-respect and community pride.

But identity politics also represents a form of political relativism, divisiveness, and despair. It has splintered groups which have common cause, and created a political discourse that makes the very notion of a common good seem like dangerous folly. Unless the leaders of identity politics can discover and embrace a set of shared values to help them nurture coalitions among different identity movements and help bridge multiculturalism and populism, identity politics will undermine its own prospects for success.[21]

Individual identity movements are beginning to understand how their own causes are intertwined, and how such links can help lead to systemic economic change. Black feminist Patricia Hill Collins writes of a "matrix of domination" made up of interlocking economic, sexual, and racial hierarchies. Other multicultural thinkers such as bell hooks and Cornel West have also crusaded against a women's or African-American movement that does not look at economic power.[22] Women and racial minorities make up the great bulk of the low-wage, temporary, and contingent labor pool—the disposable workers most at risk in the new global corporate order. Moreover, as discussed in Chapter 11, corporate ascendancy is a system which in many ways reinforces sexual and racial stratification. Women and minorities are by far the most vulnerable in the new age of economic insecurity and should be at the core of a new populist movement.[23]

Martin Luther King, Jr., anticipated this possibility and urged another route for the civil-rights movement in a prophetic 1967 speech. Asking where the civil-rights movement should go, he cast a light on the 40 million Americans who were in poverty. "You begin to ask the question," he continued, "'Who owns the oil?' You begin to ask the question, 'Who owns the iron ore?' You begin to ask the question, 'Why is it that people have to pay water bills in a world that is two-thirds water? . . . I'm not talking about communism. . . . communism forgets that life is individual. Capitalism forgets that life is social, and the kingdom of brotherhood is found neither in the thesis of communism nor the antithesis of capitalism. It is found in a higher synthesis that combines the truths of both." In his last year of life, King was trying to redirect the civil rights movement toward populism.[24]

Building bridges with the labor movement could help identity politics surmount its current class bias and move beyond the limits of current multicultural thinking. Multiculturalism, as King, Collins, and West have all argued, needs an economic and political analysis. A politics based on the analysis of culture alone is not adequate to understand culture itself, and is certainly not capable of explaining the systemic forces that are disempowering multicultural communities. Jesse Jackson has been the most powerful voice for an economically oriented multiculturalism, and his moral presence at sweatshops and factory lockouts symbolizes the populist politics that race and gender movements need to build with labor. As Jesse Jackson, Jr., writes, in the spirit of his father's thinking: "There is more racial understanding and reconciliation possible in one year of a full-employment economy than there is in three decades of talking about race on television." Jackson does not conclude that racial justice would be ensured by a change in the corporate order, but recognizes that it cannot be achieved without it.[25]

The labor movement could help identity movements find common cause in a challenge to market values, inequality, and corporate power. It could also help multiculturalists understand that the objective is not just to win women and minorities their fair place in the corporate system but to transform the system itself. Economic democracy is something very different from the more narrow pursuit of diversity and affirmative action within today's corpocracy. It also goes well beyond the goals of creating women-owned or African-American-owned businesses, challenging the idea that economic tribalism or nationalism will liberate communities. Identity politics cannot succeed under current economic arrangements; it will free no one, truly, unless it can put its energy toward restructuring the larger economy around universal democratic values.[26]

The labor movement could help empower poor and working-class women and minorities who have not found a robust enough voice in the women's movement or the civil-rights movement. By providing information and leadership, labor could help the predominantly female and minority contingent labor force to develop economic strategies that would improve their lot and that of the greater economy. As women, African Americans, and Hispanics rise to positions of prominence in the labor movement, they may be in a position to create the synergy between labor and multiculturalism that would transform both movements.[27]

Labor needs multicultural consciousness as much as multiculturalism needs class consciousness. The workforce of the twenty-first century will be, in the majority, female and nonwhite. A labor movement dominated by white males can never fully represent that labor force. If the labor movement is to democratize the larger society, it will have to start by democratizing itself. Women and minorities are most likely to infuse the labor movement with a new populist spirit and teach it the new values it needs. The labor movement needs to internalize the multicultural celebration of difference and tolerance, the feminist style of personal consciousness-raising that could invigorate labor organizing, and the politics of language, media, and cultural respect and power that are at the heart of multicultural thought.[28]

Bridging multicultural politics with the Third Sector movement could also create an electric populist synergy. The identity movements might be seen as part of the Third Sector, but they represent a very different breed of political consciousness. Multiculturalism is largely a movement of cultural critique, while the Third Sector is one of communitarian reconstruction. While identity movements speak for difference and cultural relevance, the Third Sector speaks for the community's common good.

The Third Sector, along with the labor movement, can help multiculturalism to find its universal core values. Labor's emphasis is on the universal values of economic justice and democracy, while the Third Sector teaches the universalism of love and service. Identity movements will deepen their own political analysis if they find a way to embrace both these forms of universalism. If identity politics falls back on the idea of "essentialism," which ascribes sex and race differences to biology rather than politics and culture, it will collapse into permanent fragmentation and despair. Labor and the Third Sector can help overcome essentialism; the universal values they speak for have the potential to bridge different multicultural communities and help create an awareness of common cause among them.

Multiculturalism can teach both the labor movement and the Third Sector about the dangers of ignoring or submerging differences of race or gender in the populist movement. The original Populists in the 1890s miserably failed to address America's deep racist and sexist problems, and populism today will fail again if it does not champion justice and liberation for racial minorities and women. Labor and the Left have foundered historically on a one-dimensional economic analysis which has obscured the struggles for respect and dignity—and against racism and sexism—at the heart of authentic populism. Identity movements have much to teach labor and populists about the culture wars, cultural power, and pride. They will insist that populism not become economistic and lose sight of the need for communities based on race, gender, and ethnicity to preserve their own identities within the larger movement. Populism can only grow if it becomes a kind of identity movement, in which people see the struggle for economic democracy as integral to the creation of their own identity and their own culture.[29]

Likewise, identity movements can teach the Third Sector that we cannot become nostalgic about old racist and sexist forms of community. Americans yearn for community, but not if they reproduce the tyrannies of tradition. The Third Sector and the communitarian movement, with all their fashionable talk about community and civil society, are suffering from intellectual sclerosis about what community can really mean in an age of postmodern difference. The meaning of community will have to be reinvented through a new dialogue between the Third Sector, multiculturalism, and the labor movement, each of whom has its own voice to add to the discussion.

Green Populism

Environmentalists have discovered that, unlike corporations, trees
do not have legal standing in courts. Carl Pope, executive director
of the Sierra Club, observes wryly that "some nonhuman entities
are more equal than others." The implications for the environmental movement are not reassuring. Since corporations enjoy
"virtually the full range of rights granted to people . . . corporations are allowed to spend unlimited sums to defeat environmental initiatives, because campaign spending limitations have been
ruled to interfere with their rights to free speech." He suggests
that "it is hard to argue that corporations deserve the protections
accorded to living, breathing individuals while entire ecosystems
lack the legal standing to be represented in our courts. If we're going to grant standing to fictitious entities, we could make the law
a more reliable protector of everyone's long range interests by
opening the courthouse doors to the salmon and the sequoia.[30]

Pope's argument is illuminating, in that it sees in environmentalism a basic challenge to the legal fiction of the corporation. This
is not the way we normally think about the environmental movement, or the way it typically thinks about itself. But our economic
order is at war with nature, and environmentalism leads inevitably
toward a fundamental challenge to markets as we know them. Environmentalism is gradually coming to terms with the fact that it
is a form of populism, and rapidly proliferating groups of grassroots environmentalists are linking up with unusual allies, including trade unions and inner-city community groups. The new
environmentalism—sometimes characterized as a movement for
environmental and economic justice—must systematically join
forces with the labor movement, the Third Sector, and multiculturalism to bring environmental awareness to the next century's
challenge to the imperial market.[31]

The environmental movement is already in the forefront of truly radical critiques of the market. Unlimited growth is the most sacred premise of the corporate order, but it ultimately comes a cropper when it comes up against the finite limits of nature. To allow the earth to renew itself, we need to limit environmental exploitation to reasonable levels of development: This has become the mantra of environmentalists. Ecology has thrown up the deepest challenge to the corporate world's materialist religion, arguing that it now constitutes a threat to the earth. Global warming, the extinction of species, the deforestation of continents, and the destruction of the ozone sphere have all become the most compelling popular symbols of the apocalypse that the market threatens.[32]

In a classic environmentalist manifesto, Herman Daly and John Cobb remind us that markets bump up against the all-pervasiveness of "externalities"—one of the most uncomfortable words in the mainstream economist's lexicon. "All conclusions in economic theory about the social efficacy of pure competition and the free market," Daly and Herman remind us, "are typically presumed on the absence of externalities," that is, the social costs or benefits of economic activity such as pollution costs, that the market does not take notice of. All efforts to reconcile the free market with environmentalism ultimately come to grief on the simple existence of omnipresent externalities—such as the survival of the earth.[33]

Environmentalists are recognizing that we need a new economic way of thinking that treat externalities as anything but external to economic life. As Daly and Cobb write, the very term "suggests both that the phenomena are external to the market and also that they are external to the main body of theory built on the market as an economic concept. . . . We believe that a model that would internalize 'spillover effects'—that is, the interconnections among things—into the basic theory would be a better response."[34]

Trying to make the free market take externalities into account is an intellectual oxymoron—to do so would be to change completely the nature of markets themselves. But since taking stock of externalities is the heart of environmental accounting, the environmental movement is inherently radical in its economic thinking. Daly and Cobb have called for a holistic economics in which all social and environmental costs and benefits are "internalized" within the market. This does not require a governmentally planned economy or even a major new role for government, but it does require, as discussed in the last chapter, that stakeholders are put in place to monitor such external market costs, to influence economic decisions, and to enforce a new form of social accounting. Ralph Estes, an accountant, is one of a number of scholars looking for ways to measure externalities and help corporations score their corporate social and environmental performance using a new social accounting system—the first step in building a socially responsible market.[35]

The dialogue that we need between environmentalism and the labor movement has barely started. Whether saving trees must mean killing jobs has symbolized a deep divide between the two movements. It is in large measure a class divide, with blue-collar unionists finding little common ground with environmental leaders who come mainly from privileged backgrounds and speak the language of elites.

The upper-middle-class biases of environmental leaders have seriously compromised the vision of the movement. While ecological theorists have begun to rethink the corporation and the market, the movement as a whole has focused on individual consumers as both the source of the problem and the solution. If individuals were more ecologically conscious in their lifestyles, recycled their garbage, and bought green products, we would presumably go a long way toward solving our environmental crisis.

The focus on individual lifestyle choices is hardly insignificant. Environmentalism speaks to the emptiness of a consumer society and the crisis of meaning that too much materialism engenders. Too often, labor has embraced the materialism of the market as its own cultural vision, seeking nothing but more money for its members. If the labor movement is going to become a transforming social force, it will have to lead the struggle toward a less materialistic society and help environmentalists build a more sustainable and meaningful system of values. The environmental movement and the labor movement are natural allies in working toward a consumer movement that opposes corporate ascendancy on both moral and economic terms. Consumers are not an easily organized countervailing power; but political sophistication is growing in the consumer sphere, and organized consumer power is also growing, partly through the impetus of the environmental movement. A consumer orientation must be integrated into all four movements discussed in this chapter, for we are all consumers and our buying choices are among the most personal and immediate ways we can make our values heard and help shape corporate choices.

Yet the environmental movement's focus on personal consumption, despite its great importance, deflects attention from the corporate choices and market logic that are driving the larger ecological crisis. Most pollution is created, and could be controlled, at the producer end. Moreover, since corporations so powerfully shape consumer tastes and appetites through advertising, education, and control of media, it is difficult to imagine dramatic change in consumer behavior that has not been sanctioned by corporations themselves.

Susan Seybolt has observed that environmentalism's consumer slant represents a bias rooted in the movement's class position. By focusing on personal choice, the movement mirrors America's prevailing individualism, which disassociates personal behavior from institutions and system logic. From a middle-class and elite point of view, this is a seductive way to frame environmentalism, since putting the onus on the public removes the threat from the corporations on which one's own privileges depend.[36]

The labor movement could help correct this class bias. A dialogue between labor and environmentalism could help unite the ecologist's concern about unchecked growth with the worker's need for a new type of social market. This would help generate the kind of new post-communist analysis that we need, one that would save markets but take full account of social and environmental externalities. It would also join the environmentalists' focus on nature and consumers with the labor movement's complementary focus on corporations and workers.

The environmental movement needs the labor movement to help balance its elite perspective and aid to develop a broader political analysis of the relation between corporate power and environmental degradation. The labor movement needs environmentalism to develop a longer-term perspective on the limits of growth and the needs for an economic order that is green to the core. In its daily skirmishes to protect workers, the labor movement has lost sight of workers' own long-term interests in protecting the land on which we all live. Labor needs ecological consciousness as deeply as environmentalists need class consciousness.

SIXTEEN

Why Personal Responsibility
Is Not Good Enough

Bill Clinton has helped to make fashionable a new political language of the heart. Transcending the comic cliché of "feeling our pain," Clinton exhorts us to take personal responsibility for our families, to touch the lives of our neighbors through community service, and to help spiritually renew our nation. One of my students told me that, with Clinton awash in political and sexual scandals—and a president who offered no real solutions to problems like poverty—he found Clinton's rhetoric hypocritical. But he said that the language of the heart was so deeply meaningful to him—and a spiritual politics so desperately important—that he didn't care about the hypocrisy. He just wanted to hear the words.

This one student's reaction speaks volumes about our current dilemma. As we approach the millennium, most Americans share the view that we live in an era of spiritual malaise. Even as our economy booms, so many Americans are being left behind in hopeless poverty and crime-ridden neighborhoods that our society seems to be splitting apart. Moreover, many middle-class and privileged Americans feel that their own lives lack meaning and that their own families or marriages are in trouble. The sense of moral decline is shared by liberals and conservatives alike, and the politics of individual responsibility for which Bill Clinton speaks has been embraced by virtually the whole nation.

At the end of the last century, the same feelings prevailed. America was poised to lead a global industrial revolution for a new century. Our economy was being restructured for a new era of explosive technological dynamism and growth. Yet millions of Americans were locked in poverty, politics seemed hopelessly corrupt, and a sense of spiritual emptiness and moral decline permeated the society. A politics of individual responsibility and spiritual renewal, enthusiastically embraced not only by intellectual, religious, and political leaders, but by industrialists like Andrew Carnegie, swept the nation. Many Progressives at the turn of the century shared the view of Teddy Roosevelt, who proclaimed: "We are neither for the rich man nor for the poor man as such; we are for the upright man, rich or poor." A leading historian writes that Roosevelt felt that solutions to the nation's problems depended mainly on "personal transformation of evildoers."[1]

In an era of corporate ascendancy, the very successes of business can contribute to moral and spiritual decline, as this chapter will demonstrate. Americans often turn in such periods to a politics of personal responsibility, which speaks to their fear of moral collapse and their hopes for spiritual renewal. But while a spiritual politics of responsibility can address people's deepest needs, it can also obscure the real sources of America's moral decline, and plunge us deeper into the morass. It took serious economic and political change, as well as a new moral ethos, to pull America out of the spiritual rot of the Gilded Age. We need to look at how our new spiritual crisis is linked to business and respond appropriately.

Corporate Ascendancy and Spiritual Decline

In an earlier book I wrote of the tragedy of the Ik, an African tribe reduced to desperate poverty when it was pushed off its lands. Anthropologist Colin Turnbull spent months with the Ik as they sank deeper and deeper into starvation. Turnbull met Adupa, a young girl of about six, who was so malnourished that her stomach was grossly distended and her legs and arms spindly. Her parents had decided that she had become a liability and threw her out of their hut. When she crawled back, they decided to lock her in and leave her to die. Adupa waited for them to come back with the food they had promised, but they did not return until a whole week had passed. Adupa's parents took her rotting remains, Turnbull writes, and threw them out "as one does the riper garbage a good distance away." There were no burial rites—and no tears.[2]

Turnbull describes the Ik as a loveless people. "There was simply not enough room in the life of these people," Turnbull observes, "for such luxuries as family and sentiment and love," nor for any morality beyond *marangik,* the Ik concept of goodness, which meant roughly filling one's own stomach. There are many lessons to be taken from the Ik, among them the hint that freedom from hunger is not bad for the soul. Prosperity and economic health are among the best recipes for spiritual health we have.[3]

But when corporations dominate politics and much of the rest of society, the spiritual benefits of prosperity can be overridden by the corrupting morality of the market. The great lesson of the Gilded Age is how corporate ascendancy and economic growth can go hand in hand with spiritual decline. While morality czars such as William Bennett do not talk much about it, American business—while far from the only cause—contributes in many different ways today to the moral decline of America.

Looking back on the Gilded Age, it is easy to see how the morality of unchecked materialism corrupted the soul of the nation. The extravagant wealth and conspicuous consumption of the robber barons, who spent millions on their parties and Newport summer estates, persuaded many Americans that getting rich was not only the way to be happy but the purpose of life. Money became the measure of morality itself. Herbert Spencer, the era's leading philosopher, wrote that the wealth of the rich proved that they were virtuous and that poverty was the clearest sign of moral decay: "The whole effort of nature," Spencer wrote, "is to get rid of such [the poor], to clear the world of them, and make room for better. . . . It is best that they should die."[4]

Social Darwinism and rampant materialism dominate our own era. Today's "shop till you drop" mantra symbolizes the new materialist craze. Surveys of teenage girls show that over 90 percent say that shopping is their favorite activity. For almost two decades society has been singing along with Madonna, the self-proclaimed "material girl." Both poor and rich kill for material prizes, whether the Billionaire Boys Club, the stockbrokers who murdered for big stakes on Wall Street, or the Manhattan teenagers who kill for leather jackets or an expensive pair of Nikes.[5]

A growing number of churches are locating in shopping malls—the ultimate testimony to the convergence of money and morals. Without having to put on your coat and go outside, you can leave church and step right into a McDonald's or Macy's. The worship of God and money geographically meld, and become somehow equivalent.

Corporations fuel not only extreme materialism but the hyper-individualism that is part of America's spiritual crisis. The American Dream has always embraced the virtue of self-interest, but in certain eras the Dream has become a prescription for selfishness. This is particularly likely to happen when growing prosperity is linked to growing insecurity. Permanent downsizing and the shift to disposable labor breed both chronic insecurity and hyper-individualism. When "all our jobs are contingent," as the vice president of AT&T tells his workforce, everyone becomes an entrepreneur and a survivalist. The morality of the survival of the fittest, explicitly embraced in the Gilded Age, becomes the unofficial philosophy of what Dilbert caricatures as America's new corporate jungle.

Hyperindividualism is intensified by the instability of family life. High levels of divorce create "double trouble" for many Americans, who experience both their jobs and their marriages as temporary. Even in a prosperous country, such double trouble can create the kind of terror of insecurity that can give rise to Ik-like morality. Trust in relationships of all kinds erodes, and people become more guarded. The fear of losing one's job and having nobody to rely on at home creates physical and moral exhaustion. As among the Ik, the psychological reserves necessary to care for others are depleted.

Conservative moralists such as Bennett, and liberal ones such as Amitai Etzioni, name the breakdown of family and community as the core of America's new spiritual crisis, but neither has much to say about how the corporate economy subverts both institutions. Bennett does express concern about how corporate-controlled media promote sex and violence to make money. Etzioni acknowledges that the new demands of work take time away from parenting. The links between family instability, community decline, and corporate profit-making, however, go deeper.[6]

As American wages stagnate and corporations reduce health care, pensions, and other benefits, the social contract that built the middle-class family is disappearing. Numerous studies show that financial pressures in the new corporate economy are the single biggest stress on family life, and that as both parents work longer hours in more insecure jobs, marriages and parent-child relationships suffer greatly. Juliet Schor has documented that "the average employed person is now on the job an additional 163 hours, or the equivalent of an extra month a year," compared to twenty years ago. The stress is particularly severe on women, who now average more than eighty hours a week of combined paid work, housework, and child care.[7] Sociologist Arlie Hochschild writes that working mothers are so exhausted that they talk "about sleep the way a hungry person talks about food."[8]

Corporations contribute to spiritual decline by taking over much of the socializing of children parents themselves no longer have time to do. Since television has become the major babysitter when mom and dad are out working, companies saturate their young wards with mesmerizing ads that are barely distinguishable from regular programming. At school, as noted earlier, corporations have launched the biggest sales campaign in history. The corporation is raising our children on the only values it knows: those of the market.

The breakdown of community is so transparently related to the new corporate economy that the dead silence of most communitarians about the subject is truly remarkable. All communities need an economic base, and stable communities need stable jobs and business investment. The watchword of the new corporate economy, however, is mobility. New technology makes global shifts in capital increasingly effortless, and corporations now profit by stepping up their movements of both money and people.

Sociologist William Julius Wilson has shown how America's inner cities have decayed through job disinvestment and cultural disorganization—forces that feed on each other. This is, however, only one part of the larger picture of mobility that affects suburbs as well as inner cities and has intensified social rootlessness and workers of every collar color. Environmentalist Stephen Viederman asks, in effect, whether the idea of community can survive at all in a hypermobile economy, since both families and communities depend on a commitment to place that is becoming economically dysfunctional. "Will two wage earner families likely be in sync with each other when the time to move comes? What impact will it have on the children?" he asks. "Do you, can you, love and commit to a place when you are transient?"[9]

Corporations move capital around in the global musical-chairs game that pits governments against one another and increases their bargaining power. The new mobility is not a deliberate effort to destabilize communities. But it invariably rips the fabric of community life and breeds spiritual anomie.

The new inequality bred by business is also spiritually devastating, and not just for the millions of poor children and adults. The affluent have to barricade themselves physically and morally against the reality of living well among mass poverty. In *The City of Quartz* Michael Davis writes of Los Angeles as a physical fortress and spiritual wasteland. Architecturally, the city is designed to protect the well-to-do from encounters with the poor, starting with downtown skyways, patrolled by private security guards, that allow the middle classes to stroll from building to building without ever having to walk the streets and deal with the homeless. Davis writes that park benches are designed with spikes so that poor people can't sleep on them at night. The sprinklers are kept on all night for the same reason; some restaurants even put toxins in their Dumpsters to keep hungry people from scavenging and scaring away patrons.[10]

The spiritual effects of unbridgable social gaps, which erode any sense of common good, are compounded by the corporate assault on democracy. In early 1997 Americans woke up to daily revelations of coffee-klatch White House solicitations to prospective donors who often spent the night in the Lincoln bedroom, of secret meetings between bankers and regulators in campaign fundraising sessions, and of "Lippo-suction"—the sucking of money from big foreign and domestic corporations in return for policy favors. As Clinton preached the new politics of responsibility, he seemed to be working the back rooms of Wall Street and K Street like Tammany Hall bosses a century ago.

Political corruption has waxed and waned in American history, but its crescendo in eras of corporate ascendancy is distinctive. In the Gilded Age and our own times the trading of money for votes has become institutionalized, and the elites have become transparent hucksters. When the nation's leaders have to go on television to tell Americans "I am not a crook," as Richard Nixon did, while information to the contrary comes pouring out day after day, the moral sensibilities of the nation inevitably become numbed. Clinton raged at his advisor Dick Morris that this news of scandal "dripping out day after day" had to hurt, and even he recognized that it wasn't the damage to his own image that was important but the sustained damage to the spiritual health of the nation. Leaders symbolize what the country stands for. As corruption becomes routine in Washington in both parties, it trickles down as a corrupting influence in everyone's lives. It becomes harder to resist cheating, which up to 70 percent of American college students admit to, when the president and congressional leaders are being caught with their own hands in the cookie jar.

Democracy is the ultimate casualty, and the sapping of democratic life is the most serious contribution of corporate ascendancy to our spiritual decline. As democracy ebbs, Americans retreat into private cocoons, feeling helpless to make a difference. The sense of powerlessness is not morally ennobling. In a democracy, civic participation and the belief in one's ability to contribute to the common good is the most important guarantor of public morality. When that belief fades, so too does the vision of the common good itself.

The Politics of Personal Responsibility

In 1996, close to a million African-American men joined the Reverend Louis Farrakhan in Washington. They had no demands. They were there to make a personal commitment to assume responsibility for their families and themselves. That same year, hundreds of thousands of mostly white men flocked onto football fields or stadiums in Colorado, Indiana, and Florida calling themselves Promise Keepers. They listened to evangelists and politicians who asked them to promise to support their households financially, guide their wives morally, and impose discipline on their children. The Promise Keepers swore allegiance to this as a sacred personal responsibility.

These movements are part of a new politics of responsibility that is sweeping the nation. The new politics seeks to stem the nation's decline by restoring the morality of the individual. Its central premise is that rebuilding personal responsibility is the foundation stone for solving our national problems.

This is a dramatic shift in the definition of what politics is about. For most of the twentieth century, politics has been about power, income, and the moral codes of institutions. The new politics shifts the focus toward the moral condition of the individual.

Much of the new politics, though, consists of sheer rhetoric focusing on personal morality and personal responsibility. It also overtly embraces social policies—from V-chips to school prayer to community service—that seek to promote family values and moral development. The hidden side of the new politics is an economic and political philosophy that releases corporate America or the government itself from responsibility, shifting the burden, and implicitly the blame, to individuals.

The Gilded Age saw a similar rise in emphasis on individual responsibility. Its central political philosophies—social Darwinism and laissez-faire capitalism—took for granted free-market institutions that had evolved from natural laws. The purpose of politics was to avoid the temptation to interfere with natural arrangements. What mattered was that each individual take responsibility for his or her condition. If politicians could sustain the market environment that maximized prospects for personal responsibility, the well-being of society would take care of itself.

The new politics of responsibility has diffused across the entire political spectrum. In the center, Bill Clinton, prior to his sexual scandal, became its most articulate and persuasive spokesperson. The Christian Right speaks for the new politics among millions of conservatives. Liberals who increasingly use the language of community and civil society speak for the new politics on the Left.

The new politics is no clone of the Gilded Age approach. Many of its proponents are neither social Darwinist nor laissez-faire thinkers. With the exception of sectors of the Christian Right, they are not rugged individualists. But they all accept existing market arrangements, and share a focus on personal responsibility and moral or spiritual development as key to solving our national problems.

The Reverend Robert Schuller, the televangelist preacher behind the *Hour of Power* religious program, sat next to Hillary Clinton at the 1997 State of the Union message. Schuller symbolized the president's embrace of the new politics, telling him to govern "with a pastoral heart." Former presidential advisor Dick Morris has quipped that Clinton was running for pope rather than president—referring to Clinton's new attention to issues of family values and spirituality so long dominated by the Republican Right. As Maureen Dowd of the *New York Times* writes, "Reverend Schuller and Reverend Clinton both seem to be forgetting that the President is not in charge of our souls."[11]

President Clinton's words reveal a far more communitarian language of personal responsibility than in the Gilded Age. In his second Inaugural Address, Clinton proclaimed that "each and every one of us, in our own way, must assume personal responsibility . . . not only for ourselves and our families but for our neighbors and our nation." Such communitarian language stands in sharp contrast to the individualism of the Gilded Age—and differs in political style from the style of either Farrakhan or the Promise Keepers. Clinton speaks of a link between responsibility for self and responsibility for others. But while his rhetoric includes concern for the well-being of the nation, Clinton now espouses a politics that deflects attention from the changes necessary to solve the nation's problems.

In his first term, the president made serious if flawed proposals for change, including his health-care reform package, a modest public investment budget for education and infrastructure, and tax credits for the working poor. When told that Wall Street would not tolerate his budgetary plans, Clinton is said to have exploded, incredulous that the bond markets could stymie his most serious economic initiatives.

The president concluded after the 1994 congressional elections that there was no future in fighting either Wall Street or the tide of conservatism in the nation. From 1994 to 1996 he embraced the agenda of corporate America: NAFTA, deficit reduction, smaller government, and reduced taxes. He also shifted from a concern with changing budgetary priorities and market arrangements to a preoccupation with restoring morality. In 1992 his slogan had been "It's the economy, stupid." In 1996, the new discourse was all about "values."

Clinton speaks eloquently about the importance of morality and personal responsibility, particularly in regard to race. "Obsessions cripple both those who are hated and, of course, those who hate," exclaims the president, "robbing both of what they might become. We cannot—we will not—succumb to the dark impulses that lurk in the far regions of the soul, everywhere. We shall overcome them."[12]

Clinton's language of responsibility has some of the flavor of both the civil-rights movement and the new communitarianism. It is a rhetoric of spiritual change that links personal feelings with a national problem. It speaks to one of America's deepest spiritual crises.

But as he was using these words, Clinton was ending welfare entitlements—and, according to his own government estimates, throwing another million children, mostly African-American, into poverty. The rhetoric of responsibility is largely divorced from economic realities and political policy. The president has made no substantial new commitments to help rebuild the inner cities or create employment for the African-American poor. He redefines the politics of race largely around the personal commitment to purge racism from our own souls and "embrace a new spirit of community."

This is a politics of symbolism and moral revivalism. Its purpose is to challenge individuals to do better. It relies on government as a bully pulpit rather than a countervailing power. It abandons the policies of the Progressive Era and the New Deal, but it has policy implications of its own, including a call for more police on the streets, tougher welfare conditions, and vouchers for schooling. The goal is to encourage moral development and personal responsibility, with the assumption that the well-being of the larger community will follow.

The rhetoric is sincere, uplifting, and important. But when it goes hand in hand with policies of neglect and abandonment, it betrays itself and hints at the fatal flaws of the new politics. Moral commitments will not employ the inner-city poor. That will take both new economic and social policies and shifts in power arrangements and morality at the pinnacles of corporate America. While he did propose some new policies involving important economic reforms—such as extension of Medicare and new child-care funding—the president in his second term abandoned serious concern with market reform and turned to such matters as educational standards, drugs and crime, deadbeat dads, and personal responsibility for oneself and one's family. These are far from insignificant issues, but they shift the rhetorical terrain of politics from market arrangements to personal morality.

The tacit assumption is that existing market arrangements do not require fundamental change. The new politics continues to deal with issues of the economy, but without challenging corporate dominance or the free-market consensus that binds both parties in the wake of the end of the Cold War. This is the New Democrats' real innovation: the decisive rejection of the New Deal effort to redress corporate power. The economic agenda of the new politics varies considerably from the Christian Right to the Clintonian center to the communitarian Left, but they all seek policies that pursue a presumed common good within the framework of the market.

In the new politics, government is expected to do *less* for citizens, while they are expected to do more for themselves. Here, Clintonism meets Gingrichism in a new bipartisan consensus about values. The president has a more activist vision of government, but he largely accepts the notion that the direction of government should be to decrease dependency on the state. The president proclaims that "the era of big government is over." He means that the government will assume fewer responsibilities, in the name of promoting responsibility itself.

The president's new politics has some common ground with the rhetorical movements for responsibility to both his right and his left. The Christian Right is the theocratic version of the new politics. Alabama judge Roy Moore, who was ordered by higher courts to remove his hand-carved plaques of the Ten Commandments from his courtroom, expresses the Christian Right's political credo. "As a circuit judge, my biggest problems I see all stem from the same thing," says Judge Moore. "The increase in crime among juveniles, illiteracy problems, corruption in public office, all stem from a loss of personal morality. That morality is directly related to the acknowledgment of God."[13]

About 25 percent of American voters now identify with the Christian Right. Its most important organization is the Christian Coalition, led by the Reverend Pat Robertson. A major force in the Republican Party, the Christian Coalition now speaks for millions of Americans who believe that spiritual rot and the collapse of traditional values lie at the root of the nation's problems. They are revolutionaries, as Barry Goldwater describes them, because they believe that the nation's problems require a spiritual conversion on the part of every citizen, ideally nourished by a society restructured under biblical law.

The Christian Right shares with Clinton the focus on morality and personal responsibility. Cal Thomas, a national journalist long identified with the Christian Right, suggests that churches and synagogues should take over the welfare system "because these institutions deal with the hearts and souls of men and women." He writes, "Only the churches could reach root causes of poverty," most of all the collapse of personal responsibility.[14]

The Christian Right's success—which has waned since Clinton co-opted its theme—is partly what converted Clinton to the politics of morality. Robertson, along with Jerry Falwell, the founder of the Moral Majority, created a paradigm shift in American politics even before the Reagan era, showing that millions of Americans responded to the view that a collapse of traditional values was dragging the country down. Reagan was the first president to capture that theme and govern on a mandate of traditional values.

Clinton calculated correctly that in the new political era he could get elected only by taking the "values" theme away from the Republicans and making it a centerpiece of the new Democratic agenda.

The Christian Right's approach, however, adds a heavy accent on spirituality. At the 1992 Republican convention in Houston Robertson said that "Since I have come to Houston, I have been asked repeatedly to define traditional values. I say very simply, to me and to most Republicans, traditional values start with faith in Almighty God." Robertson also makes clear that family values and spirituality converge in the new Christian politics: "To us, there was only one family, that ordained by the Bible, with husband, wife, and children."[15]

Whether saving souls is the business of politicians is an open question, but there is no doubt that some of the success of the Christian Right lies in its attunement to the spiritual malaise of our times. The Christian Right offers moral absolutes to a population feeling increasingly adrift both economically and spiritually. Many Americans find comfort and support in a movement that unashamedly addresses their hungers for meaning and moral certitude.

But the astonishing wealth of Robertson and many other televangelical Christian Right leaders, who are generously endowed by corporate leaders and foundations, suggests additional reasons for its rise. The values that the Christian Right promotes are unabashedly those of the market. Scholar Sara Diamond writes that "The Christian Right supports capitalism in all its forms." A theocratic biblical kingdom proposed by elements of the Christian Right, would let the market and churches worry about social welfare and the state focus only on keeping order. Christian Reconstructionists, an extremist sect that influences many parts of the movement, would abolish public schools and federal taxation. The explicit embrace by Robertson of the free market as God-inspired has helped unleash a flood of financial support from sectors of business and the media. While corporate America is not the prime mover of the Christian Right, it is one of its principal sponsors and beneficiaries.

The foot soldiers of the Christian Right are Americans deeply buffeted by the new global economy. Very much as Hitler did in 1920s Germany, the Christian Right helps channel the economic frustrations and insecurities of the declining middle class toward racial scapegoats. White supremacy and militia movements attract white males threatened by African Americans or by women who compete with them for scarce jobs. In Robertson's discussion of the New World Order and Patrick Buchanan's call for protectionism, there is some explicit attention to economic anxieties. But the new political paradigm shifts the focus away from corporations and economic arrangements to the culture wars and the spiritual war inside the human soul.

In the 1990s, a host of new conservative groups—dubbed compassionate conservatives or Comcons—have emerged as another expression of the new politics on the Right. Rooted in well-endowed conservative institutes like the Heritage Institute, they are more likely to use the secular language of civil society than the spiritual discourse of the Christian Right. But they share with their conservative spiritual cousins—and with the new politics on all sides of the political spectrum—a central focus on what they perceive as the breakdown of personal responsibility.

For the Comcons, politics must now be fundamentally about the rebuilding of character and personal morality. Part of the task, as conservative theoreticians like Richard John Neuhaas and Peter Berger have written, is institutional: to shrink government so that family, neighborhood, and church can flower as the civil institutions most capable of generating moral development. This view they share with many civil-society advocates on the Left, as discussed below. But their central political concern, like that of the Christian Right, is to help create the conditions for a nationwide spiritual conversion. As Republican congressman John Ashcroft, a

Comcon leader, puts it, "We think government needs to do more than feed the body. The soul and mind need to be addressed."[16]

The new cultural and theocratic politics of the Right is partly a reaction to multiculturalism, which can be seen as a comparable expression on the Left of the new politics. Multiculturalism focuses on building self-respect and cultural identity. It does not entirely neglect issues of power, since it focuses on hierarchies of sex and race. But multiculturalism has helped redefine power itself, away from the "old paradigm" concern with economic power toward a new postmodern concern with linguistic and other forms of cultural authority.

The redefinition of power—and ultimately the movement away from power as the key political issue—is ironically now being championed by large sectors of the Left as well as the Right. Historically, the Left has been the one tradition in America to focus like a laser on corporate power. But the multicultural Left, centrally concerned with questions of identity, has contributed to the larger national shift toward a cultural politics. Themes of personal respect and race or gender pride overshadow the politics of the market.

The identity movements seek to claim their rightful place in the national cultural pantheon. Issues of racial and sexual identity have magnetic attraction in a culture undergoing a generic crisis of values and the spirit. Part of the success of these movements, as of the Christian Right, has been to offer the promise of spiritual meaning to large sectors of the population who have been denied respect and a sense of purpose or community in our materialistic and individualistic culture.

In 1997, Jesse Jackson, a leader of multicultural politics who is acutely aware of its limits, called for a new civil-rights movement focused on economic opportunity. He emphasized that the spiritual crises of minority communities are deeply intertwined with their economic disenfranchisement. Cultural respect is an important antidote to spiritual distress and helps mobilize people politically. But multiculturalism has preoccupied itself with cultural respect and identity while tending to abandon traditional Left concerns with corporate power, class inequality, and democracy.

Multiculturalism is one of two main currents that are turning the Left toward cultural politics. The other is a broad array of movements that speak for civil society, communitarianism, and a religious Left. They differ in many ways, but they all represent a Left response to a perceived moral or spiritual crisis, and constitute an embryonic Left politics of personal transformation and moral commitment. The implications, as with the new politics generally, are at once hopeful and profoundly distressing.

In the last chapter, I described these movements under the rubric of the Third Sector. They are the Left's effort to speak the language of the heart, emphasizing personal responsibility, service to others, community building, and spiritual meaning. While the Right has begun to use the language of civil society, such talk is already particularly strong on the Left, and is almost universal among many of the new Third Sector groups. They argue that the Left must move beyond its traditional concern with adversarial politics and class enemies and learn to speak for the common good.[17]

There is something deeply refreshing in this new Left perspective, which is a genuine departure from classic Left orthodoxy. By ceding to the Right issues of values and spirituality, the Left had lost its capacity to speak to ordinary citizens. Americans are preoccupied with economic insecurity, but the moral and spiritual problems of their lives are closely intertwined with their economic problems and are just as compelling. The emerging Left politics of the heart moves beyond purely economic terms to help the Left speak to the problems of family, community, and faith that are central to millions of Americans.

Moreover, this is a Left that for the first time is taking up the theme of personal responsibility in a serious way. For most of this century, the Left has interpreted almost all problems—from crime to community decline to inequality—as problems of "the system." Championing democratization and redistribution, Leftists have been historically unreceptive to the idea that individuals had to assume any responsibility for their plight. They have also believed that economic solutions would solve our national problems without requiring any explicit attention to the moral or spiritual needs of individuals.

This alienated the Left from most Americans, who have a deep belief in the need for personal responsibility. It also tended to obscure gaps between many Leftists' own political rhetoric and their personal conduct. The new moral and spiritual discourse on the Left has the potential to bring the Left back into a real dialogue with a broader spectrum of America, and to make its own political practice more personally authentic.

But the embryonic Left politics of the heart has its own dangers. Of great concern is the tendency of many communitarians, religious Leftists, and liberal advocates of civil society to overlook the need for structural changes in the market and corporate order that have long been the focus of the Left. In the name of a new common good, significant sectors of the Left now see the critique of corporations and elites as divisive and adversarial, essentially subversive of the civil community that we so desperately need. This can lead to a repudiation of class conflict and, at its extreme, toward an abandonment of the concern with power itself.

The new movements for civil society keep a safe distance from political challenges to the corporation. Communitarians such as Amitai Etzioni write of the importance of moral development and personal responsibility, which can only be nurtured by families and churches and must ultimately be personal choices made by individuals. In his communitarian manifesto, Etzioni never discusses how the corporate economy is undermining communities, nor do the members of his Communitarian Network discuss corporate power. Champions of civil society tend to emphasize civic involvement at the local level, which can create a new public life but does not pose any serious challenge to current economic arrangements. Many of the community-based Third Sector groups even look to corporations for funding, and do not understand corporate power as a threat to their own communities. Those on the Spiritual Left, such as Michael Lerner and Jim Wallis, have been more attentive to the way the market undermines civility, community, and spirituality. But the Spiritual Left has, with some important exceptions, tended to practice a therapeutic politics, in which concerns for personal growth and community override any serious concern with challenges to the corporate status quo.[18]

The effort to create personal empowerment doesn't necessarily conflict with a call for political mobilization, indeed it can enhance mobilization since the individual who feels more self-respect and power is more capable of acting assertively. But because common-good ideologies have a history of rejecting challenges to institutional authority as uncivil and divisive, the moral development and empowerment of the individual has often been disassociated from political change and become an end in itself. This is the great failure of the new politics on all sides of the political spectrum. It confuses moral development, community building, and personal empowerment with political change—or takes one as a substitute for the other. It is part of a long American political legacy—starting with the Puritans—that has viewed moral and spiritual transformation as the only way to solve our political problems.

The Left—along with the new Democrats and the new Right—is beginning to fall into the trap of the very political individualism it has long criticized. Personal change and empowerment can spark social movements. But political individualism assumes that the moral or spiritual transformation of individuals is the goal of politics—a deeply flawed and distinctively American perception. Personal change does not necessarily create institutional change. And a society of morally developed or spiritual individuals can remain profoundly unjust.

We need only think back to slavery to confirm this notion. Many slaveowners—including such leaders and moral philosophers as George Washington, Thomas Jefferson, and James Madison—were preoccupied with civic and moral issues, and many were deeply religious. They were capable of love toward their families and even their slaves. The moral sensibilities of some led to deep reservations about the slave system, but most kept their slaves and could not envisage egalitarian relations among the races. But the just politics of the era had to move toward the abolition of slavery itself—something that demanded a confrontation not only with one's conscience but with all the institutional supports of the slave system. The cultivation of personal responsibility among slaveowners—many of whom were seen as the moral pillars of their communities—was not the answer.

Abolitionism grew partly out of evangelical religious movements, which fueled moral revulsion against slavery. Leaps in personal and moral awareness, then as now, are necessary for major political change. But to assume a political form, they must bring about not only changes in the consciousness and behavior of individuals, but an educated collective challenge to economic and political institutions. A few slaveholders freed their slaves voluntarily out of personal conscience, but this was not and could not be the essence of an antislavery politics. Abolitionism required a restructuring of the entire economy of both the North and the South, something which only the Civil War ultimately made possible. Abolitionism was an inherently moral and spiritual movement, but had it restricted itself to changes in individual conscience and responsibility, it would not have been a political movement at all—and certainly could not have ended slavery.

From Therapy to Politics

None of this implies that the new politics of the individual—and the new political language of the heart—is worthless. In an era of spiritual malaise and mass citizen demoralization, it plays a crucial role. We need a political discourse that speaks to the heart and gives individuals a sense of responsibility and hope.

As more and more Americans sink into the passive identity of the couch potato, it will take an inspirational politics to reengage them in public life. Americans have become deeply cynical, and are retreating in droves from politics. As they "bowl alone," as Robert Putnam describes the new American lifestyle, or cocoon alone in the desolate privacy of their television room, they are losing hope in anything but private gratification.

The new politics is finding purchase with a nation in despair. It suggests the possibility of getting beyond personal depression and finding a sense of personal power and meaning. A nation of couch potatoes desperately needs a politics of personal empowerment. Such personal change must accompany any serious movement for economic and social justice.

The new politics is beginning to create a shared language across the political spectrum for such personal transformation. By emphasizing the need for personal responsibility, moral development, spiritual revitalization and service to others, it is providing much-needed public acknowledgment of the national crisis of personal demoralization. Up to this point, people have largely responded to their personal crises in purely privatized ways. For the privileged, the route out has been through psychotherapy or Prozac. For the masses who cannot afford psychiatrists sports, Hollywood, and drugs on the street have been the therapies of choice.

The new responsibility politics is, in essence, a new form of collective therapy. It has the merits of taking the national moral and spiritual crisis out of the psychiatrist's office or the confessional and into the public domain. This is a step forward. It is the first stage in recognizing that the moral and spiritual crisis of our times is not purely personal. It affirms the social character of private despair and hints that our sense of personal powerlessness has social roots.

The new politics, however, remains essentially therapeutic. It views the shared crisis of the spirit as ultimately rooted in a failure of individual responsibility. It points to personal growth and spiritual transformation as the principal way out. And it rests on the notion that if individuals take responsibility and empower themselves morally and spiritually, they will have solved the nation's problems or will know how to do so.

There is the rub. Psychological moral empowerment doesn't necessarily help us to understand the economic and political arrangements that have contributed to the problems of both our pocketbooks and our spirit. Spiritual enlightenment is not the same thing as political understanding. Finding a personal moral path— and committing to a life of personal responsibility—is something different from collectively finding the solution to the nation's economic, political, and spiritual problems.

In short, therapy is no substitute for political education and action. Americans need a crash education in the economic, social, political, and spiritual problems of the market. They need to understand the system of corporate ascendancy—including its economic, political, and moral sides—that has been described in these pages. And they need to think seriously about the institutional alternatives that offer the possibility of a shift from the culture of greed to one of community, and from a system of corporate to popular sovereignty.

The new politics of responsibility can help kindle hope in alternatives and belief in one's own ability to make a difference. But to translate personal empowerment into social change is the most difficult step in the politics we need. First, Americans will have to realize that personal change is not enough. Second, they will have to undertake the discipline of a serious education in the workings of the corporate economy and how it contributes to our problems. Third, they will have to lay out the alternatives—from public chartering of the corporation to employee ownership to the construction of a social market—that can bring a more just social order while preserving the dynamism of the economy. Fourth, they will have to commit to the social movements that can bring these more just institutions into being.

Creating new institutions *does* depend on deep underlying changes in values. Moving beyond a corporate-dominated world will require toppling the gods of consumerism and hypermaterialism, and building a new culture in which human values take precedence over market priorities. We need a politics not less concerned with morality but one bent on bringing about real moral transformation, that is, one that changes the codes and practices of corporations and governments as well as individuals. Today's politics of responsibility will not achieve that end, but the politics that will is no less concerned with morality—it simply recognizes that it takes institutional as well as personal change to bring new values into the world.

The new politics of the heart is a preamble. It can lay the groundwork, but in its present form discourages movement toward any of the four steps that will take us beyond corporate sovereignty toward democracy.

In the dark days of the Gilded Age, Americans found a way, beyond social Darwinism and the politics of individual responsibility advanced by the robber barons, to better their lot. The populists recognized that personal responsibility could only survive when corporations and governments assumed their own responsibility and were made accountable to the people. Surely if they could come to this recognition, so can Americans today. As it was at the end of the last century, our own challenge is to lay the foundation of a new struggle for democracy. This is America's longest and greatest drama—and must define the new century as it has the one to which we now say good-bye.

Epilogue

What You Can Do Now

After listening to and being persuaded by many of the ideas I present here, people often bring me down to earth with a simple comment. Yes, I think you're right, and I want to do something. But what is it that I can do? Here, in a nutshell, is what I answer.

1. **Practice Self-Awareness:** Reflect deeply and often about your own place in the corporate world. How do you participate in it? How does the corporate world shape your life and values—and those of your family? Do your corporate roles as worker, manager, consumer, or shareholder make you a better person? Is corporate morality your morality? How does the corporation benefit you and how does it oppress or control you? From your place in the corporate world, how do you benefit or hurt others?

2. **Educate Yourself and Others:** Join a group to read and talk about the corporation and your lives. The nineteenth-century populists met in each others' kitchens to read about and discuss their problems, while sponsoring traveling lecturers to speak in their communities. Form your own group from your workplace, church, or community. Let this be both a consciousness-raising group about your own experiences as employee, consumer, or shareholder, and an educational group for reading and analyzing

corporate power, economic democracy, and the corporate high road.

3. Just Say No: Many communities are organizing to prevent corporations from taking over their schools, hospitals, or social services. Think of the battles to save community hospitals from giant for-profit chains such as Columbia HCA. Consider the fact that corporations addicted to short-term profits may be providing the curricula for your kids at school or determining what drugs or treatment your doctor can provide. Join community efforts—and you will surely find them in your town or city—to keep corporations and the market mentality out of spheres in your life where they don't belong.

4. Buy Smart: Use your power as a consumer wisely. Buy union-labor or "no sweat" clothes, but make sure the labels mean what they say: no sweatshops. Boycott corporations that abuse workers or the environment. Students at Duke, Brown, and other universities have persuaded their schools not to buy products—from caps to sweatshirts—from vendors who do not sign codes of ethical conduct. Get your city or state to use their own massive consumer power by passing selective purchasing laws, such as the Massachusetts Burma law that imposes a 10 percent penalty on any vendor to the state doing business in the outrageous dictatorship of Burma today. Twenty-nine cities have joined Massachusetts, and Vermont may soon add its name.

5. Create Good Money: If you are an investor—small or large—think of where your money is going and how you can invest it to enhance your values and citizenship as well as your wallet. Invest in socially conscious companies and you may want to examine socially responsible investment funds such as Franklin Research or Development in Boston or a small company called Good Money—which puts out an informative guide you can find

on the Web. Pressure your church, union, or pension fund to use a socially conscious approach in their own investment decisions.

6. **Get Your Company On the High Road:** You and your company should join Business for Social Responsibility, headquartered in Washington, D.C., or other business groups committed to high road practice. You can get lots of practical ideas from them about what to do, and they will benefit from your views about how to move the corporate responsibility movement beyond its current limits toward positive populism. Think of one practical business initiative your company could take that would truly improve the lives of your fellow workers or the community and fight for it.

7. **Support Economic Alternatives:** Support worker-owned businesses, community-owned enterprises, small, locally owned businesses, governmental and nongovernmental enterprises, and nonprofits—all part of the growing alternatives to corporate America. Tell people about them. Work for them. Lobby for government tax-breaks for them. Corporations survive only by accepting vast corporate welfare—the alternatives need public support too.

8. **Unite:** UNITE is a coalition of labor unions in the needle trade industry seeking to end sweatshops. Support it with time or money as a symbol of your endorsement of a labor movement that fights for social justice rather than just more money for its members. Think about the kind of union you could support in your workplace—which may be quite different from a traditional union—and get involved in efforts to organize such positive unions or other worker organizations. Pay attention to the AFL-CIO under its new leadership, read their new publications, and if you like what they're saying, send them money and support them in their new organizing efforts among part-timers (as at UPS),

low-paid service workers, office workers, and even professionals such as doctors and middle managers.

9. **Be a "Civil Society" Activist:** Think of one corporation that is making your community a less civil place to live. Join others who are seeking to "civilize" it, close it down, or get it out of your community. Almost every major corporation—from Microsoft to Wal-Mart—has been confronted by nationwide coalitions of community groups seeking to preserve their own civility and autonomy. Join their efforts.

10. **Vote Populist:** Believe it or not, there are politicians in both the Democratic and Republican parties who are voicing populist concerns—about downsizing, economic insecurity, big money in politics, inequality, corporate mergers and monopolies, and corporate welfare. Throw your voice and vote behind those with the most forceful and positive message. Look also at the small new parties—such as the New Party or the Greens—which are speaking more directly about corporate power and economic democracy. Try your hand at writing a positive populist platform and send it to your local newspaper or Senators and Representatives.

11. **Join a Populist Organization:** Join one of the many consumer groups, unions, churches, or new explicitly populist groups—such as the Alliance for Democracy, Friends of the Earth, Public Citizen, and United for a Fair Economy. Find out about these organizations on the World Wide Web, get their literature, call them, and join them on the issues they are fighting for—from campaign finance reform to new corporate charters to a fair tax code.

12. **Own Your Own Job:** Thousands of corporations are offering forms of worker ownership through Employee Stock Ownership Plans (ESOP) and retirement options. Make sure your corporation is

one of them and fight to make sure the ownership is truly meaningful—giving a voice and a vote, not just a dividend payment.
Write for more information to the Center on Employee Ownership
in Oakland, California, a fount of useful information for businesses
and workers interested in worker ownership.

13. **Support Women at Work:** Think of the millions of
young women all over the world forced to work in degrading conditions within the corporate controlled export zones of the Third
World. They make the clothes you wear and assemble the stereos
you listen to. Think also of the working women here at home—
including thousands thrown off welfare—who suffer most in the
new world of temp and part-time labor. If you are already a feminist, make sure your favorite women's organization has not forgotten these working women. Rethink your own feminist values
in the light of your understanding of the corporation, and make
sure you are not just thinking about middle class women. Help
develop and support—with your money and time—a populist
feminism.

14. **Join the Race to the Top:** Think about the global race to
the bottom and the proposals advanced here to create a race to the
top. Join forces with the hundreds of grassroots groups—you can
find them on the Web—which are fighting the MAI, promoting in-
clusion of labor and environmental standards in NAFTA and the
WTO, and demanding that corporations and nations respect human
rights and democracy over profits. Choose one campaign—for example, the struggle against MAI—and join with others who are trying to get their city councils to pass a resolution against MAI as
undermining local, state, and federal sovereignty.

15. **Stand Up for Your Rights:** Corporations are taking away
your rights and constitutionalizing new ones of their own. These
may be as simple as your right to go to the bathroom at work or
to keep your e-mail private. Or as complex as the corporations'

new right to give billions of dollars to political candidates as a form of First Amendment free speech. Stand up for your rights in the workplace and the community. Write to your local newspapers about how you feel about corporations reading workers' e-mail or using the Bill of Rights to defend their corruption of politics with big money. Send the positive message that corporations which empower workers and vest them with rights will be more productive as well as more democratic.

16. **Join the Campaign for a Living Wage:** Communities all over the nation are fighting for "liveable wages" enforced by their city governments. Populist activists in this campaign are outraged that millions of Americans work forty hours or more and remain poor. In Baltimore, Minneapolis, and other cities, the city council has passed an ordinance requiring that all employers doing business with the city pay a minimum wage adequate to pull a family out of poverty. Get your city on board.

17. **Bust the Trusts:** Even *Business Week* is asking its readership whether it's time to dismantle the Microsoft monopoly. When banks get as big as the near-trillion-dollar Citicorp-Travelers merger, even conservatives get scared. Many long-distance companies are assailing the local phone companies' monopoly. Join one of the many consumer and populist groups—led most visibly by Ralph Nader—that are leading a new campaign to recharter and potentially dismantle the huge transnational corporate monopolies that now sit astride the world.

18. **Take Democracy Seriously:** You are lucky to live in a country that embraces the value of democracy. If your right to vote were taken away in your community, you would be frightened. But your right to vote at work is no less important to your well-being, so you have to become a champion of economic democracy. Demand your stakeholder right to vote in the workplace through any means possible: ownership, unionization, professional associ-

ation, team representation. Talk about it frequently and seriously enough that others will listen. As corporate power expands to control much of government itself, your constitutional right to vote outside the workplace becomes increasingly meaningless as well. You will have to fight to reclaim a meaningful vote in a political system where both parties speak the language of business. This means supporting social movements, political candidates, and populist parties who speak openly about the dangers of corporate sovereignty, and who propose concrete plans for making democracy real, both in the corporation and in the nation at large.

NOTES

Introduction: The New Problem with No Name

1. Betty Friedan, *The Feminine Mystique* (New York: Norton, 1963).
2. Ethel Klein and Guy Molyneux, "Corporate Irresponsibility: There Ought to Be Some Laws" (New York: Preamble Center for Public Policy, July 29, 1996), p. 20.
3. *Ibid.*
4. Friedan, *Feminine Mystique*, p. 21.

1: The End of the Century

1. *Human Development Report* (Oxford, 1966).
2. Edward N. Wolff, *Top Heavy: A Study of the Increasing Inequality of Wealth in America* (New York: 20th Century Fund, 1995). Lawrence Mischel and Jared Bernstein, *State of Working America, 1996–1997* (Armonk, NY: M. E. Sharpe, 1997).
3. James Fallows, "A Talk with Bill Clinton," *Atlantic,* October 1996, (20–26), p. 22.
4. For discussion of the Gilded Age, I have relied most heavily on Matthew Josephson, *The Robber Barons: The Great American Capitalists, 1861–1901;* Sidney Fine, *Laissez Faire and the General Welfare State: A Study of Conflict in American Thought, 1865–1901* (Ann Arbor: University of Michigan Press, 1956); and Gabriel Kolko, *Railroads and Regulation, 1877–1901* (Westport, CT: Greenwood Press, 1976).
5. Elise O'Shaughnessy, "The New Establishment," *Vanity Fair* 10/94, (209–229), p. 214.
6. Josephson, *Robber Barons,* p. 316.

7. Cited in Harvey Wasserman, *Harvey Wasserman's History of the United States* (New York: Harper and Row, 1972).
8. O'Shaughnessy, *Establishment,* p. 225.
9. *Ibid.,* p. 228.
10. Wasserman, *United States,* p. 24.
11. O'Shaughnessy, *Establishment,* p. 228.
12. Robert Reich, "America's Broken Social Contract," *Boston Globe,* January 19, 1997: E7.
13. Cited in Richard Abrams (ed.) *The Issues of the Populist and Progressive Eras* (Columbia, SC: University of South Carolina Press, 1969), p. 33.
14. Wasserman, *United States,* p. 31.
15. Richard Hofstadter, *The Progressive Movement* (Englewood Cliffs, NJ: Prentice-Hall, 1963), pp. 2, 35.
16. Indira Lakshmana, *Boston Globe,* June 6, 1995, pp. 1, 10.
17. Josephson, *Robber Barons,* p. 371.
18. *Ibid.,* pp. 363, 372–73.
19. Wasserman, *United States,* pp. 32–33.
20. Cited in Howard Zinn, *The People's History of the United States* (New York: Harper & Row, 1980), p. 367.
21. Cited in Wasserman, *United States,* p. 30.
22. Cited in Wasserman, *United States,* p. 25.
23. Josephson, *Robber Barons,* p. 359.
24. Wasserman, *United States,* p. 47.

2: The Curse of the Robber Barons

1. On the role of regulation today and in the Gilded Age, see Martin J. Sklar, *The Corporate Reconstruction of American Capitalism, 1890–1916* (Cambridge: Cambridge University Press, 1991) and Gabriel Kolko, *The Triumph of Conservatism* (New York: Free Press, 1969).
2. John Kenneth Galbraith, *American Capitalism: The Concept of Countervailing Power* (Boston: Houghton Miflin, 1951), p. 116.
3. *Ibid.,* p. 121.
4. *Ibid.,* p. 122.
5. *Ibid.,* pp. 122ff.
6. *Ibid.,* pp. 124–25.
7. Adolf Berle and Gardner Means, *The Modern Corporation and Private Property* (New York: Harcourt Brace and Co., 1967), pp. 210–11.
8. See Scott Bowman, *The Modern Corporation and American Political Thought* (University Park, PA: University of Pennsylvania Press, 1995), pp. 203ff.
9. Berle, *Modern Corporation,* pp. 210–11.

10. See Chapters 7 and 8 as well as Kolko, *Conservatism,* and Bowman, *Modern Corporation,* especially Chapter 5.

11. See Tom Kochan, Harry C. Katz, and Robert B. McKersie, *The Transformation of American Industrial Relations* (Ithaca, NY: ILR Press, 1994).

12. See Kochan et al., *Transformation.* See also Stanley Aronowitz, *Working Class Hero: A New Strategy for Labor* (New York: Pilgrim Press, 1983); Thomas Geoghegan, *Which Side Are You On?* (HarperCollins, 1991), and Jeremy Brecher and Tim Costello, *Global Village or Global Pillage?* (Boston: South End Press, 1994).

13. Michael Useem, *Investor Capitalism: How Money Managers Are Changing the Face of American Capitalism* (New York: HarperCollins, 1996). See also Useem, *Executive Defense: Shareholder Power and Corporate Restructuring* (Cambridge, MA: Harvard University Press, 1993).

14. See Josephson, *Robber Barons,* and Kolko, *Railroads.*

15. Alfred Chandler has written the most important account of the relation between the rise of the corporation and changes in scale of production, suggesting that only corporations can capture the economies of scale that larger markets make possible. See Alfred Chandler, *The Invisible Hand* (Cambridge, MA: Harvard University Press, 1977) and Alfred Chandler, *Scale and Scope* (Cambridge, MA: Harvard University Press, 1991).

16. See Chandler, *Scale.*

17. Kolko, *Railroads.* See also Gabriel Kolko, *Main Currents in American History* (New York: Pantheon, 1984), pp. 6ff.

18. For a discussion of how unions are beginning to globalize, see Brecher and Costello, *Global Village.*

19. See Paul Krugman, *Pop Internationalism* (Cambridge, MA: MIT Press, 1994).

20. Brecher and Costello, *Global Village.*

21. See Jeremy Rifkin, *The End of Work: The Decline of the Global Labor Force and the Dawn of the Post-Market Era* (New York: Putnam, 1995). See also Stanley Aronowitz and William Difazio, *The Jobless Future: Sci-Tech and the Dogma of Work* (Minneapolis, MN: University of Minnesota Press, 1995).

3: The Mouse, Mickey Mouse, and Baby Bells

1. James Gleick, "Making Microsoft Safe for Capitalism," *The New York Times Magazine,* November 5, 1995 (50–57; 64), p. 53.

2. Quoted in *Ibid.,* p. 51.

3. *Ibid.,* p. 52.

4. Quoted in *Ibid.,* p. 51.

5. *Ibid.,* p. 50.

6. *Ibid.,* p. 52.
7. *Ibid.,* p. 54.
8. *Ibid.,* p. 64.
9. Bill Gates, "Microsoft Says It's Going After the Internet," *New York Times,* December 8, 1995, pp. D1; 5.
10. Quoted in *Business Week,* July 15, 1996, p. 57. See also Schlender, "Whose Internet Is It Anyway?" *Fortune,* December 11, 1995.
11. James Gleick, "Making Microsoft Safe for Capitalism," p. 56.
12. Stephan Labaton, "Bill Gates, Meet Your Adversary, the Antitrust Chief," *New York Times,* December 22, 1997, (D1–7).
13. Sarah Anderson and John Cavanagh, *The Top 200* (Washington, D.C.: Institute for Policy Studies, 1997), pp. 1–2, 5.
14. Grant McConnell, *Private Power and American Democracy* (New York: Alfred Knopf, 1965), p. 5.
15. Charles Reich, *Opposing the System* (New York: Putnam, 1995), pp. 3, 31.
16. For a discussion of the rise of corporate influence in politics, and the highly organized character it assumed in the 1970s and 1980s, see Michael Useem, *The Inner Circle: Large Corporations and the Rise of Business Political Activity in the US and the UK* (New York: Oxford University Press, 1984).
17. Peter Drucker, *New Society,* pp. 44–45, 203.
18. For an excellent discussion of Berle's view of the corporation as a political but nonstatist institution, and of the contradictions within Berle's view of the public/private distinction, see Bowman, *Modern Corporation,* pp. 209–217. See also Barry Gozeman, "Understanding the Roots of Publicness," in Brenda Sutton (ed.), *The Legitimate Corporation: Essential Readings in Business Ethics and Corporate Governance* (Cambridge, MA: Basil Blackwell, 1993).
19. On the origins of this melding of corporation and government, see M. Sklar, *Corporate Reconstruction.* See also Kolko, *Conservatism.*
20. See Adolf Berle, *The 20th Century Capitalist Revolution,* pp. 145ff.
21. The biggest corporations are decentralizing, but that is quite different than suggesting that they are becoming smaller or less powerful, which is not supported by the evidence. See David L. Birch, *Job Creation in America: How Our Smallest Companies Put the Most People to Work* (New York: Free Press, 1986); Tom Peters, *Liberation Management: Necessary Disorganization for the Nanosecond Nineties* (New York: Knopf, 1992); and Bennett Harrison, *Lean and Mean* (New York: Basic Books, 1994).
22. *American Almanac,* 1994, p. 550.
23. Nancy Folbre, *The New Field Guide to the U.S. Economy* (New York: The New Press, 1995), pp. 110.

24. Harrison, *Lean and Mean,* p. 45.
25. *Ibid.,* p. 47.
26. See Harrison, *Lean and Mean,* p. 47. See also David Korten, *When Corporations Rule the World* (San Francisco: Kumarian Press and Berrett Koehler, 1995).
27. Paul Samuelson, cited in David Warsh, "Goodbye to Bal Harbour," *Boston Globe,* September 1, 1996, p. E2.
28. Robert Bork, quoted in the *Wall Street Journal,* February 27, 1997, p. 1.
29. Joel Klein quoted in Labaton, "Bill Gates," p. 7. For a review of antitrust movements and policy historically, see Rudolph J. R. Peritz, *Competition Policy in America, 1888–1992* (New York: Oxford University Press, 1996). See also Roger D. Blair and Jeffrey L. Harrison, *Monoposony: Antitrust Law and Economics* (Princeton: Princeton University Press, 1993). See also Thomas Karier, *Beyond Competition: The Economics of Mergers and Monopoly Power* (Armonk, NY: M. E. Sharpe, 1993). Also Kurt Rudolf Minow and Harry Maurer, *Webs of Power: International Cartels and the World Economy* (Boston: Houghton Mifflin, 1982).
30. Several different business reference volumes document changing market share concentrations in each major industry. See especially *Market Share Reporter* (Detroit, MI: Gale Research, 1998). See also Korten, *Corporations Rule,* p. 23.
31. Steven Pearlstein, *Washington Post Weekly,* December 11–17, 1996, p. 9.
32. Walter V. Shipley quoted in "Will the New Chase be greater than its parts?" *New York Times,* March 29, 1996, pp. D3–4.
33. George W. Stocking and Myron W. Watkins, *Monopoly and Free Enterprise* (New York: The 20th Century Fund, 1951), pp. 505–6.
34. See Peritz, *Competition.*
35. The definitive 1990s text on the social threat that network capitalism creates is Harrison, *Lean and Mean.*
36. Kolko, *Railroads.*
37. On the history of regulation in the Gilded Age and the Progressive Era, see Kolko, *Conservatism.*
38. Kolko, *Currents,* p. 6.
39. This theme is documented and developed extensively in Chapter 8.
40. Joshua Shenk, *Washington Monthly,* June 1995. James Boyle, "Sold Out," *New York Times,* March 31, 1996, p. 15.
41. Steven Pearlstein, *Washington Post Weekly,* December 3, 1995, p. 14.
42. Louis Gerstein, quoted in *Business Week,* September 11, 1995, p. 35.

43. Ivan G. Seidenberg, quoted in the *New York Times,* February 5, 1996.

44. James O'Boyle, *US News and World Report,* August 14, 1995, p. 43.

4: Companies That Run America

1. *Wall Street Journal,* August 29, 1995, p. C1.
2. Peter Truell and Laura M. Holson, "2 Giants Make Giant Shadow," *The New York Times,* April 7, 1998, p. D1.
3. Korten, *Corporations Rule.* See also Robert Kuttner, *Everything for Sale* (NY: Knopf, 1997).
4. Korten, *Corporations Rule,* p. 2.
5. Kevin Phillips, *Arrogant Capital* (Boston: Little Brown, 1994), p. 84.
6. *Ibid.,* p. 87.
7. *Wall Street Journal,* August 29, 1995, pp. A1–2.
8. Bernard Wysocki, Jr. "Improved Distribution Not Better Production is Key Goal in Merger," *Wall Street Journal,* August 25, 1995, pp. A1–2.
9. George Taber, "Remaking an Industry," *Time,* September 4, 1995, pp. 24–5.
10. Elyse Tanouye, "Merck's Medco Unit Moves 'On Track' Chairman Gilmartin Assures Analysts," *Wall Street Journal,* December 13, 1995, p. B6.
11. *Market Share Reporter,* 1998. See also Korten, *Corporations Rule,* p. 223.
12. Korten, *Corporations Rule,* p. 228.
12. *Statistical Abstracts,* 1993–94, p. 550.
13. *Ibid.,* p. 541.
14. Harrison, *Lean and Mean,* p. 47.

5: Bye, Bye, American Pie

1. Reported on *Marketplace,* National Public Radio, December 26, 1995.
2. Richard T. Curtin, quoted in *New York Times,* November 20, 1994, p. 7. See also *Time,* November 22, 1993, p. 35. See also Beth Belton, "Downsizing leaves legacy of insecurity," *USA Today,* August 29, 1997, pp. 1, 1b.
3. Louis Uchitelle, "The Losing Class," *New York Times,* November 20, 1994, p. A6.
4. Bill Bradley, quoted in *Boston Globe,* November 31, 1993, p. A5.
5. Florence Skelly, quoted in *The New York Times,* November 20, 1994, p. 1.
6. Herbert Spencer, *Social Statics* (New York: Appleton and Co., 1864), pp. 414–5. William Graham Sumner, "The Concentration of Wealth,"

in Stow Pearson (ed.), *Social Darwinism: Selected Essays of William Graham Sumner* (Englewood Cliffs, NJ: Prentice-Hall, 1963). See also Richard Rubenstein, *The Age of Triage* (Boston: Beacon Press, 1983), pp. 220–21.

7. Quoted in Josephson, *Robber Barons,* pp. 364, 374.

8. For a recent reinterpretation of the New Deal, see David Plotke, *Building a Democratic Political Order: Reshaping American Liberalism in the 1930s and 1940s* (New York: Cambridge University Press, 1996).

9. See Barry Bluestone and Irving Bluestone, *Negotiating the Future* (New York: Basic Books, 1992), Chapter 2.

10. See Bluestones, *Negotiating,* Chapters 1–3.

11. See Paul Osterman, *Employment Futures* (New York: Oxford University Press, 1988).

12. The GM model is described in detail by Harry Katz, *Shifting Gears: Changing Relations in the U.S. Automobile Industry* (Cambridge, MA: MIT Press, 1985).

13. See Osterman, *Employment,* chapters 3 and 4.

14. For a quintessential view of the postwar era as exceptionalist, see Robert Samuelson, *The Good Life and Its Discontents: The American Dream in the Age of Entitlement* (New York: Times Books, 1996). For a brief critique of the exceptionalist thesis as ideology, see James Rinehart, "The Ideology of Competitiveness," in Kevin Danaher, *Corporations Are Gonna Get Your Momma* (Monroe, ME: Common Courage Press, 1997).

15. See Russ Eckel, *The Silent Dust Bowl: The New Industrial Migrant Work Force,* Unpublished Ph.D. Dissertation (Boston College Department of Sociology, 1994).

16. See Bluestone and Bluestone, *Negotiating,* Chapter 3.

17. Verena Dobnik, "Group Cites Abuses by Nike Subcontractors," *Boston Globe,* February 28, 1997, p. B2. G. Paschal Zachary, "Just Blew It," *In These Times,* July 28, 1997, (7–9), p. 7.

18. William Bridges, "The End of the Job," *Fortune,* September 19, 1994, (62–74), p. 62. See also William Bridges, *Jobshift* (Boston: Addison Wesley, 1994).

19. Virginia L. duRivage, Françoise J. Carre, and Chris Tilly, "Making Labor Law Work for Part-Time and Contingent Workers," *Russell Sage Foundation Working Paper #88,* 1996. Dorothy Sue Cobble, "Making Postindustrial Unionism Possible," in Sheldon Friedman, Richard W. Hurd, Rudolph A. Oswald, and Ronald L. Seeber (eds.), *Restoring the Promise of American Labor Law* (Ithaca, NY: ILR Press), 285–302. See also Debra Osnowitz, "Policy as Strategy: Labor Law and the Contingent Work Force" (Boston, 1996).

20. See Polly Callaghan and Heidi Hartmann, *Contingent Work: A Chart Book on Part-Time and Temporary Employment* (Washington, D.C.: Economic Policy Institute, 1991).

21. DuRivage et al., "Labor Law." This discussion is also based on conversations with Tim Costello, a Boston-based labor organizer and writer, and with Debra Osnowitz, who has written illuminating papers on the legal problems and new risks faced by contingent workers. See Osnowitz, "Policy as Strategy."

22. See Richard Belous, *The Contingent Economy* (Washington, D.C.: National Planning Association, 1989), Chapters 3 and 4. See also Osterman, *Employment.*

23. It has proved extremely difficult to get precise national data on the numbers of contractors and other contingent workers, partly because the Labor Department has only recently been collecting data on some categories and partly because companies often use different classifications and do not keep accurate records. For data now several years old, see Callaghan and Hartmann, *Contingent Work.* On part-timers particularly, see Chris Tilly, *Half a Job: Bad and Good Part-Time Jobs in a Changing Labor Market* (Philadelphia: Temple University Press, 1996). For recent data, see Thomas Allison, "The Contingent Workforce," *Occupational Outlook Quarterly,* Spring, 1996, pp. 45–48.

24. Lester Thurow, quoted in Steven Pearlstein, *Washington Post Weekly,* December 18–24, 1996, p. 10.

25. See Belous, *Contingent.*

26. See Tily, *Half a Job.* See also Lonnie Golden and Eileen Appelbaum, "What Was Driving the 1982–1988 boom in Temporary Employment: Preference of Workers or Decisions and Power of Employers?" *American Journal of Economics and Sociology,* 51(4), 1992 (473–83).

27. Cited in *Boston Globe,* April 3, 1994, p. 18.

28. *Boston Globe,* December 31, 1995, p. 56.

29. Bob Herbert, "A Worker's Rebellion," *New York Times,* August 7, 1997, p. A39. Steven Greenhouse, "High Stakes for 2 Titans," *New York Times,* August 5, 1997 (A1, A14).

30. Dirk Johnson, "Angry Voices of Pickets Reflect Sense of Concern," *New York Times,* August 6, 1997, p. A16.

31. Greenhouse, "High Stakes," *New York Times,* p. A14.

32. Chris Tilly, "Beyond the Strike," *Boston Globe,* August 10, 1997 (D1, 5) p. 5.

33. Jane Slaughter, "Face-off at UPS," *In These Times,* August 11, 1997 (6–7).

34. American Management Association, "Summary of Key Findings," *1995 AMA Survey: Corporate Downsizing, Job Elimination and Job Cre-*

ation (New York: American Management Association, 1995). See also Louis Uchitelle and N. R. Kleinfield, "On the Battlefields of Business, Millions of Casualties," Part I of series, "The Downsizing of America," *New York Times,* March 3, 1996.

35. James Meadows quoted in Edmund L. Andrews, "Don't Go Away Mad, Just Go Away," *New York Times,* February 13, 1996 (D1, 6).
36. Kevin Becraft, quoted in *Business Week,* October 17, 1994, p. 77.
37. Bridges, "The End," p. 64.
38. *Ibid.*
39. American Management, "Key Findings."
40. Quoted in Alex Markels and Matt Murray, "Call It Dumbsizing," *Wall Street Journal,* May 14, 1996, p. 1.
41. James Medoff, quoted in *Boston Globe,* December 31, 1995, p. 56.
42. A growing number of labor scholars are seeking to conceptualize the form of a new labor movement in a contingent economy. See duRivage et al., "Labor Law." See also Cobble, "Postindustrial Unionism." See also Osnowitz, "Policy as Strategy."
43. Paul Fireman, quoted in Joel Makower, *Beyond the Bottom Line* (New York: Simon and Schuster, 1994), p. 178.
44. For the full text of these and other corporate mission statements, see Robert Waterman, *What America Does Right.* (New York: Norton, 1994), pp. 87, 140.
45. See, for example, Eileen Appelbaum and Rosemary Batt, *The New American Workplace: Transforming Work Systems in the United States* (Ithaca, NY: ILR Press, 1994).
46. Michael Useem argues that the new power of giant pension and mutual funds, and of the money managers at their helm, suggests a qualitative shift toward a new economic paradigm that he calls "investor capitalism." See Useem, *Investor Capitalism.* See also Useem, *Executive Defense.*
47. Cited in Useem, *Investor Capitalism.*

6: The Making of the Corporate Mystique

1. See Richard L. Grossman and Frank T. Adams, *Taking Care of Business: Citizenship and the Charter of Incorporation* (Cambridge, MA: Charter, Ink. [a publication of the Program on Corporation, Law, and Democracy], 1995).
2. Bowman, *Modern Corporation,* pp. 38ff.
3. Report of the Packer Commission, cited in Goodrich, Carter (eds.), *The Government and the Economy, 1783–1861* (Indianapolis: Bobbs-Merrill Co., 1967), p. 374.

4. The Virginia Supreme Court cited in Morton Horwitz, *The Transformation of American Law, 1780–1860* (Cambridge, MA: Harvard University Press, 1977), p. 112.

5. Grossman and Adams, *Taking Care,* pp. 8–9.

6. *Ibid.,* p. 8.

7. Joseph Story quoted in Edwin Merrick Dodd, *American Business Corporations Until 1860* (Cambridge, MA: Harvard University Press, 1934), p. 60.

8. Cited in Grossman and Adams, *Taking Care,* p. 14. *See also* James Madison, "Bank of the United States," Congressional Speech, February 2, 1791.

9. U. S. Supreme Court, *Dodge v. Woolsey,* cited in Dodd, *Corporations,* p. 130.

10. *Ibid.,* p. 101.

11. Arthur W. Machen quoted in Horwitz, *Transformation,* p. 103.

12. Horwitz, *Transformation,* p. 74.

13. As far back as the famous Dartmouth case, the Marshall court, as noted earlier, had begun to lay the foundation of corporate personhood by viewing the corporation as possessing "immortality, and . . . individuality; properties by which a perpetual succession of many persons are considered as the same and may act as a single individual." Marshall wrote of the corporation as a "legal person" whose charter represented a contract protected under the Constitution. John Marshall quoted in Bowman, *Modern Corporation,* p. 44.

14. This he considered even more sacred than the Constitution itself: "There is, as it were, back of the written Constitution, *an unwritten Constitution* . . . which guarantees and well protects all the absolute rights of the people. The government can exercise no power to impair or deny them." Quoted in Fine, *Laissez Faire,* p. 128.

15. *Ibid.,* p. 142.

16. Kent Greenfield, "From Rights to Regulatory Theory in Corporate Law," (Boston College Law School, 1996), p. 17.

17. Bowman, *Modern Corporation,* pp. 57–58.

18. Quoted in Horwitz, *Transformation,* p. 84.

19. Ralph Nader, Mark Green, and Joel Seligman, *Taming the Giant Corporation* (New York: Norton, 1976), p. 44ff.

20. *Ibid.,* p. 47.

21. Quoted in Nader, *Taming,* p. 48.

22. Quoted in Nader, *Taming,* p. 51.

23. Nader, *Taming,* p. 50.

24. *Ibid.,* p. 52.

7: Reinventing the Mystique

1. Berle and Means, *Modern Corporation,* p. 8.
2. *Ibid.,* p. 355.
3. *Ibid.,* p. 356.
4. Quoted in Henry Butler and Larry Ribstein, *The Corporation and the Constitution* (Washington, D.C.: The AEI Press, 1995), p. 33.
5. *Ibid.,* pp. 33–34.
6. William T. Allen, "Our Schizophrenic Conception of the Business Corporation," *Cardozo Law Review* 143 (2), 1992, (262–81), p. 277. See also the discussion of the corporation as a social entity in Margaret Blair, *Ownership and Control* (Washington, D.C.: The Brookings Institute, 1996), pp. 210 ff.
7. Milton Friedman, "The Social Responsibility of Business Is to Increase Its Profits," *New York Times Magazine,* September 13, 1970.
8. Daniel Fischel and Frank Easterbrook, *The Economic Structure of Corporate Law* (Cambridge, MA: Harvard University Press, 1991).
9. See M. Blair, *Ownership,* and Bernie Black, *Proceedings of the Conference on Law and Economics,* New York University, 1996.
10. Daniel Fischel, "The Corporate Governance Movement," 35 *Vanderbilt Law Review,* 1259, 1982, 1273–74.
11. Butler and Ribstein, *Corporation,* p. 20.
12. Richard Epstein, *Takings: Private Property and the Power of Eminent Domain* (Cambridge, MA: Harvard University Press, 1987), pp. 12–13.
13. Kent Greenfield, "From Rights to Regulatory Theory in Corporate Law," (Boston: Boston College Law School, 1996), p. 17.
14. *Ibid.,* pp. 16–17.
15. Robert Monks, "Growing Corporate Governance: From George III to George Bush," in Brenda Sutton (ed.), *The Legitimate Corporation* (Cambridge, MA: Basil Blackwell, 1993), (165–77), p. 172.
16. *Ibid.,* p. 171.
17. Robert L. Carter, quoted in Bowman, *Modern Corporation,* p. 136.
18. *Ibid.,* p. 136.
19. *Ibid.,* p. 137.
20. Monks, "Corporate Governance," pp. 170–71.
21. David Millon, "Personifying the Corporate Body," 2 *Graven Images,* 1995, (116–17), p. 116. Frederic Maitland, the great English legal theorist of the turn of the last century, argued that the idea of the corporation as an entity dates all the way back to Roman law. Maitland noted that the entity notion attracted conservative theorists who liked the picture of the corporation as an organic natural association as well as liberal theorists who embraced the idea of a corporate citizen with its own social rights and responsibilities. With the rise of fascist cor-

poratism in Italy and Germany, however, both conservative and liberal notions of a corporationist entity fell into disfavor. See Aviam Soifer, *Law and the Company We Keep* (Cambridge, MA: Harvard University Press, 1995), pp. 73ff. See also Horwitz, *Transformation,* especially chapter 3. See also Millon, "Personifying."

22. Rachel Burstein, "Paid Protection: Why Monsanto and other industry giants love EPA regulations," *Mother Jones,* January/February 1997, p. 42.

23. Kolko, *Conservatism.*

24. Henry P. Davison, quoted in Kolko, *Currents,* p. 13.

25. *Ibid.,* p. 6. Kolko calls the system "political capitalism," by which he means a regime in which corporations rely on state regulation and other forms of state intervention to solve market problems they cannot resolve on their own. See Kolko, *Conservatism.*

26. Howard Schweber, "The Duties of the Postmodern Corporation" (McLean, VA: Odyssey Forum, 1996), p. 10.

27. *Ibid.*

28. Bowman, *Modern Corporation,* p. 141.

8: The Dependent Corporation

1. Ralph Nader quoted in "Stop Corporate Welfare," Interview by Monika Bauerlein, printed on the Internet, January 2, 1996, p. 1.

2. John Kasich, quoted in the *Wall Street Journal,* December 18, 1996, p. A22.

3. Johanna Schneider, quoted in the *Wall Street Journal,* December 18, 1996, p. A22.

4. Nader, quoted in "Corporate Welfare," p. 1.

5. Stephen Moore and Dean Stansel, "Ending Corporate Welfare as We Know It," Cato Institute; 1995, p. 4.

6. Ann McBride, Public Correspondence from Common Cause, 1996, 1997.

7. Moore and Stansel, "Corporate Welfare," p. 15.

8. "Cut and Invest," Public Policy Institute, Report No. 23, Washington, D.C., 1996.

9. Theodore Forstmann, quoted in Moore and Stansel, "Corporate Welfare," p. 11.

10. "Cut and Invest," p. 4.

11. Moore and Stansel, "Corporate Welfare," p. 11.

12. *Ibid.,* p. 12.

13. James O'Connor, *The Corporations and the State* (New York: Harper Colophon, 1974). See especially Chapter 6. See also James O'Connor, *The Fiscal Crisis of the State* (New York: St. Martin's Press, 1973).

14. O'Connor, *Corporations,* p. 126.
15. *Ibid.,* pp. 126–7.
16. Ralph Nader, quoted in "Corporate Welfare," p. 2.
17. Ralph Nader, quoted in "Corporate Welfare," p. 3.
18. Don Tyson, quoted in *National Review,* February 20, 1995.
19. Robert D. Brown, quoted in Kathryn Mulvey, Letter from INFACT, 1996, p. 1.
20. Archibald Cox, Public Correspondence from Common Cause, January, 1997.
21. Jeff Gerth, "Business Gains with the Democrats," *New York Times,* B7, December 15, 1996.
22. Leslie Wayne, "Loopholes Allow Presidential Race to Set a Record," *New York Times,* December 8, 1996, (1, 26), p. 26.
23. For a useful discussion of the *Buckley* case, see Bowman, *Modern Corporation,* pp. 156–7.
24. See the discussion in Bowman, *Modern Corporation,* p. 157.
25. Cited in Bowman, *Modern Corporation,* p. 158.
26. Cited in Bowman, *Modern Corporation,* p. 161.
27. Cited in Bowman, *Modern Corporation,* p. 158.
28. David F. Linowes, *Privatization: Report of the President's Commission on Privatization* (Washington, D.C., 1988), p. 251.
29. See the discussion of recent privatization efforts in Robert Kuttner, *Everything for Sale* (New York: Knopf, 1996).

9: Five Reasons Americans Don't Think about Corporate Power and Why They Should

1. Jason DeParle, "Class is No Longer a Four Letter Word," *The New York Times Magazine,* March 17, 1996 (40–43), p. 43. See also Howard Fineman, "Extreme Measures," *Newsweek.* March 4, 1996 (20–27).
2. Alan Brinkley, "A Swaggering Tradition: Buchanan belongs to a long line of fiery populists who burn themselves out," *Newsweek,* March 4, 1996, (28–9), p. 28. *Wall Street Journal,* February 22, 1996, p. 26.
3. See Richard Rosenfeld, *American Aurora* (New York: St. Martin's Press, 1997).
4. Henry Jackson, quoted in Sidney Fine, *Laissez Faire,* p. 132.
5. Francis Fukuyama, *The National Interest,* 1989, pp. 3, 4.
6. Lester Thurow, *Head to Head* (New York: Morrow, 1993).
7. This view of unabashed American free-market superiority is also propagated by influential business leaders abroad, particularly in the Bundesbank and other important German corporate elites. But it is not shared by many other business leaders on the Continent, nor, obviously, by the public in France, Italy, and other European coun-

tries, which in the late 1990s are electing Labor, Social Democratic, or Socialist governments to protect their welfare-state economies.

8. Ethel Klein and Guy Molyneux, "Corporate Irresponsibility," July 29, 1996, p. 1.

9. Juliet Schor, *The Overworked American* (New York: Basic Books, 1993); Robert Putnam, "Bowling Alone," *The American Prospect,* 1996.

10. Cited in Wasserman, *United States,* p. 72.

11. For an insightful historical assessment of the Left's democratic project in the United States, see Richard Flacks, *Making History* (New York: Columbia University Press, 1988). For the best short study of populism, see Lawrence Goodwyn, *The Populist Moment* (New York: Oxford University Press, 1978).

10: How to Be Politically Hopeful for the Next Century

1. For a discussion of corporate rhetoric and practice of social responsibility, see Makower, *Bottom Line.*

2. See especially Richard Hofstadter,*The Age of Reform* (New York: Random House, 1955).

3. Goodwyn offers not only the best brief interpretation of the Gilded Age populist movement, but an illuminating critical bibliographical essay showing how historians have helped to discredit the American public's view of populism. See Goodwyn, *Populist Moment.*

4. See Michael Kazin, *The Populist Persuasion* (New York: Basic Books, 1995).

5. See Hofstadter, *Reform,* and Kazin, *Populist Persuasion.*

6. Wasserman, *United States,* pp. 74, 77.

7. *Ibid.,* p. 77.

8. *Ibid.,* p. 77.

9. Lawrence Goodwyn, *Populist Moment,* p. 296.

10. *Ibid.*

11. For the beset analyses in this vein of the Progressive Movement, see Kolko, *Conservatism;* M. Sklar, *Corporate Reconstruction,* and James Weinstein, *The Liberal Ideal in the Corporate State* (Boston: Beacon Press, 1968).

12. As in the Gilded Age, we are witnessing at the grassroots level a proliferation of new economic alternatives, from community-owned banks and development councils to employee-owned companies to new community-based local currencies. We are also seeing a variety of efforts to work both against and with corporations to make them more accountable to workers and communities, as in the case of unions and community groups working with large banks on development projects mandated by the Community Reinvestment Act.

11: Why You Shouldn't Be Liberal or Conservative

1. This involves an entirely different approach than the forms of populist political rhetoric that have surfaced through much of the twentieth century. See Kazin, *Populist Persuasion.*

2. See Virginia L. duRivage (ed.) *New Policies for the Part-Time and Contingent Workforce* (Armonk, NY: M. E. Sharpe, 1992). See also Osnowitz, "Policy."

3. Quoted in Louis Uchitelle, "A Top Economist Switches His View on Productivity," *New York Times,* May 8, 1996, p. D2.

4. Ethel Klein and Guy Molyneux, "Corporate Irresponsibility: There Ought to Be Some Laws," July 29, 1996, p. 18.

5. *Ibid.,* p. 36.

6. See the discussion of these legislative initiatives by Jeremy Brecher, *Countering Corporate Downsizing* (New York: The Preamble Collaborative, 1996), pp. 8, 12.

7. The discussion of the Massachusetts initiative is based on conversation with its director, Tim Costello, a longtime labor activist and writer.

8. For a careful statistical analysis of the growing gap at all levels, see Sheldon Danziger and Peter Gottschalk, *America Unequal* (Cambridge, MA: Harvard University Press, 1995). See also Mischel and Bernstein, *Working America.* On wage inequality, see Richard B. Freeman and Lawrence F. Katz, "Rising Wage Inequality: The United States vs. Other Advanced Countries," in Richard B. Freeman (ed.) *Working Under Different Rules* (New York: Russell Sage Foundation, 1994). For a discussion of the wealth gap, see Edward Wolfe, *A Study of the Increasing Inequality of Wealth in America* (New York: 20th Century Fund Report, 1995). Easily understood data on the gap is available from United For A Fair Economy, a public-interest group based in Boston. See *The Growing Divide: Inequality and the Roots of Economic Insecurity* (Boston: United for a Fair Economy, March 1997). For another popular, graphic presentation of the data see also Nancy Folbre, *Field Guide.*

9. For a comparison of American inequality with that in other countries, see Timothy M. Smeeding and John Coder, *Income Inequality in Rich Countries during the 1980s—Working Paper No. 88* (Syracuse, NY: Luxembourg Income Study, 1993). On child poverty, see Arloc Sherman, *Wasting America's Future: Report on Child Poverty* (Washington, D.C.: Children's Defense Fund, 1994). Regarding income trends, see "Income, Poverty, and Valuation of Noncash Benefits," *US Department of Commerce, Current Population Reports, Series P60-188,* 1993. See also Mischel and Bernstein, *Working America.*

10. For a discussion of wage inequality and the effect of unions on both

wages and the wage gap, see Richard B. Freeman, "How Labor Fares in Advanced Economies," in Freeman (ed.), *Different Rules,* pp. 1–29. See also Richard B. Freeman and James L. Medoff, *What Do Unions Do?* (New York: Basic Books, 1984). For an overview on wage- and income-inequality trends, see Lawrence Burton, Robert Havecman, Owen O'Donnell, *Recent Trends in US Male Work and Wage Patterns* (Madison: Institute for Research on Poverty, University of Wisconsin, 1995).

11. For documentation of the effects of contingent work on wages and inequality, see Callaghan and Hartmann, *Contingent Work.* See also Mischel and Bernstein, *Working America.*

12. See Kevin Phillips, *The Politics of Rich and Poor* (New York: Random House, 1990). See also Donald L. Barlett and James B. Steele, *America: Who Really Pays the Taxes?* (New York: Simon and Schuster, 1994).

13. See Richard B. Freeman, "Why are Workers Faring Poorly in NLRB Representation Elections?" in Thomas Kochan (ed.), *Challenges and Choices Facing American Unions* (Cambridge, MA: MIT Press, 1985). See also Richard B. Freeman and James L. Medoff, *What Do Unions Do?*

14. For a readable historical overview of how tax policy has affected inequality, see Barlett and Steele, *Who Really Pays?* See also Mischel and Bernstein, *Working America.*

15. Archibald Cox, Public Correspondence from Common Cause, 1996.

16. David Rosenbaum, "In Political Money Game, The Year of Big Loopholes," *New York Times,* December 26, 1996, pp. 1, D9.

17. See Bowman, *Modern Corporation,* pp. 154–68.

18. See the discussion of corporate influence on politics and on the workings of the Business Council in Michael Useem, *Inner Circle.* See also Phillips, *Arrogant Capital.*

19. The literature on the gendered and racialized dimension of the economy is vast but fragmented. For an excellent historical approach, focusing on black women, see Jacqueline Jones, *Labor of Love, Labor of Sorrow* (New York: Vintage, 1995).

20. Annette Fuentes and Barbara Ehrenreich, *Women in the Global Factory* (Boston: South End Press, 1992).

21. Quoted in M. Blair, *Ownership,* p. 102.

22. For an informed discussion of the shareholder revolution from the shareholder's perspective, see Robert A. G. Monks and Nell Minow, *Watching the Watchers: Corporate Governance for the 21st Century* (Cambridge, MA: Blackwell, 1995).

23. For the most definitive discussion of how shareholder activists have begun to shape the priorities of corporations, see Useem, *Investor Capitalism.*

24. Berle and Means, *Modern Corporation,* pp. 333ff.
25. Useem, *Investor Capitalism,* pp. 84ff.
26. *Ibid.,* p. 91.

12: What's Right and Wrong with Corporate Responsibility

1. Joseph Pereira, "Split Personality: Social Responsibility and Need for Low Cost Clash at Stride Rite," *Wall Street Journal,* May 28, 1993, pp. 1–7 in reprint of story from Internet.
2. Hiatt helped found Business for Social Responsibility (BSR), the national association of corporations and other businesses dedicated to ideals of responsibility. BSR commissioned Joel Makower to write a book about the principles and practices of the movement, from which I have drawn heavily in this chapter. See Makower, *Bottom Line.* The quotation from Hiatt is from p. 52.
3. Pereira, "Split Personality," p. 4.
4. *Ibid.*
5. *Ibid.,* p. 6.
6. Gerald Levin, quoted in Makower, *Bottom Line,* p. 23.
7. William Norris, quoted in Makower, *Bottom Line,* p. 25.
8. For a useful discussion of the Saturn model, see Bluestone and Bluestone, *Negotiating,* especially chapter 8. For a discussion of the surge in employee ownership, see Joseph Blasi and Douglas Kruze, *The New Owners: The Mass Emergence of Employee Ownership in Public Companies and What It Means to American Business* (New York: Harper Business, 1991).
9. This argument is made explicitly by Makower and, in a more scholarly mode, by Jeffrey Pfeffer, *Competitive Advantage Through People: Unleashing the Power of the Work Force* (Boston: Harvard Business School Press, 1994).
10. Bob Dunn, quoted in Makower, *Bottom Line,* p. 229.
11. Robert Waterman, *America,* pp. 91–92.
12. Quoted in Makower, *Bottom Line,* pp. 57–58.
13. For a summary of this research, see Makower, *Bottom Line.*
14. See Severyn Bruyn, *A Future for the American Economy* (Stanford, CA: Stanford University Press, 1991). See also Sandra A. Waddock and Samuel B. Graves, "The Corporate Social Performance-financial Performance Link," *Strategic Management Journal,* 18 (4), 1997, (303–319); Sandra A. Waddock and Samuel B. Graves, "Quality of Management and Quality of Stakeholder Relations: Are They Synonymous?" *Business and Society,* 36 (3), 1997, September (250–279); Moses L. Pava and Joshua Krausz, "The Association between Corporate Social-Responsibility and Financial Performance: The Paradox of

Social Cost," *Journal of Business Ethics,* 15: 1996 (321–357); Jennifer J. Griffin and John F. Mahon, "The Corporate Social Performance and Corporate Financial Performance Debate: Twenty-five Years of Incomparable Research," *Business and Society,* 36 (1), March 1997 (5–31); John B. Guerard, Jr., "Is There a Cost to Being Socially Responsible in Investing?" *The Journal of Investing,* 6 (2) 1997, (11–18); and Sally Hamilton, Hope Jo, and Meir Statman, "Doing Well while Doing Good? The Investment Performance of Socially Responsible Mutual Funds," *Financial Analysts Journal,* November/December 1993 (62–66).

15. Quoted in Makower, *Bottom Line,* p. 31.

16. Quoted in Makower, *Bottom Line,* p. 14.

17. See Robert Putnam, Robert Leonardi, and Raffaella Nanetti, *Making Democracy Work: Civic Traditions in Modern Italy* (Princeton, NJ: Princeton University Press, 1992) and James Coleman, *The Foundations of Social Theory* (Cambridge, MA: Harvard University Press, 1994). See also Thurow, *Head.*

18. Makower, *Bottom Line,* p. 13.

19. *Ibid.,* p. 271.

20. *Ibid.,* p. 31.

21. For literally hundreds of examples, see, in addition to Makower's account, Jeffrey Pfeffer, *Competitive Advantage.* See also Waterman, *America.*

22. Quoted in Makower, *Bottom Line,* p. 14.

23. Milton Friedman, "Social Responsibility."

24. Robert Kuttner, "Taking Care of Business," *The American Prospect,* July–August 1996, (6–8), pp. 7–8.

25. Bernard Avishai, "Social Contract, Version 2.0," *The American Prospect,* July–August 1996, (28–34) p. 29.

26. For an excellent introduction to the American Plan, see Elly Leary, *The American Plan* (New Directions Press, 1994). For a historical account of "welfare capitalism," both before and after the New Deal, see Sanford Jacoby, *Modern Manors: Welfare Capitalism Since the New Deal* (Princeton, NJ: Princeton University Press, 1997).

27. For a robust argument about the uncoupling of the interests of global corporations from those of their host societies, see Robert Reich, *The Work of Nations* (New York: Knopf, 1991). See also Brecher and Costello, *Global Village.*

28. For the best description of the deep flaws in most ESOP governance structures, which essentially prevent real authority from devolving to the worker-owners, see Blasi and Kruze, *New Owners,* especially Chapter 4.

29. The disregard for conflicting interests helps explain why responsibility advocates rarely address the need for powerful unions. If one as-

sumes a corporate common good that workers and managers fully share, there is no need for the adversarial representation that unions mobilize. The responsibility movement has thus tended to present itself as an alternative to the labor movement rather than its advocate.

30. Responsibility advocates would be well advised to read the classic works of political theory that explore economic democracy. These would include Carole Pateman, *Participation and Democratic Theory* (Cambridge: Cambridge University Press, 1970) and Robert Dahl, *A Preface to Economic Democracy* (Cambridge: Polity Press, 1985).

31. See Joel Rogers and Joshua Cohen, *Associations and Democracy* (London: Verso, 1995). See also Bernard Barber, *Strong Democracy* (Berkeley, CA: University of California Press, 1984).

32. There are good reasons to believe that corporate responsibility can become a meaningful movement only when driven by powerful unions and community groups working to help reshape the depoliticized version advanced by the executives.

33. The idea of a socially responsible macroeconomic policy is rarely articulated by corporate executives, but is not uncommon among labor-union leaders, another hint of the importance of bringing in unions and other stakeholder groups as key new participants in a transformed corporate responsibility movement. See John Sweeney with David Kusnet, *America Needs a Raise: Fighting for Economic Security and Social Justice* (New York: Houghton Mifflin, 1996).

34. This argument has been advanced forcefully in the article by Avishai, "Compact."

1 3: How to be Against Corporate Power and For Business

1. Positive populism is an embryonic and still inchoate social movement arising from within and across several different existing social movements, as discussed in chapter 14. The changes discussed in this chapter examine ideas and proposals that are beginning to emerge from these movements. I try here both to reflect and help develop the most promising new thinking.

2. George Soros, "The Capitalist Threat," *Atlantic Monthly,* April 1997, p. 45.

3. For a provocative scholarly effort to intellectualize this new balance between markets, government, and civil society, see Joshua Cohen and Joel Rogers, *Associations and Democracy* (London: Verso, 1995). See also Kuttner, *Everything.* Also Samuel Bowles and Herbert Gintis, *Democracy and Capitalism* (New York: Basic Books, 1986).

4. Kuttner, *Everything,* p. 47.

5. *Ibid.,* p. 53.

6. For a useful extended critique of free market dogma, see Kuttner, *Everything*.

7. Alan Wolfe, *Whose Keeper?* (Berkeley, CA: University of California Press, 1987).

8. Kuttner, *Everything*, p. 18.

9. For a discussion of the concept of the social market, which was used originally to describe developments in post–World War II Germany, but has now been developed by American theorists as an alternative to free market economics, see Bruyn, *Future*. See also Charles Derber, *The Wilding of America* (New York: St. Martin's Press, 1996), chapter 8.

10. The stakeholder statutes reflect the growing interest in theories of stakeholder capitalism as an alternative to American-style shareholder capitalism. A general case for the stakeholder model has been advanced by a number of management theorists; see Russell L. Ackoff, *The Democratic Corporation* (New York: Oxford University Press, 1994) and Abbass F. Alkhafaji, *A Stakeholder Approach to Corporate Governance* (New York: Quorum Books, 1989). An extensive legal literature on stakeholder statutes is beginning to emerge. For a lay audience, there is a useful brief discussion by M. Blair, *Ownership*. For a review of the legal literature and an overview of legal debates about stakeholder statutes, see Lawrence E. Mitchell, "A Theoretical and Practical Framework for Enforcing Corporate Constituency Statutes," *Texas Law Review*, Vol. 70, No. 3, February 1992 (579–641). See also Steven M. H. Wallman, "The Proper Interpretation of Corporate Constituency Statutes and Formulation of Director Duties," *Stetson Law Review*, Vol. 21, 1991 (163–193).

11. This language was introduced as an amendment to the Massachusetts Incorporate Statute by Senator Lois Pines in 1996.

12. For a discussion of the German model, see Walter Muller-Jentsch, "Germany: From Collective Voice to Co-Management," in Joel Rogers and Wolfgang Streeck (eds.), *Works Councils: Consultation, Representation and Cooperation in Industrial Relations* (Chicago: University of Chicago Press, 1995). See also Robert J. Kuhne, *Co-Determination in Business* (New York: Praeger, 1980).

13. For a discussion of stakeholder models which are attracting attention among management itself, see Ackoff, *Democratic Corporation* and Alkhafaji, *Stakeholder Approach*.

14. For discussion of the European employee-representation model as well as concrete proposals regarding how to create employee representation in the United States along the lines of works-council systems in Europe, see Rogers and Streeck (eds.), *Works Councils*. See also Paul Weiler, *Governing the Workplace: The Future of Labor and Employment Law* (Cambridge, MA: Harvard University Press, 1990).

15. A variety of populist thinkers and organizations have begun to develop a new movement focused on corporate charters. Ralph Nader raised the concept over two decades ago, arguing strongly for federal chartering. Richard Grossman, founder and president of the Center for Corporations, Law and Democracy in Provincetown, MA, deserves much of the credit for inspiring new interest in the idea and catalyzing conversations about it among grassroots groups, such as churches, unions, and student organizations. See Grossman and Adams, *Taking Care.*

16. The flurry of legislative initiatives for R corporations in 1996, coming in the wake of populist anger stirred up by Pat Buchanan, has not led on the federal level to sustained debate or concrete new laws. A variety of legislative initiatives at the state level has had more teeth and more success. For a detailed description, see Jeremey Brecher, *Corporate Downsizing: A Survey of Proposals to Halt Layoffs and Job Degradation* (Washington, D.C.: The Preamble Collaborative, 1996).

17. See Ralph Nader, Mark Green, and Joel Seligman, *Taming.*

18. These include not only the First Amendment, but the Fourth Amendment, the Fifth Amendment, and the Ninth Amendment, to name a few.

19. See Bowman, *Modern Corporation,* pp. 154ff. See also Grossman and Adams, *Taking Care.*

20. I am grateful to Kent Greenfield, a legal scholar concerned with corporate accountability, for the suggestion about the potential value of public reviews of corporate charters, an idea that has also been proposed by Richard Grossman on the basis of his historical examination of the nineteenth-century charter system. See Grossman and Adams, *Taking Care.*

21. For a discussion of the European models of public-interest representation on corporate boards, see Jonathan P. Charkham, *Keeping Good Company: A Study of Corporate Governance in Five Countries* (New York: Oxford University Press, 1994). See also Kuhne, *Co-Determination.*

22. Christopher Stone, *Where the Law Ends* (New York: Harper and Row, 1975).

23. This discussion of Web Converting is based on personal conversation with Vice President Charles Edmunson, other employees including Rob Zacharias, and on the extensive written documentation of its management vision and practice provided by Web.

24. Most current forms of employee ownership, based on 401K retirement plans, stock options, or ESOPs do not challenge corporate property rights, since they assign new employee rights only on the basis of and in proportion to employee shareholdings. For an important critique of current forms of ESOP governance, see Blasi and Kruze, *New Owners,*

chapter 4. See also David Ellerman, *The Democratic Worker-Owned Firm* (London: Unwin, 1990).

25. The most recent employee ownership is drawn from the Employee Ownership Report, July/August 1997, pp. 7–8, produced by the Center for Employee Ownership in San Francisco, a leading technical-assistance and advocacy institute. Data from the early 1990s is drawn from Blasi and Kruse, *New Owners*.

26. Blasi and Cruse, *New Owners*, chapter 4.

27. For an excellent discussion of cooperativism, see David Korten, *Envisioning a Post-Corporate World*. (San Francisco: Berrett-Koehler Publishers, 1999, forthcoming).

28. Theorists of economic democracy who pay useful attention to macro-level approaches include Samuel Bowles, David M. Gordon, and Thomas E. Weiskopf, *After the Waste Land: A Democratic Economics for the Year 2000* (Armonk, NY: M. E. Sharpe, 1990). See also Paul Hirst, *Associative Democracy: New Forms of Economic and Social Governance* (Amherst, MA: University of Massachusetts Press, 1994).

29. Brecher and Costello, *Global Village*. Also John Cavanagh and Robin Broad, "Global Reach: Workers Fight the Multinationals," in Danaher (ed.), *Corporations*.

30. See Bruyn, *Future*.

31. For important historical accounts of these national debates about the corporation, see especially M. Sklar, *Corporate Reconstruction* and Bowman, *Modern Corporation*.

32. For a useful discussion of this theme, see Bowman, *Modern Corporation*, pp. 174ff.

33. This perspective is advanced forcefully today by Korten, *Corporations Rule*.

34. The leading managerial exponent of this notion of radical corporate decentralization has been Tom Peters. See Peters, *Liberation*. See also Peters, *The Tom Peters Seminar* (New York: Vintage, 1994).

35. While there is a vast business literature promoting corporate decentralization and arguing that only the small company can be agile enough to survive and compete, theorists within the business world rarely promote governmental, antitrust, or populist action to speed the process along. The assumption is that market forces will get the job done more efficiently.

14: The Global Populist

1. Corporate Europe Observatory, "Maigalomania: Citizens and the Environment Sacrificed to Corporate Investment." February, 1998.

2. Anderson and Cavanagh, *Top 200.*

3. Corporate Europe Observatory, "Maigalomania." See also United States Council for International Business, *A Guide to the Multilateral Agreement on Investment* (January 1996). See also The Preamble Collaborative, "The Multilateral Agreement on Investment: Basic Facts." (Washington, D.C., 1997).

4. For an excellent discussion of the Ethyl case and all aspects of the MAI, see Maude Barlow and Tony Clarke, *MAI* (New York: Stoddart Publishing Co., 1998).

5. "House Letter on MAI," signed by Congressman David Bonior, Ronald Dellums, John Tierney et al., November 5, 1997, cited in *Inside U.S. Trade,* November 14, 1997.

6. Scott Nova, cited in R. C. Longworth, "New Rules for Global Investment," *Chicago Tribune,* December 4, 1997, p. 1.

7. Howard Wachtel, "Labor's Stake in the WTO," *The American Prospect,* March/April 1998 (34–38), p. 36.

8. William Greider, *One World, Ready or Not* (New York: Simon and Schuster, 1997).

9. Jeffrey Sachs, "The IMF and the Asian Flu," *The American Prospect.* March/April, 1998, (16–21), pp. 17, 21.

10. See Greider, *One World,* for a brilliant analysis both of the global capital markets and regulatory regimes which might redirect them toward the public interest.

11. The public's failure to understand markets as political and historical accomplishments is one of the great obstacles to the new populism. Populists must thus press for educational reform in the schools at all levels to analyze markets in historical and institutional terms. Populism depends both on the explosion of the myth of markets as "natural" and the recognition of the historical role of corporations as key players in constructing the political and legal architecture of the national markets a century ago and the global market today.

12. Fischer and Stiglitz, cited in Louis Uchitelle, "IMF May Be Closer To Lending-Curb Idea," *The New York Times,* February 3, 1998, p. D4.

13. Greider, *One World,* p. 317.

14. *Ibid.,* pp. 316ff.

15. David Lewitt, *Campaign to Stop the MAI and Promote Positive Alternatives* (Cambridge, MA: Alliance for Democracy, January 8, 1998).

16. For a good discussion of the global dimension of chartering, see Brecher and Costello, *Global Village,* p. 140. See especially chapters 7 and 8.

17. *Ibid.*

18. Richard McCormick, Letter to President Clinton, January 13, 1997.

19. *Ibid.*

20. *Ibid.*

15: The Four Movements to Join

1. John Sweeney, "Response to Jeremy Brecher and Tim Costello," *Labor Research Review* #24, 1996 (27–29), p. 27. See also Sweeney and Kusnet, *Raise.*

2. Sweeney, "Response," p. 27.

3. *Ibid.*

4. Sam Dillon, "After Four Years of NAFTA, Labor Is Forging Cross-Border Ties," *The New York Times,* December 20, 1997 (A1–7) p. A1.

5. I draw here on the insightful thinking of Tim Costello, a longtime labor activist with the kind of innovative vision that the labor movement desperately needs. See Jeremy Brecher and Tim Costello, "A 'New Labor Movement' in the Shell of the Old?" *Labor Research Review* #24, 1996, (5–26).

6. The most intriguing argument for this new form of associational unionism has been developed by Charles Heckscher. See Heckscher, *The New Unionism* (New York: Basic Books, 1988).

7. See the collection of essays by Rogers and Streeck (eds.), *Works Councils.* See also Paul Weiler, *Governing the Workplace* (Cambridge, MA: Harvard University Press, 1990). See also Joel Rogers and Richard B. Freeman, "Who Speaks for Us? Employee Representation in a Non-union Labor Market," in Bruce Kaufman and Morris M. Kleiner (eds.), *Employee Representation: Alternatives and Future Directions* (Madison, WI: Industrial Relations Research Association, 1993).

8. Critics of cooperation say that it will undermine a new aggressive labor movement, but examples from Sweden, Germany, and other European countries, however, suggest that certain forms of cooperation may strengthen labor as a robust political actor for social justice. See Bluestone and Bluestone, *Negotiating,* for the case for cooperation. For a discussion of the European model, see Robert Kuttner, *The Economic Illusion* (Boston: Houghton Mifflin, 1984). Also Rogers and Streeck (eds.), *Works Councils.*

9. For a useful discussion of the German system, see Herman Knudsen, *Employee Participation in Europe.* London: Sage, 1995. See also Rogers and Streeck (eds.), *Works Councils.*

10. See Bluestone and Bluestone, *Negotiating.*

11. Rifkin's most extended treatment of the Third Sector is in the final section of Rifkin, *End Work.*

12. Jeremy Rifkin in "Roundtable: Election '96 and the Future of Lesser-Evil Politics," *Tikkun,* September 1996, Vol. 8, No. 3, pp. 11, 14.

13. *Ibid.,* p. 13.

14. For a more extensive discussion of the City Year conversations, see Charles Derber, "National Service: The Sixties Meet the Nineties,"

Tikkun, September, 1996, Vol. 8, No. 3, pp. 19–21. See also my exchange with Daniel Yankelovich on the same subject in *Tikkun,* Vol. 8, No. 3, pp. 21ff.

15. See Amitai Etzioni, *The Spirit of Community* (New York: Morrow, 1993).

16. For a more expansive critique of the communitarian movement in this spirit, see Charles Derber, "Coming Glued: Communitarian versus Communitarianism of the Professional Middle Class," in Charles Derber et al., *What's Left?* (Amherst, MA: University of Massachusetts Press, 1995).

17. For a discussion of the role of religion in nineteenth-century labor and populist movements, see Terence Powderly, *Thirty Years of Labor, 1859–1889* (Columbus, OH: Excelsior Publishing, 1889). See also Philip Foner, *History of the Labor Movement in the United States* (New York: New World Publishers, 1955).

18. On religion and populism, see Harry Boyte, who has also been an important voice in tying together Third Sector ideas with labor struggles and populist politics. See Harry Boyte, *Commonwealth* (New York: Free Press, 1990).

19. John Sweeney, both in his writings and his efforts to reach out to progressive sectors of the religious community, has begun this dialogue. See Sweeney, *Raise.*

20. See Stanley Aronowitz, *The Politics of Identity: Class, Culture, and Social Movements* (New York: Routledge, 1992).

21. A well-known critique of identity politics from this perspective has been advanced by Todd Gitlin, *The Twilight of Our Common Dreams* (New York: Henry Holt, 1995). See also Charles Derber, "Four Futures of the Left" in Derber et al., *What's Left?*

22. See the concluding chapter of Patricia Hill Collins, *Black Feminist Thought* (New York: Routledge, 1991). See also Cornel West, *Prophetic Reflections: Notes on Race and Power in America* (Monroe, Maine: Common Courage Press, 1993). See also bell hooks, *Feminist Theory: From Margin to Center* (Boston: South End Press, 1984).

23. For accessible data on the percentage of women and minority groups who are low-wage or poor, see Mischel and Bernstein, *Working America.* For government data showing the percentage of poor people who are female or minority, see *Income, Poverty, and Valuation of Noncash Benefits: 1993.* For comparable data on the race and gender composition of the contingent labor force, see Callaghan and Hartmann, *Contingent Work.*

24. Martin Luther King, Jr. quoted in *Boston Globe,* January 20, 1997, p. A4.

25. Jesse Jackson, Jr., "Why Race Dialogue Stutters," *New Republic*, March 31, 1997 (22–24), p. 24.
26. See Todd Gitlin, *Twilight*, for one perspective on this theme.
27. For an outstanding discussion of how the labor movement, the women's movement, and multicultural movements can enrich each other, see Sharon Kurtz, *All Kinds of Justice: Labor and Identity Politics*, Unpublished Ph.D. Dissertation (Boston: Boston College, 1994).
28. See *Labor and Identity*.
29. Richard Flacks has shown that left and populist movements have only succeeded historically when they have spoken powerfully to the psychological needs for belonging and the larger identity needs of their members. See Flacks, *Making History*.
30. Carl Pope, "The Salmon and the Sequoia," *Sierra Magazine*, November/December, 1996, p. 14.
31. For an inventory of the new populist environmental ideas and organizations, see the special issue of *In These Times* dealing with the emergence of a new environmental movement linked to economic democracy and social justice. See *In These Times*, July 28–August 10, 1997.
32. For examples of environmental thinking that seriously challenge existing market theory, see Petra Kelly, *Thinking Green* (Berkeley, CA: Parallax Press, 1994). See also Rudolf Bahro, *Socialism and Survival* (London: Heretic Books, 1982).
33. See Herman E. Daly and John B. Cobb, Jr., *For the Common Good* (Boston: Beacon Press, 1989), p. 55.
34. *Ibid.*, pp. 52–53.
35. See Ralph Estes, *Why Good People Do Bad Things* (San Francisco: Berrett-Kohler, 1996).
36. Susan Seybolt, "Environmentalism and Individualism," (Boston, 1994).

16: Why Personal Responsibility Is Not Good Enough

1. Kolko, *Conservatism*, pp. 70, 111.
2. Colin Turnbull, *The Mountain People* (New York: Simon and Schuster, 1987), p. 132.
3. *Ibid.*
4. Spencer, *Social Statics*, p. 55.
5. See Derber, *Wilding*.
6. Amitai Etzioni, *Community*.
7. Juliet Schor, *The Overworked American* (New York: Basic Books, 1992), pp. 29, 21.

8. Arlie Hochschild, *The Second Shift: Working Parents and the Revolution at Home* (New York: Viking Penguin, 1989), p. 9.
9. Stephen Viederman, "Challenge of Sustainability," 1994, pp. 8–9.
10. Mike Davis, *City of Quartz* (New York: Vintage, 1992), especially chapter 4.
11. Maureen Dowd, "Greener $$$ and Pastures," *New York Times,* February 13, 1997, p. A33.
12. William Jefferson Clinton, Second Inaugural, January, 1997.
13. Rick Bragg, "Judge Faces Deadline on Religious Display," *New York Times,* February 13, 1997, p. A14.
14. Cal Thomas, quoted in Chip Berlet (ed.), *Eyes Right: Challenging the Right Wing Backlash* (Boston: South End Press, 1995), p. 17.
15. The Reverend Pat Robertson, quoted in Berlet, *Eyes Right,* p. 34.
16. Quoted in David Brooks, "Compassionate Conservatives: Can They Reinvent the Right?" *Washington Post Weekly,* February 24, 1997, pp. 22–23.
17. Among the writers who have helped create the theoretical foundation for this transition are Alan Wolfe, *Whose Keeper?* (Berkeley, CA: University of California Press, 1989), Jeremy Rifkin, *End Work,* and Michael Lerner, *The Politics of Meaning* (New York: Addison Wesley, 1996). Robert Putnam, *Making Democracy Work* (Princeton, NJ: Princeton University Press, 1993).
18. See Etzioni, *Community,* and my earlier critique of the failure of communitarians, notably Etzioni and his colleagues, to address issues of power and the market. See Charles Derber, "Left Communitarians versus Communitarians of the Professional Middle Class," in Derber et al., *What's Left?* See also Lerner, *Meaning,* and Jim Wallis, *The Soul of Politics* (New York: New Press, 1994).

INDEX